THE
North and West Illustrated

—FOR—

TOURIST, BUSINESS AND PLEASURE TRAVEL.

THE POPULAR RESORTS OF

California, Nevada, Idaho, Montana, Utah, Wyoming, Colorado, Nebraska, Dakota, Iowa, Illinois, Wisconsin, Northern Michigan and Minnesota.

A GUIDE TO THE LAKES AND RIVERS, TO THE PLAINS AND MOUNTAINS, TO THE RESORTS OF BIRDS, GAME ANIMALS AND FISHES; AND HINTS FOR THE COMMERCIAL TRAVELER, THE THEATRE MANAGER, THE LAND HUNTER AND THE EMIGRANT.

COMPILED BY W. H. STENNETT,
General Passenger Agent Chicago & North-Western Railway Co.

PUBLISHED BY THE

Chicago & North-Western Railway Co.

Entered according to Act of Congress, in the year 1876,
By W. H. STENNETT,
In the Office of the Librarian of Congress, at Washington, D. C.

CHICAGO & NORTH-WESTERN RAILWAY

General Officers, etc.

ALBERT KEEP	President	Chicago.
M. L. SYKES, Jr.	Vice-President, Secretary and Treasurer, 52 Wall Street	New York.
MARVIN HUGHITT	General Manager	Chicago.
MARVIN HUGHITT	General Superintendent	"
H. C. WICKER	General Freight Agent	"
C. G. EDDY	Assistant General Freight Agent	"
W. S. MELLEN	Assistant General Freight Agent	"
W. H. STENNETT	General Passenger Agent	"
W. A. THRALL	General Ticket Agent	"
E. H. JOHNSON	Chief Engineer	"
B. C. COOK	General Solicitor	"
M. M. KIRKMAN	Local Treasurer and General Accountant	"
J. B. REDFIELD	Assistant Secretary and Auditor	"
JASON H. CARPENTER	Purchasing Agent	"
N. A. PHILLIPS	General Baggage Agent	"
W. F. FITCH	General Claim Agent	"
G. H. THAYER	Superintendent of Telegraph	"
G. P. GOODWIN	Land Commissioner	"
F. M. LUCE	Car Accountant	"

Division Superintendents.

EDWARD J. CUYLER	Sup't Galena Division and Freeport and Fox River Lines	Chicago.
J. S. OLIVER	Sup't Iowa Division and Iowa Midland Ry.	Clinton, Iowa.
A. A. HOBART	Sup't Wis. and Milwaukee and Kenosha & Rockford Div's	Chicago.
C. A. SWINEFORD	Sup't Madison Division	Baraboo, Wis.
S. SANBORN	Sup't Winona & St. Peter R. R.	Winona, Minn.
W. B. LINSLEY	Sup't Peninsular Division	Escanaba, Mich.

General Agents, etc.

L. F. BOOTH	General Eastern Agent, 415 Broadway, New York.
H. P. STANWOOD	General Agent, 121 Montgomery Street, San Francisco.
C. E. MOODY	General Agent, Milwaukee, Wis.
CHARLES ATKINS	General Agent, Council Bluffs and Omaha.
GEO. L. HARRISON	New England Agent, 5 State Street, Boston, Mass.
C. H. KNAPP	General Agent, Winona, Minn.

Traveling Agents.

V. M. CAME	Chicago, Ill.	G. L. HARRISON........5 State Street, Boston, Mass
E. B. SPAIN	Buffalo, N. Y.	J. H. MOUNTAIN.......Omaha, Neb.
H. A. POWER	Baltimore, Md.	

IMPORTANT TO WEST BOUND EMIGRANTS.

Emigrant Trains are not run on the Chicago & North-Western Railway. Emigrants on this line are carried on the regular first class Express Trains, and make the same time as passengers who hold first class tickets. The cars on this line that are used by emigrants are good, clean, well lighted coaches, with upholstered seats and backs, and are as good as the coaches furnished by many roads to first class passengers.

EMIGRANT TRAINS WEST OF OMAHA.—The trains carrying Emigrants on the Union and Central Pacific roads, west of Omaha, are made up of comfortable coaches, nicely cushioned, and far better in every way than the emigrant cars of the Atlantic Seaboard Roads. The passengers are not crowded in the cars, but have plenty of room. Sleeping cars do not accompany these trains, and the only sleeping facilities offered are those that may be found in any passenger coach. The time of these trains is about twelve miles per hour, which, making the time from Omaha to San Francisco by Emigrant trains about eight to nine days, gives passengers by them ample time to see the country as they move through it. Emigrants can get meals at the regular "Eating Stations" along the line, or they can carry cooked provisions with them, and buy coffee or tea at the eating houses, and eat on the train. Emigrants' movables can go on the same train taken by emigrants from Omaha, as through freight cars are attached to emigrant trains.

NEITHER second class passengers nor emigrants can have Pullman Sleeping Car accommodations, and in this lies about all the restrictions that are placed on them. These classes of passengers are taken care of and protected in every way possible by the agents and employees of the Company.

EMIGRANT TICKETS—Are limited as to time, being good between Chicago and Omaha for eight (8) days from and including day of sale. At Omaha you exchange this ticket for one of the Union Pacific Railroad issue; good for nine days from and including day of exchange. No "stop over checks" are issued on second class or emigrant tickets. Each member of any party going west by rail, must have a regular passage ticket, as no car charters are recognized or will be by the Pacific roads. *No cars are chartered by this Company* or by ANY other line for carrying passengers to points west of Omaha, as the Union and Central Pacific Railroads exact their full schedule rates from all roads ticketing over their lines, without any reference to the number in one party ticketed. The only exception to this rule is made in favor of excursionists who may wish to avail themselves of the first class round trip tickets at the rates and conditions named by the Pacific Roads west of Omaha. The difference in time between Express and Emigrant Trains from Omaha to San Francisco is about five days.

Emigrants are not allowed to travel in the same freight cars with their effects. Where parties of twenty-five or upwards are travelling together, a special passenger car can be secured so as to keep the party together, without extra cost, but no reduction from the rate can be made, no matter how large the party may be.

In all cases possible, buy your Through Tickets from the local Ticket Agent nearest your home. You will in almost all cases save money by so doing, and can then be certain of getting the tickets you desire. In all cases see that your Tickets between Chicago and Omaha read via Chicago & North-Western Railway.

NEW YORK OFFICE: No. 415 Broadway. BOSTON OFFICE: No. 5 State Street.
MILWAUKEE CITY TICKET OFFICE: 102 Wisconsin Street.
ST. PAUL TICKET OFFICE: Corner Third and Jackson Streets.
CHICAGO TICKET OFFICES: 62 Clark Street, under Sherman House; 75 Canal, corner Madison Street; Kinzie Street Depot, corner West Kinzie and Canal Sts.; Wells Street Depot, corner Wells and Kinzie Sts.
OMAHA TICKET OFFICES: 245 Farnham Street, corner Fourteenth, and at Union Pacific Depot.
COUNCIL BLUFFS TICKET OFFICES: Corner Broadway and Pearl Sts., and at C. & N.-W. R'y Depot.
SAN FRANCISCO OFFICE: 121 Montgomery Street.

The Puzzled Traveler.

"I should like to know where this Chicago & North-Western Railway does *not* solicit business for," said Judge Mason a few days ago to a certain ticket agent at Boston, "for," said he, "last fall my friend John Wilson came here to buy a ticket to San Francisco, en route for Japan, and he was told that the Chicago & North-Western Railway was the Chicago link in the TRANS-CONTINENTAL LINE; that it was the first road built to the Missouri River to connect with the great Pacific roads, and to complete the OVERLAND ROUTE; that it is the only line running Pullman Drawing-Room Palace Cars between Chicago and Omaha, ('and that is true to-day' "chipped in" the ticket agent), and that if he wanted to travel on the best and safest road in the country, he must get his ticket by this route. He accepted the story as true, bought his tickets, and wrote me from 'Friscoe that he would advise all of his friends to try this route if they were going to the "Golden State." Later in the season Doctor Dillon was called by telegraph to St. Paul to see "Bill" King, an old chum of the Doctor's. The Doctor went to New York, and dropping into a railway ticket office on Broadway, asked for a ticket to St. Paul, Minn. What do you think he was told? Cannot guess? Well, that if he wanted to ride in Pullman Sleepers all the way to St. Paul, that he must go over the Chicago & North-Western Railway Company's Chicago, Madison & St. Paul Line, as it was the only line that run these celebrated cars between Chicago and St. Paul, or in any part of Wisconsin or Minnesota. Of course he bought his tickets by that route, returned by the same route, and has ever since been talking about the splendid time he had, what an excellent route it is, and how well he was taken care of and used by every one he met connected with the line. He lauds the scenery along the route, and names that in the vicinity of Madison and the "Devil's Lake," as being something really wonderful. In July last, when my wife and daughter were planning their summer trip, they wished for information about Marquette, Lake Superior, and the routes thereto. Coming here you told them there was only one railroad running to that country, and that it was the Chicago & North-Western Line, and that it run through Milwaukee, Fond du Lac, Green Bay, etc. Now to-day I come here and want to get to New Ulm, in Central Minnesota, where I have lands that need looking after, and you tell me the only way I can get there from Chicago is over the Chicago & North-Western Railway. This beats anything I have ever heard. Here is Omaha and San Francisco directly west of Chicago, Marquette 400 miles north of Chicago, St. Paul 400 miles northwest of Chicago, and New Ulm lying about half way between St. Paul and Omaha, and fully 450 miles from Chicago, and you say go by the Chicago & North-Western Railway if you would reach any or all of them. I would like to know how all this can be true!" "My dear sir," said the genial ticket agent, "your story is all true. The Chicago & North-Western Railway is a great institution, and has lines radiating from Chicago like the fingers on the human hand, and reaching all important points in the West, North and Northwest." Taking down his map he showed the "puzzled traveler" something of the various lines we propose to describe.

Dialogues similar to the above may be heard daily in some ticket office in or out of Boston. It is then to make clear to other puzzled travelers a few facts about this great road, and to show you where it is, what it is, and what it can do for you, that this little book is written. We describe routes of travel that are owned and operated by the Chicago & North-Western Railway Company, and those closely identified with its interests and that form its immediate connections. All points named in the book can be reached directly by this line, and to the larger proportion it is the only route by which they can be reached.

The index published herewith will be found to be full, and can be consulted with profit not only by travelers but by railway ticket sellers everywhere. The pages it refers you to will give you such information and advice as may be of great value to you in determining the route you should take to reach the desired destination.

General Passenger Department.   THE COMPILER.
CHICAGO & NORTH-WESTERN RAILWAY,
    Chicago, Ill.

CONTENTS.

	PAGE		PAGE
Across the Mississippi	15	Montana	34
American Fork R. R.	34	New Zealand	35
Australia	35	Northwestern Union Ry.	112
British Columbia	39	North Wisconsin Ry.	84
Burlington, Cedar Rapids & Minnesota Ry.	19	Omaha & California Line	7
Burlington & Missouri, of Nebraska	32	Omaha & Northwestern R. R.	32
Central Railroad of Iowa	20	Oregon	39
Chippewa Falls & Western Ry.	87	Red River Valley of the North	92
Cheap Lands for the Farmer	68	Rich Lands at Low Rates	88
Chicago, Dubuque & La Crosse	15	Rockford, Rock Island & St. Louis R. R.	14
Chicago, Dubuque & Minnesota Ry	15	Routes	1
Chicago, Madison & St. Paul Line	76	Route to Black Hills	25
Chicago, Green Bay & Lake Superior Line	48	Route to China and Japan	35
Colorado	32	Route to Green Lake	60
Commutation Rates, Galena Division	9	Route to St. Paul and Minneapolis	78
Commutation Rates, Milwaukee Division	103	Route to the Pacific Coast	35
Commutation Rates, Wisconsin Division	50	Sagaunash Mineral Springs	107
Concluding Remarks	119	Sheboygan & Fond du Lac, R. R.	38, 115
Consolidation	5	Silver and Copper Mines	73, 74
Cortland & Sycamore R. R.	11	Sioux City & Pacific R. R.	23
Dakota Southern R. R.	21	Southern Minnesota R. R.	16
Davenport & St. Paul Ry.	16	Sparta and vicinity	96
Des Moines & Ft. Dodge R. R.	21	Stanwood & Tipton R. R.	17
Des Moines & Minnesota R. R.	21	St. Paul & Pacific Ry.	93
Elroy Route	76	Suburban Trains Milwaukee Division	103
Fine Lands at Low Rates	98	Synopsis of Game Laws	116
Freeport & Dubuque Line	42	The Geysers of California	88
From Marquette to Duluth	74	The Geysers of Montana	85
From Kenosha to Rockford	115	The Northern Pacific Ry.	91
Galena Division Chicago & North-Western Ry.	9	The Westward Line	3
Game Laws	116	The Winona & St. Peter Ry.	98
Green Bay & Minnesota R. R.	66	Toledo & Northwestern R. R.	20
Historical	1	To Sparta, Winona, and beyond	96
Idaho	34	To the North and Northwest	48
Iron Mines and Furnaces	23	Up the Lake Shore	113
Kansas City, St. Joseph & Council Bluffs R. R.	32	Utah Central Ry.	33
Kenosha & Rockford R. R.	115	Utah Northern Ry.	33
La Crosse, Trempealeau & Prescott R. R.	97	Virginia & Truckee R. R.	35
Lake Geneva Line	45	Washington Territory	39
Lake Superior & Mississippi R. R.	91	Waukegan Magnesian Mineral Springs	106
Lake Tahoe	38	Western Union R. R.	14
Manitoba	93	Westward Again	35
McAllister Mineral Springs	107	West Wisconsin R. R.	86
Mileage	1	Wisconsin	53
Milwaukee	108	Wisconsin Central R. R.	63
Milwaukee Division	103	Wisconsin Valley R. R.	86
Milwaukee, Lake Shore & Western R. R.	113	Yosemite	36
Minnesota	89	Yosemite, Routes to the	109

ILLUSTRATIONS.

NO.		PAGE	NO.		PAGE
1	Agnes Park	29	42	McAllister Springs	101
2	Amphitheatre, Echo Canon	40	43	Milwaukee in 1835	102
3	Arlington Heights	43	44	Mineral Dock	51
4	Ayer's Hotel	45	45	Minneopa Falls	88
5	Beaumont House	62	46	Minneopa Falls in Winter	89
6	Castle Rock	83	47	Mineral Springs, Sparta	80
7	City Aqueduct	85	48	Near Evanston	92
8	Cliff House and Seal Rocks	108	49	Northwestern Hotel	58
9	Clinton, Iowa	15	50	Oak Grove House	76
10	Cook's Hotel	49	51	Oakwood House	46
11	Council Bluffs and Omaha Bridge	31	52	On the Baraboo	67
12	Custer's Park	30	53	On the St. Croix	70
13	Devil's Gate, Weber Canon	88	54	Perch Lake	82
14	Dixon, Ill.	13	55	Public School	44
15	Dubuque's Grave	115	56	Pulpit Rock	69
16	Eagle Point	117	57	Pyramid Rock	64
17	Elkhart Lake	105	58	Rock River University	14
18	Falls of Minnehaha	72	59	Routes to the Yosemite	109
19	Falls of St. Anthony	73	60	Sherwood Forest	47
20	Ferry Hall	95	61	Sioux Falls	23
21	First National Hotel	49	62	Skillet Creek	66
22	Gitche Gumme	59	63	Stephenson County Court House	41
23	Glen Flora Hotel	100	64	Table Rock	26
24	Grand Central Hotel	82	65	Teal Lake	52
25	Great Salt Lake	112	66	The Buttes, Winona	85
26	Hanging Rock	113	67	The Chapel, Mt. Vernon	18
27	Head of the Boyer	22	68	The Cliff House	65
28	Highland Hall	97	69	The Dalles of St. Croix	71
29	Ingraham's Gold Fish Pond	98	70	The Dalles of the St. Louis	79
30	In the Yosemite	110, 111	71	The Mills, Minneapolis	74
31	Iron Mines and Ore Train	53	72	The Point	57
32	Ishpeming—its hotel	54	73	The State Capitol, Sacramento	106
33	Lake Dells	104	74	The Tabernacle, Salt Lake City	36
34	Lake Forest Academy	94	75	Trout Falls	81
35	Lake Forest Seminary	93	76	Turkey River Bluff	118
36	Lake Minnetonka	77	77	Walker House	34
37	Lake Minnetonka (2d)	78	78	Warner House	84
38	Lake Side Hotel	63	79	White Bear Lake	75
39	Magone Falls	48	80	Whiting House	42
40	Mankato	90	81	Winona	87
41	Marquette	61	82	Willow River Falls	68

INDEX.

PLACE AND STATE.	PAGE	PLACE AND STATE.	PAGE	PLACE AND STATE.	PAGE
Ableman's, Wis	85	Blairstown, Ia	19	Clinton Junction, Wis	55
Ackley, Ia	20	Blencoe, Ia	24	Clintonville, Ill	42
Addison, Ill	10	Bloomington, Ill	13	Cloverdale, Cal	35
Afton, Wis	78	Blue Cut, Iowa	41	Clyman, Wis	56
Albany, Ill	14	Bluff Side, Wis	98	Coleta, Ill	14
Albany, Oregon	40	Boise City, Idaho	34	Colfax, Cal	35
Albany, Wis	79	Boone, Ia	21	Colo, Ia	20
Albert Lea, Minn	16, 100	Boonesboro, Ia	21	Colorado Springs, Col	33
Albia, Iowa	20	Bowmanville, Ill	103	Columbus, Neb	32
Alden, Ill	116	Bozeman, Mont	34	Columbus, Wis	56
Alden, Minn	16	Brainerd, Minn	92	Como, Ill	14
Alexandria, Minn	93	Brandon, Wis	56	Concord, Minn	99
Algonquin, Ill	45	Breckenridge, Minn	94	Cordova, Ill	14
Allen's Grove, Wis	54	Bristol, Wis	116	Corinne, Utah	34
Alma, Minn	101	Brodhead, Wis	78	Cortland, Ill	11
Almont, Ia	41	Brookfield, Wis	55	Coteau, Minn	102
Amboy, Ill	13	Brooklyn, Wis	79	Cottage Hill, Ill	10
Ames, Ia	21	Brookside, Wis	67	Cottonwood, Minn	102
Amherst, Wis	63, 67	Brownsville, Minn	16	Council Bluffs, Ia	30
Anamosa, Ia	41	Bryan, Wy. Ter	33	Council Hill, Ill	44
Ankeny, Iowa	21	Bryant, Ia	41	Courtland, Minn	102
Anoka, Minn	95	Buena Vista, Ia	16	Covington, Neb	24
Antioch, Ill	105	Burlington, Wis	55	Crescent, Ia	30
Apple River, Ill	44	Burnett Junction, Wis	56	Creston, Ill	12
Appleton, Wis	63	Burns, Minn	102	Crete, Neb	32
Arcadia, Ia	22	Byron, Minn	99	Crookston, Minn	95
Arcadia, Wis	67	Byron, Wis	56	Crowell, Neb	29
Argenta, Mont	34			Crystal Lake, Ill	45, 52
Argona, Ia	24	Calamine, Wis	13		
Argyle, Ill	116	Calamus, Ia	16	Dakota City, Neb	24, 29
Arlington Heights, Ill	50	Caledonia, Ill	116	Dalles City, Oregon	40
Ashland, Neb	32	Caledonia, Minn	93	Dane, Wis	80
Ashton, Ill	12	Calhoun, Neb	29	Darien, Wis	55
Astoria, Oregon	40	Calienta, Cal	35	Darlington, Wis	55
Auburn, Cal	35	California Junction, Ia	24	Davenport, Ia	14, 16, 17
Auckland, N. Z	35	Calistoga, Cal	35	Davis, Wis	55
Audubon, Minn	93	Calvary, Ill	103	Davis Junction, Iowa	25
Audubon Lake, Minn	93	Camanche, Ia	16	Dartford, Wis	58
Augusta, Wis	86	Camp Douglas, Wis	86	Dayton, Minn	95
Austin, Ill	10	Canfield, Ill	50	Decatur, Neb	24, 29
Austin, Minn	19	Canon City, Col	33	Deer Lodge, Mont	34
Aztalan, Wis	56	Canton, Ill	41	DeKalb, Ill	11
		Capron, Ill	116	Delavan, Wis	55
Bagley, Mich	69	Carroll, Ia	22	Delaware, Ia	17
Baker City, Idaho	34	Carroll, Mont	93	Delevan, Minn	16
Baldwin, Ia	41	Carson, Nev	35	Delhi, Ia	17
Baldwin, Wis	88	Carpenterville, Ill	45	Deloit, Ia	23
Bangor, Wis	97	Cary, Ill	52	Delmar Junction, Ia	16
Baraboo, Wis	85	Cascade, W. T	40	Dement, Ill	12
Barrington, Ill	51	Castana, Ia	23, 24	Denison, Ia	23
Barton, Wis	112	Cataract, Wis	97	Denver, Col	33
Bassetts, Wis	116	Cavoits, Wis	68	DePere, Wis	65
Batavia, Ill	11	Cazenovia, Wis	85	Des Moines, Ia	21
Battle Creek, Neb	30	Cedar Falls, Ia	19	DeSoto, Neb	32
Battle Mountain, Nev	35	Cedar Lake, Minn	90	Desplaines, Ill	50
Bayfield, Minn	73	Cedar Rapids, Ia	18	Detroit, Minn	93
Bay View, Wis	108	Center Junction, Ia	41	Devil's Lake, Wis	81
Bear Valley, Minn	99	Centralia, Wis	86	DeWitt, Ia	16
Beatrice, Neb	32	Central City, Col	33	Dexterville, Wis	67
Beaver, Ia	21	Centreville, Utah	34	Dheinsville, Wis	112
Beaver, Minn	102	Ceresco, Wis	58	Dixon, Ill	12
Beaver Dam, Wis	56	Charlotte, Ia	41	Dodge Center, Minn	99
Becker, Minn	95	Chatfield, Minn	99	Dodge City, Minn	100
Belle Plaine, Ill	103	Chelsea, Ia	19	Dover, Minn	99
Belle Plaine, Ia	19	Chemung, Ill	116	Dowville, Ia	23
Bellevue, Ia	16	Cherry Valley, Ill	43	Dubuque, Ia	13, 16, 19, 44
Belgium, Wis	113	Chester, Minn	99	Duck Creek, Wis	67
Beloit, Wis	78	Chester, Wis	56	Duluth, Minn	73, 91
Belvidere, Ill	43	Cheyenne, Wyo	32, 33	Dundas, Minn	100
Benton, Ill	107	Chippewa Falls, Wis	87	Dundee, Ill	45, 113
Berlin, Wis	56	Claremont, Minn	99	Dunlap, Ia	23
Bertram, Ia	18	Clarence, Ia	17	Dunleith, Ill	44
Birch Creek, Mich	69	Clarksville, Ia	19	Durand, Wis	55
Big Lake, Minn	95	Clayton, Ia	16	Dutch Flat, Cal	35
Big Suamico, Wis	67	Clear Creek, Wis	112	Dysart, Ia	19
Bismark, Dak	93	Clear Lake, Minn	95		
Blackberry, Ill	11	Clear Water, Minn	95	Eagle, Wis	55
Black Hawk, Col	33	Clermont, Ia	19	Eagle Lake, Minn	101
Black River Falls, Wis	86	Cleveland, Minn	101	East Side, Ia	22
Blair, Neb	24, 29	Clinton, Ia	15	Eau Claire, Wis	86

(5)

PLACE AND STATE.	PAGE	PLACE AND STATE.	PAGE	PLACE AND STATE.	PAGE
Eddyville, Ia	20	Gilberts, Ill	42	Jamestown, Neb	29
Eden, Wis	113	Gill's Landing, Wis	62, 64	Janesville, Minn	101
Edgerton, Wis	55	Gilroy, Cal	35	Janesville, Wis	55
Eldora, Ia	20	Glenbeulah, Wis	115	Jefferson, Wis	56
Eldorado, Wis	58	Glencoe, Ill	104	Johnson, Wis	55
Eldridge, Ia	16, 17	Glendale, Wis	96	Johnson Centre, Wis	55
Elgin, Ill	42	Glen Flora, Ill	105	Johnson's Creek, Wis	56
Elgin, Minn	99	Glidden, Ia	22	Judd, Wis	78
Elk Grove, Ill	50	Glyndon, Minn	93	Julesburg, Neb	32
Elkhart Lake, Wis	115	Gold Hill, Col	33	Junction, Ill	10
Elkhorn, Wis	55	Gold Hill, Nev	35	Juneau, Wis	56
Elko, Nev	35	Golden City, Col	33		
Elk Point, Dak	24, 25	Goose Lake, Ia	41	Kandiyohi, Minn	94
Elkport, Ia	16	Gordon's Ferry, Ia	16	Kasota, Minn	101
Elk River Junction, Ia	16	Gower's Ferry, Ia	17	Kasson, Minn	99
Elk River, Minn	95	Grand Detour, Ill	13	Kaukauna, Wis	65
Elmhurst, Ill	10	Grand Island, Neb	32	Kaysville, Utah	34
Elroy, Wis	86	Grand Junction, Ia	21	Kearney, Neb	32
Emerald Grove, Wis	55	Grand Mound, Ia	16	Kekaska, Wis	56
Empire City, Oregon	40	Grand Rapids, Wis	67	Kelley, Iowa	21
Escanaba, Mich	69	Granite Falls, Minn	102	Kelton, Utah	34
Eugene City, Oregon	40	Granville, Wis	112	Kendalls, Wis	96
Eureka, Wis	62	Greeley, Col	32, 33	Kenosha, Wis	107
Evans, Col	32, 33	Green Bay, Wis	65	Kewaskum, Wis	112
Evanston, Ill	103	Green Bay Junction, Wis	86	Kingston, Minn	95
Evansville, Wis	79	Green Lake, Wis	58	Kirkwood, Wis	85
Evanston, Wyo	33	Green River, Wyo	33	Kishwaukee, Ill	52
Everett, Neb	29	Grinnell, Ia	21	Kloman, Mich	69
Excelsior, Minn	90	Grundy Centre, Ia	20	Kohlsville, Wis	112
Eyota, Minn	99	Guttenberg, Ia	16	Koshkonong, Wis	55
Fairfax, Ia	19	Hainesville, Ill	105	Lac-qui-parle, Minn	102
Fairhaven, Minn	95	Hammond, Wis	88	La Crescent, Minn	16
Faribault, Minn	100	Hampton, Ill	14	La Crosse, Wis	16, 98
Farley, Ia	19	Hampton, Ia	20	La Fox, Ill	11
Farmington, Utah	34	Hancock, Mich	74	La Salle, Ill	13
Fargo, Minn	93	Hanover, Wis	78	Lake Benton, Minn	102
Fayette, Ia	17	Harlem, Ill	4, 10	Lake City, Minn	99
Fergus Falls, Minn	93	Harper's Ferry, Ia	16	Lake Forest, Ill	105
Fish Creek, Minn	97	Harvard, Ill	52	Lake Geneva, Wis	46
Flagg, Ill	12	Havana, Minn	99	Lake Kampeska, Minn	102
Florence, Neb	32	Haven, Iowa	19	Lake Michigamme, Mich	72
Fond du Lac, Minn	91	Havelock, Ill	103	Lake Mills, Wis	56
Fond du Lac, Wis	56	Hawley, Minn	93	Lake Shetek, Minn	102
Fontanelle, Neb	29	Hebron, Ill	116	Lake Side, Ill	104
Footville, Wis	78	Hebron, Wis	116	Lake View, Ill	103
Fort Abercrombie, Minn	93	Helena, Ia	19	Lake Walusa, Wis	79
Fort Atkinson, Wis	55	Helena, Mont	34	Lake Zurich, Ill	51
Fort Benton, Mont	93	Herman, Neb	24, 29	Lamartine, Wis	58
Fort Dodge, Ia	21	Hersey, Wis	97	Lamoille, Ia	20
Fort Fred Steel, Wyo	33	Heytmans, Ia	17	Lanark, Ill	14, 45
Fort Garry, B. N. A	93	Highland Park, Ill	104	Lane, Ill	12
Fort Howard, Wis	65	Highwood, Ill	105	Lanesboro, Minn	16
Fort Sanders, Wyo	33	Hillsborough, Wis	85	L'Anse, Mich	72
Fort Seward, Minn	93	Hinckley, Minn	91	Lansing, Ia	16
Fort Sully, Dak	102	Honey Creek, Ia	30	La Porte, Ia	19
Fort Thompson, Dak	102	Houghton, Mich	74	Laporte, Neb	30
Fort Totten, Dak	93	Hollister, Cal	35	Laramie, Wyo	33
Fort Wadsworth, Dak	93	Hong Kong, China	35	Lathrop, Cal	35
Fox Lake, Wis	56	Honolulu, S. I	35	Lavelle, Wis	85
Fox River, Wis	116	Hokah, Minn	16	Lawrence, Ill	53
Forreston, Ill	13	Hopkinton, Ia	17	Le Grand, Ia	20
Forest City, Minn	95	Hooper, Neb	29	Leavenworth, Minn	102
Forest Lake, Minn	91	Houston, Minn	16	Lee Centre, Ill	12
Franklin, Ill	12	Hudson, Wis	88	Lehi, Utah	34
Frazier City, Minn	93	Huntley, Ill	42	Lena, Ill	13, 44
Fredericksburg, Ill	10	Humboldt, Nev	35	Lewiston, Minn	99
Freeborn, Minn	100			Libertyville, Ill	105
Freeport, Ill	44	Iberia, Minn	102	Lindwerm, Wis	112
Fremont, Neb	24, 29	Idaho City, Idaho	34	Lincoln, Neb	32
Fremont, Wis	62	Idaho Springs, Col	33	Lincoln, Minn	99
Fulton, Ill	14	Ida Grove, Ia	24	Linn, Ia	19
		Independence, Ia	19	Lisbon, Ia	17
Galena, Ill	13, 44	Iowa Centre, Ia	21	Liscomb, Ia	20
Galt, Ill	14	Irving Park, Ill	50	Litchfield, Minn	94
Garden Prairie, Ill	43	Ironton, Wis	85	Little Chute, Wis	65
Galesville, Wis	98	Ishpeming, Mich	70	Little Kaukauna, Wis	65
Garry Owen, Ia	41	Isle Royale, Mich	71	Little Suamico, Wis	67
Gayville, Dak	26	Itaska, Minn	95	Little Sioux, Ia	24
Geneva, Ill	10	Ives Station, Wis	108	Litchfield, Minn	94
Genoa, Wis	46, 116			Lodi, Ill	11
Genoa Junction, Wis	46, 116	Jackson, Wis	112	Lodi, Wis	81
Georgetown, Col	33	Jacksonville, Oregon	40	Logan, Ia	23
Germantown, Wis	112	Jamestown, Minn	93	Logan, Neb	29

Index.

PLACE AND STATE.	PAGE	PLACE AND STATE.	PAGE	PLACE AND STATE.	PAGE
Logan, Utah	33	Moline, Ill.	14	Orford, Wis.	78
Logansville, Wis.	85	Montrose, Ill.	50	Orangeville, Ill.	44
Lombard, Ill.	10	Montour, Ia.	20	Oroville, Cal.	35
Lone Tree, Neb.	32	Mondamin, Ia.	24	Oshkosh, Wis.	61
Long Prairie, Minn.	93	Monmouth, Ia.	41	Oshawa, Minn.	102
Los Angeles, Cal.	35	Monticello, Ia.	17, 19	Oskaloosa, Iowa.	20
Loudon, Ia.	17	Monticello, Minn.	95	Osterdock, Ia.	16
Low Moor, Ia.	16	Monroe, Wis.	44, 78	Osceola, Ill.	45
Lowell, Wis.	56	Monterey, Cal.	35	Oto, Ia.	24
Luzerne, Ia.	19	Moorhead, Minn.	93	Otter Tail City, Minn.	93
Lyle, Minn.	19	Morris, Minn.	94	Ottumwa, Ia.	20
Lyons, Ia.	41	Morrison, Ill.	14	Owatonna, Minn.	99
Lyons, Neb	29	Mount Carroll, Ill.	14, 45	Owego, Minn.	93
Lytles, Wis.	98	Mount Vernon, Ia.	17	Oxford Mills, Ia.	17
Lyndon, Ill.	14	Mount Prospect, Ill.	50	Ozark, Ia.	41
		Munster, Wis.	116	O'Neill City, Neb.	30
Madison, Neb.	30				
Madison, Wis.	79	Nachusa, Ill.	12	Palatine, Ill.	50
Magnolia, Wis.	78	Napa, Cal.	35	Palisade, Nev.	35
Malade, Idaho	34	Nashville, Ia.	41	Palmyra, Wis.	55
Malone, Ia.	16	Nederland, Col.	33	Paola, Wis.	79
Malta, Ill.	12	Neenah, Wis.	63	Park Ridge, Ill.	50
Manitoba, B. N. A.	93	Negaunee, Mich.	70	Parkers, Minn.	93
Manitou, Col.	33	Nelson, Ill.	13	Pecatonica, Ill.	43
Manitowoc, Wis.	113	Neleigh City, Neb.	30	Pembina, Dak.	93
Mankato, Minn.	101	Neosho, Wis.	56	Pensaukee, Wis.	67
Mankato Junction, Minn.	101	Nevada, Ia.	20	Perham, Minn.	93
Mantorville, Minn.	99	New Cassel, Wis.	112	Peshtigo, Wis.	68
Maple, Neb	29	New Glarus, Wis.	79	Petaluma, Cal.	35
Maplewood, Ill	50	New Hampshire, Ill.	42	Pewaukee, Wis.	56
Mapleton, Ia.	24	New Jefferson, Ia.	21	Pine City, Minn.	91
Maquoketa, Ia.	16, 41	New London, Wis.	62, 66	Pine Creek, Wis.	98
Marengo, Ill	43	New Sharon, Iowa	20	Pine Island, Minn.	99
Marinette, Wis.	69	New Ulm, Minn.	102	Plainview, Minn.	99
Marion, Minn.	99	Newton, Ia.	20	Plank Road, Ill.	50
Marion, Ia.	19	Newton, Neb.	32	Platteville, Wis.	13
Marshall, Minn.	102	Nicollet, Minn.	102	Pleasant Grove, Minn.	99
Marshall, Wis.	56	Nickerson, Neb.	29	Pleasant Prairie, Wis.	116
Marshalltown, Ia.	20	Niles, Cal.	35	Plover, Wis.	67
Marshfield, Wis.	63	Nora, Ill.	13, 44	Plum River, Ill.	44
Marshland, Minn.	98	Nora Junction, Ia.	19	Plymouth, Wis.	115
Marquette, Mich.	71	Nordland, Minn.	102	Pokegama Falls, Minn.	92
Marysville, Cal.	35	Norfolk, Neb.	30	Polk City, Ia	21
Mason City, Ia.	20	Normal, Ill.	13	Polo, Ill	13
Mazeppa, Minn.	99	Norman, Minn.	93	Poplar Grove, Ill.	116
Massillon, Ia.	17	North Evanston, Ill.	103	Portage Lake, Mich.	74
Mauston, Wis.	85	North Freedom, Wis.	85	Portage, Wis.	56
Mayville, Wis.	56	North McGregor, Ia.	16	Port Byron, Ill.	14
Mayfield, Wis.	112	North Pacific Junction, Minn.	91	Port Townsend, W. T.	40
Maywood, Ill.	10	North Platte, Neb.	32	Port Washington, Wis.	113
McGregor, Ia.	16	Northfield, Minn.	100	Portland, Oregon.	35
McHenry, Ill.	45	Northport, Wis.	62	Portlandville, Iowa.	24, 25
McGilroy's Ferry, Wis.	98	Northwood, Ia.	20	Postville, Ia.	19
McConnell's Grove, Ill.	44	Norway, Ia.	19	Poynette, Wis.	81
Mechanicsville, Ia.	17	Norwalk, Wis.	96	Prairie, Minn.	102
Meckling, Dak.	26	Norwood, Ill.	50	Prairie aux Isle, Minn.	98
Medford, Minn.	100			Prairie du Chien, Wis.	16
Melrose, Ill.	10	Oak Center, Wis.	56	Prairie du Sac, Wis.	81
Melrose, Minn.	97	Oak Creek, Wis.	108	Princeton, Minn.	95
Melbourne, Aust.	35	Oak Park, Ill.	10	Princeton, Wis.	61
Menasha, Wis.	63	Oakdale, Neb.	30	Prospect Park, Ill.	10
Mendota, Wis.	80	Oakfield, Wis.	56	Prophetstown, Ill.	14
Menomonee, Mich.	69	Oakland, Neb.	29	Provo, Utah.	34
Menomonee, Wis.	88	Oconto, Wis.	67	Puget Sound, Oregon.	35
Menomonee Falls, Wis.	112	Oconomowoc, Wis.	56		
Meriden, Minn.	100	Ogden, Ia.	21	Quarry, Ia.	20
Merrimac, Wis.	81	Ogden, Utah.	33		
Merrillan, Wis.	67	Ogdensburg, Wis.	67	Racine, Wis.	107
Midway, Ia.	21	Okaman, Minn.	101	Racine Junction, Wis.	107
Midway, Wis.	98	Okee, Wis.	81	Ramsey, Minn.	16
Milburne, Ill.	105	Olmsted, Minn.	99	Ravenswood, Ill	103
Millidgeville, Ill.	14	Olympia, W. T.	40	Ravinia, Ill.	104
Mill Rock, Iowa.	41	Omro, Wis.	56, 62	Rawlings, Wyo.	33
Milton Junction, Wis.	55	Omaha, Neb.	32	Redding, Cal.	39
Milwaukee, Wis.	108	Onawa, Ia.	24	Red Wing, Minn.	99
Minnesota Junction, Wis.	56	Oualaska, Wis.	97	Redwood Falls, Minn.	94, 102
Mindoro, Wis.	97	Onslow, Ia.	41	Reedsburg, Wis.	85
Mineral Point, Wis.	13	Ontario, Ia	21	Reno, Nev.	35
Minonk, Ill.	13	Ontario, Wis.	85	Richmond, Ill.	46
Minnesota City, Minn.	99	Ontonagon, Mich.	74	Richwood, Wis.	56
Minneapolis, Minn.	90	Oregon City, Oregon.	40	Ridgefield, Ill.	52
Missouri Valley Junction, Ia.	23	Oregon, Wis.	79	Ridgeland, Ill.	10
Modale, Ia.	24	Oronoko, Minn.	99	Ridott, Ill.	44
Moingona, Ia.	21	Orono, Minn.	95	Ringwood, Ill.	45

PLACE AND STATE.	PAGE	PLACE AND STATE.	PAGE	PLACE AND STATE.	PAGE
Ripon, Wis.	58	Spring Valley, Wis.	85	Walden, Ia.	17
River Forest, Ill.	10	Springfield, Wis.	55	Wallace, Mich.	69
River Sioux, Ia.	24	Springville, Ia.	19	Walla Walla, Wash. Ter.	40
Rochelle, Ill.	12	Stanton, Neb.	30	Wallula, W. T.	40
Rochester, Ia.	17	Stanwood, Ia.	17	Wall Lake, Ia.	22
Rochester, Minn.	99	State Centre, Ia.	20	Walnut Grove, Minn.	102
Rockfield, Ill.	19	State Hospital, Wis.	62	Waltham, Ia.	19
Rockfield, Wis.	112	State Line, Ill.	107	Warren, Ill.	13, 44
Rockford, Ill.	43	State Line, Minn.	102	Waseca, Minn.	100
Rock Island, Ill.	14	St. Anthony, Minn.	94	Watab, Minn.	96
Rock Island Junction, Ill.	14	St. Cloud, Minn.	96	Waterloo, Ia.	19
Rockton, Wis.	55	St. Charles, Ill.	10	Waterloo, Wis.	56
Rogers Park, Ill.	103	St. Charles, Minn.	99	Waterman's Mills, Ill.	44
Rome Corners, Wis.	79	St. Francis, Minn.	95	Watertown, Wis.	56
Roscoe, Ill.	78	St. Francis, Wis.	108	Watkins, Ia.	19
Rosehill, Ill.	103	St. Helena, Cal.	35	Wauconda, Ill.	51
Roseburgh, Oregon	40	St. Ignace Island, L. S.	71	Waukegan, Ill.	105
Rosendale, Wis.	58	St. Mary, Wis.	61, 97	Waukesha, Wis.	55
Round Grove, Ill.	14	St. Paul, Minn.	89	Waunakee, Wis.	80
Royalton, Wis.	62, 67	St. Peter, Minn.	101	Waupacca, Wis.	63
Rush City, Minn.	91	Steamboat Rock, Ia.	20	Waupeton, Ia.	16
Rushford, Minn.	16	Steilacoom, W. T.	40	Waupun, Wis.	56
		Sterling, Ill.	13	Wausau, Wis.	86
Sabula, Ia.	15	Stephenson, Mich.	69	Wayne, Ill.	42
Sacramento, Cal.	35	Stevenstown, Wis.	98	Wayne Centre, Ill.	42
Salem, Oregon	40	Stevens' Point, Wis.	63	Wayzata, Minn.	94
Salem, Wis.	116	Stillwater, Minn.	91	Webster City, Ia.	19
Salinas, Cal.	35	Stockton, Cal.	35	Wells, Minn.	16
Salix, Ia.	24	Stockton, Minn.	99	Welton, Iowa	16
Salt Lake City, Utah	33	Stoughton, Wis.	55	Wenona, Ill.	13
San Diego, Cal.	35	Summit, Wis.	96	West Bend, Wis.	112
San Francisco, Cal.	35	Summerdale, Ill.	103	West Menasha, Wis.	63
San Jose, Cal.	35	Sun Prairie, Wis.	56	West Pensaukee, Wis.	67
Santa Barbara, Cal.	35	Superior City, Wis.	73	West Point, Neb.	24, 29
Santa Clara, Cal.	35	Swede Point, Ia.	21	West Rapids, Ia.	19
Santa Cruz, Cal.	35	Sycamore, Ill.	11	West Salem, Wis.	97
Santa Rosa, Cal.	35	Sydney, Australia	35	West Side, Ia.	22
Santiago, Minn.	95	Syene, Wis.	79	West Union, Ia.	19
Saratoga, Minn.	102			Weyauwega, Wis.	62, 63
Sargeant's Bluff, Ia.	24	Tacoma, Oregon	35	Wheaton, Ill.	10
Sauk City, Wis.	81	Tama, Ia.	19	Wheatland, Ia.	16
Sauk Rapids, Minn.	95	Taylor, Ill.	12	Wheeling, Ill.	50
Savanna, Ill.	14, 45	Tekama, Neb.	24, 29	Whitewater, Wis.	55
Saylor, Ia.	21	Thompson, Minn.	91	White Bear Lake, Minn.	91
Scales Mound, Ill.	44	Tipton, Ia.	17	Whiting, Ia.	24
Scandinavia, Wis.	67	Toana, Utah	35	Wilmar, Minn.	94
Schuyler, Neb.	32	Toledo, Ia.	20	Wilmette, Ill.	104
Scranton, Ia.	21	Tomah, Wis.	86	Wilmot, Wis.	116
Scribner, Neb.	29	Toronto, Ia.	17	Wilton, Ia.	17
Seattle, Oregon	40	Traer, Ia.	20	Wilton, Minn.	96
Seymour, Wis.	66	Trempealeau, Wis.	98	Winfield, Ill.	10
Shannon, Ill.	14, 45	Truckee, Cal.	35	Winnebago, Ill.	43
Sharon, Wis.	54	Turkey River, Ia.	16	Winnebago, Minn.	16
Shawano, Wis.	62, 65	Turner, Ill.	10	Winneconne, Wis.	56, 62
Sheboygan, Wis.	113	Twin Lakes, Ill.	46, 53	Winnemucca, Nev.	35
Sheldahl, Ia.	21	Two Rivers, Wis.	113	Winnepeg, Manitoba.	93
Shellsburg, Ia.	19			Winnetka, Ill.	104
Shell Rock, Ia.	19	Udina, Iowa	42	Winona, Minn.	98
Shiocton, Wis.	66	Umatilla, Oregon	40	Winona Junction, Wis.	97
Shopiere, Wis.	55	Union, Ill.	43	Wisconsin Valley Junc., Wis.	96
Sidney, Neb.	32	Union, Ia.	20	Wisner, Neb.	24, 29
Silver City, Idaho.	34	Union Centre, Wis.	85	Wonowoc, Wis.	85
Silver City, Nev.	35	Union Grove, Ill.	14	Woodbine, Ia.	23
Sioux City, Ia.	24	Utica, Minn.	99	Woodside, Wis.	88
Sioux Falls City, Dak.	24, 25			Woodstock, Ill.	52
Sioux St. Marie, Mich.	71	Vail, Ia.	23	Woodworth, Wis.	116
Sleepy Eye Lake, Minn.	102	Vancouvers Island, B. C.	35	Worcester, Wis.	63
Sloan, Ia.	24	Vandyne, Wis.	61	Worthington, Minn.	101
Smithland, Ia.	24	Vermillion, Dak.	24, 25	Wrightstown, Wis.	65
Snelles, Wis.	62	Verona, Wis.	79	Wyoming, Ia.	17, 41
Soledad, Cal.	35	Victor, Ia.	19	Wyoming, Minn.	91
South Caledonia, Ill.	116	Victoria, B. C.	35, 40		
South Evanston, Ill.	103	Vinton, Ia.	19	Yankton, Dak.	24, 25
Sparta, Wis.	96	Viola, Ia.	19	Yellow Creek, Ill.	44
Spaulding, Mich.	69	Virginia City, Mont.	34	Yellow Medicine, Minn.	94
Spechts Ferry, Ia.	16	Virginia City, Nev.	35	Yokohama, Japan.	35
Spring Creek, Ia.	20	Viroqua, Wis.	97	Young America, Wis.	112
Spring Green, Wis.	85	Volga City, Ia.	16		
Spring Hill, Ill.	14			Zumbro, Minn.	99
Spring Valley, Minn.	16, 99	Wadsworth, Nev.	35	Zwingle, Ia.	41

THE CHICAGO & NORTH-WESTERN RAILWAY.

WHERE IT IS, AND WHAT IT IS.

HISTORICAL.

We do not propose to trouble you much with figures, but merely give you at this time the mileage owned and operated exclusively by this Company, and the mileage owned and operated entirely or mainly by this Company.

Lines owned and operated exclusively by this Company.

Chicago to Council Bluffs and Omaha	492.00	Chicago Cut-off and Branches	18.03
Stanwood to Tipton	8.50	Clinton to Anamosa, Iowa	72.40
Chicago to Freeport	121.00	Chicago to Ishpeming, (Marquette), including branches	463.82
Elgin to Lake Geneva	44.50		
Geneva, Ill. to St. Charles, Ill.	2.40	Milwaukee to Fond du Lac	63.30
Geneva, Ill. to Batavia	3.00	Winona to Lake Kampeska	330.25
Belvidere, via Madison and Elroy, to Winona	228.60		
Kenosha to Rockford	72.40	Total Miles	2,003.70
Chicago to Milwaukee	85.00		

Routes owned and operated entirely or mainly by this Company.

Omaha and California Line	492	Lake Geneva Line	85
Chicago, Madison & St. Paul Line, (Elroy Route)	409	Clinton and Anamosa	72
Green Bay and Lake Superior Line	470	Kenosha and Rockford Line	72
Elroy, Winona and Lake Kampeska Line	623	Stanwood & Tipton Railroad	9
Sioux City and Yankton Line	603	Geneva and St. Charles Line	3
Dubuque and La Crosse (via Clinton) Line	315	Geneva and Batavia Line	2
Freeport Line and Dubuque	121	Chicago "Cut-off" and Branches	18
Chicago and Milwaukee Line	85		
Milwaukee and Fond du Lac Line	63	Total Miles	3,442

We wish to describe to you the commencement, growth, and present *status* of the Company, and give you short descriptions of the country, cities, towns, villages and stations it passes through, and to note in passing any special items that may be thought of interest to those not fully familiar with our great Western land. This Company owns and operates—

First—The shortest, oldest and best line between Chicago and Council Bluffs and Omaha, and the first that formed a connection with the Union Pacific for Nebraska, Colorado, Wyoming, Utah, Idaho, Montana, Nevada, California, Oregon, and the Pacific Coast. This is known as the OMAHA AND CALIFORNIA LINE, or THE GREAT TRANS-CONTINENTAL OVERLAND ROUTE.

Second—The best and most direct route to Madison, St. Paul, Minneapolis, and for all points beyond. This line is new, and as such has been equipped with everything tending to comfort, speed and safety, that modern invention has placed in the hands of the progressive Railroad Manager. This line is known as "The Elroy Route."

Third—The ONLY line from Chicago to Fond du Lac, Green Bay, Escanaba, Negaunee, Marquette and L'Anse, by which the traveler can reach the shores of Lake Superior *by rail*.

Fourth—The only line from Chicago to Freeport, and, via Freeport, to Galena, Dunleith, Dubuque, and points West. This is one of the oldest and best lines in the West, and for many years was the only rail line by which the traveler from the Lakes could reach the Mississippi river.

Fifth—The only line from Chicago to Sparta, Winona, Rochester, St. Peter, New Ulm, Marshall, and Lake Kampeska, Dakota. This line is 623 miles long, and runs through Illinois, Wisconsin, Minnesota, and into Dakota.

Sixth—A line from Kenosha to Rockford, which is the only route through that part of the country.

Seventh—The old and popular route from Chicago to Milwaukee. This is the only line between these cities that runs along the Lake Shore, and offers to the traveler the benefit of the Lake views, and access to the many beautiful cities, towns and villages along its shores.

Eighth—A line from Clinton, Iowa, to Anamosa. This was formerly known as the Iowa Midland Railroad, and runs through the garden of Iowa.

Ninth—Numerous branches, which open up routes off the main line of travel.

As we get further along you will see that even these form but a proportion of the lines controlled by this great Company. Owning at this time over two thousand miles of railroad, it may readily be conjectured that the present Company were not the builders of the whole of it. This is true. The present line is the final result of a series of grand consolidations. Beginning, then, with the earlier built portion of the *original* Chicago & North-Western Railway, we find that on January 16th, 1836, the Galena & Chicago Union Railway Co. was incorporated by the State of Illinois, with power to construct a railroad from Chicago to Galena, and lateral lines as they might deem advisable, and to "*unite*" with any other railroad company already chartered or that might be chartered, and to build lines to connect with these lines or any other. In 1847 they began to build, and by January, 1850, had finished to Elgin, 42 miles. Under charters above named, and previous to 1854, the G. & C. U. Co. had built a branch line from Belvidere, Ill. to Beloit, on the border of Wisconsin, a distance of 21 miles, and in 1854, they leased the Beloit & Madison Railway, a line projected and partly built from Beloit towards Madison, 47 miles. In 1847, the officers of the G. & C. U. Co. visited Janesville, and other places in Wisconsin, soliciting aid to construct their projected lines, and incited by promises of co-operation, on August 19, 1848, an act was procured incorporating the Beloit & Madison Railway, *named above*, which was chartered to be built from Beloit, via Janesville, Madison and La Crosse, to a point on Mississippi river near St. Paul, and also from Janesville to Fond du Lac. February 9th, 1850, the name of the Madison & Beloit Railway Co. was changed to that of The Rock River Valley Union Railroad Company. The line from Janesville was not pushed by this Company, as the people had been led to believe it would be, and as a result of the dissatisfaction a charter was approved February 12, 1851, incorporating "The Illinois & Wisconsin Railroad Co.," with power to build a railroad from Chicago north to the Illinois State line, and to consolidate with any line in Wisconsin. March 10th, 1855, this last named line was by act of Legislature of Wisconsin consolidated with the Rock River Valley Union Railroad Co., and authorized to take such name for the new company as the Board of Directors might see fit. On March 30th, 1855, this consolidation was perfected, and the conscolidated company was named The Chicago, St. Paul & Fond du Lac Railroad Co. Here, then, we have the origin of the first portion of the present Wisconsin Division of Chicago & North-Western Railway.

"The object and desire of the Chicago, St. Paul & Fond du Lac Railroad Co. from the beginning, was the extension of their line from Janesville northwest via Madison and La Crosse to St. Paul, and from Janesville north along the valley of Rock river to Fond du Lac, and to the great iron and copper regions of Lake Superior." During the first four years of its existence, it succeeded in building a line (broad gauge, 6 feet) from Chicago to the Wisconsin State line at Sharon, and in the meantime The Rock River Valley Union Railroad Co. had built 30 miles of its road from Fond du Lac towards Minnesota (then La Crosse) Junction. The consolidated company proceeded as fast as possible to close up the gap between the two pieces of road, and completed it in 1859, thus forming a continuous line from Chicago via Janesville and Watertown to Fond du Lac, 176 miles. In June, 1856, by the almost unaided efforts of the Chicago, St. Paul & Fond du Lac Railroad, Congress was induced to make a grant of land to the State of Wisconsin, to aid in completing its lines of road. At an extra session of the Legislature of Wisconsin, held in September or October, 1856, a contest arose over this grant, and the result was the land upon the northwestern line was given to the La Crosse & Milwaukee Railroad Co., and the lands on the northern line were given to the Wisconsin & Lake Superior Railroad Co., a corporation that was chartered by this Legislature for the express purpose of giving it this land grant! The Chicago, St. Paul & Fond du Lac Railway was thus deprived of the grant of lands which had been obtained for the State of Wisconsin by its efforts! By Acts of February 12 and 28, 1857, the Wisconsin & Lake Superior Railway and the Chicago, St. Paul & Fond du Lac Railway Cos., were authorized to consolidate, and on March 5, 1857, the companies were consolidated under name of Chicago, St. Paul & Fond du Lac Railroad Co., and thus secured the land grant of six (6) sections (3,840 acres) per mile along its line in Wisconsin.

In 1857 came the great financial revulsion, which at once put a stop to further construction of this with many other lines of railway. In February, 1859, in Illinois, and in March, (and October), 1859, the Legislatures authorized reorganization of the company, and on June 6th a new company was organized, under the name of Chicago & North-Western Railway Co., to which was passed all the franchises and rights of the then defunct Chicago, St. Paul & Fond du Lac Railway Co. Here, then, is the real beginning of the present great corporation that is now known by the above name. On April 10, 1861, this Company was authorized to build a line from Fond du Lac via Fort Howard or Green Bay to the north line of Wisconsin, at the Menomonee river. During 1859 the road was completed to Oshkosh, (194 miles); in 1860 and '61 to Appleton, 20 miles further north; and in 1862 the line was extended to Fort Howard, (Green Bay), forming a line 242 miles long. In 1862-3, The Kenosha, Rockford & Rock River Railroad, running from Kenosha westwardly, was completed, 72 miles, to Rockford, on the Galena & Chicago Union Road, and to prevent its falling into unfriendly hands, it was purchased by the Chicago & North-Western Railway Co. in 1863, and operated as the Kenosha Division. To secure the business of the Upper Peninsula of Michigan, The Peninsula Railroad Co. was incorporated in 1861, and authorized to build a road from Escanaba on Little Bay Des Noquet, to Marquette, on Lake Superior. The company was organized in 1862, work commenced in 1863, and the road completed to the Jackson Mines, at the village of Negaunee, where it formed a junction with the Marquette, Houghton & Ontonagon Railroad, 12 miles from Marquette. In October, 1864, this line was consolidated with the Chicago & North-Western Railway, and was designated "The Peninsula Division."

A line of steamboats was established by the Green Bay Transit Company, to ply between Green Bay and Escanaba, and form the connection between the two pieces of railroad. This brings the history of the line down to the date of the Grand Consolidation that was effected between the Chicago & North-Western and Galena & Chicago Union Railways, and offers a chance to give the history of the last named of these roads.

THE LINE WESTWARD.

The Galena & Chicago Union Railroad Co. was incorporated January 16, 1836, and was provided with a "saving clause" in its charter, whereby the contemplated road *might* be made a "*good turnpike*" instead of a railroad!

Whether hesitating over *which* it should be, or simply waiting for the "Star of Empire," it exhibited no especial vitality for some time, and ten years after its organization, we find the Directors of the Company seriously discussing the policy of turning their attention *backward* from the wilds of Illinois, and first building their road *eastward* to meet the Michigan Central Road, which was then halting at New Buffalo. They however did decide to venture *westward*, and the first ten miles of road, Chicago to Harlem, was completed December 30, 1848, extended to Elgin, January 22, 1850, to Rockford, August 2, 1852, and to Freeport, September 1, 1853. At this point the superior advantages of T rail became apparent, and the "strap rail," with which the road had been built, was taken up, and the T iron rail put down. This again, with the further march of improvement, has given place to the *steel* rail, with which the line is now laid.

Before the completion of the road to the Fox river, the Chief Engineer placed on the records of the Company a prophetic "estimate," to the effect that when completed to that point, the resources of the country might furnish business sufficient for "two trains each way for two-thirds of the year, and one train each way for one-third of the year." That prophet (whose "eye is not dimmed") may now count more than 20 regular trains each way daily passing over this line. When the line to Freeport had been in operation about a year, the Company decided to seek a more direct line to the Mississippi, and acting upon this decision, the road from Turner Junction to the Mississippi river was completed to Dixon, December 4, 1854, extended to Sterling, July 22, 1855, to Morrison, September 23, 1855, and the Mississippi river, December 10, 1855.

FROM THE MISSISSIPPI WESTWARD.

The Chicago, Iowa & Nebraska Railroad Co. completed in 1858 a line from Clinton to Cedar Rapids, and leased it to the G. & C. U. Co., July 3, 1862. The Cedar Rapids & Mo. River Railroad Co. commenced the construction of a road from Cedar Rapids westward, of which the first 27 miles were completed in 1860, and extended from time to time, until having 40 miles completed, it also was leased to the G. & C. U. Co., July 8th, 1862. These Iowa roads, together with the roads built by the G. & C. Co., came under the management of the Chicago & North-Western Railway Co., by consolidation, June 2, 1864. The extension of the road through Iowa was continued and finally completed to the Missouri river March 15, 1867, ready to join the Union Pacific in its march toward the Pacific Ocean.

During the building of the Dixon Air Line, as the road was designated that ran from Junction, 30 miles west of Chicago, the G. & C. U. absorbed and consolidated with its other charters, that of the Mississippi & Rock River Junction Railroad Co., which company had been chartered by the State of Illinois, on February 15, 1851. The consolidation was effected January 9th, 1855. In 1854 the G. & C. U. Co. built a line from Belvidere to Beloit, as we have already stated in an earlier portion of this sketch, and in 1854 entered into an arrangement with the Beloit & Madison Railroad Co., which owned a line between these points. Some time prior to 1857, the G. & C. U. Co. became identified with the Fox River Valley Railroad, which was being built northwardly up the valley of Fox river, and towards the Wisconsin State Line. This road was finally reorganized, absorbed by the G. & C. U. Co., and its name changed to that of The Elgin & State Line Railroad. It was extended from Elgin to Richmond, near the north line of Illinois, and was 33 miles long. It now forms a portion of the Chicago & North-Western Railway line to Lake Geneva. About this time the G. & C. U. Co. bought the St. Charles & Mississippi Air Line Railway, of which only 9 miles, from Chicago to Harlem (now Oak Park) was ever built. This then brings down the history of the G. & C. U. Co. to the date of the grand consolidation.

In 1861 the directory of the Chicago & North-Western Railway was composed of—
W. B. Ogden, (Pres.), Geo. Smith, both of Chicago; Perry H. Smith, (Vice-Pres.), of

Appleton; M. C. Darling, of Fond du Lac; A. L. Prichard, of Watertown; J. J. R. Pease, of Janesville; W. A. Booth, Lowell Holbrook, David Dows, C. S. Seyton, H. H. Boody, and Austin Baldwin, of New York; and G. M. Bartholomew, of Hartford, Conn. It then owned 29 locomotives and 19 passenger cars, and its operating expenses for the year were only $258,657.74. In 1861-2-3, George L. Dunlap was Superintendent, C. S. Tappan, General Freight Agent, and E. De Witt Robinson, its General Ticket Agent. In 1861-2, its earnings were $849,719.27, and in 1862-3, $1,083,054.05.

The great iron bridge that connects the Iowa lines with those in Illinois, was begun in 1864. The Union Pacific Railway was also commenced at Omaha this year, and by June, 1865, 100 miles were completed. The Central Pacific Railroad was completed in 1864 from Sacramento to Clipper Gap, 44 miles, and 12 miles further by September 1, 1865. The total mileage of the roads owned by the G. & C. U. Co. at the time of the consolidation was as follows: Chicago to Freeport, 121 miles; Chicago to Dixon, 138 miles; Beloit Branch, 21 miles; St. Charles & Mississippi Air Line, 9 miles; Elgin to Richmond, and a short line at Elgin, 35 miles. Total, 324 miles, of which 30 miles, Chicago to Turner Junction, (now Junction) was really double track. Its leased lines completed were Clinton, Ia. to Cedar Rapids, 82 miles, (Chicago, Iowa & Nebraska Railroad); Cedar Rapids to Nevada, 122 miles, (Cedar Rapids & Missouri River Railroad); and Beloit to Madison, 47 miles, (Beloit & Madison Railroad.) Total leased lines then finished, 251 miles.

THE CONSOLIDATION.

"The long-continued, unwise and injurious competition which existed between the Galena & Chicago Union Railroad and Chicago & North-Western Railway Companies, at their several points of contact, and which seemed to be chronic and not likely to terminate, and which induced the companies to give much of their time and attention to the control or construction of inferior, rival and illegitimate lines, naturally gave rise to proposals for the consolidation of these lines, as the only certain and permanent remedy for loss of earnings and increase of expenses, resulting from the senseless, but apparently unavoidable, competition which existed." The stockholders consented to the consolidation, and on June 2, 1864, it was virtually effected and carried out; and on February 15, 1865, was approved and ratified by legislative enactments, and the new corporation was named The Chicago & North-Western Railway Co. From this time (October, 1865,) forward, we have to deal with the history of but one company.

About this time the Directory of the Company, to secure its interests, and prevent its falling into hostile hands, found that it was essential to obtain control of a line from Chicago to Milwaukee, and The Chicago & Milwaukee Railroad was secured. This line, connecting the cities of Chicago and Milwaukee, was commenced at each end at about the same time, but under two corporations—The Chicago & Milwaukee Railroad Co., incorporated February 17, 1851, building the line from Chicago to the State Line, 45 miles; and the Milwaukee & Chicago Railroad Co., incorporated March 12, 1851, building the line from Milwaukee to State Line, 40 miles. Both lines were completed in 1855, and run in connection until June 5, 1863, when they were consolidated, under the name of The Chicago & Milwaukee Railroad Co., and which came under the management of the Chicago & North-Western Railway Co., by perpetual lease, May 2, 1866. M. L. Sykes, Jun., now joined the Chicago & North-Western Railway. This year found C. S. Tappan, General Freight Agent, and B. F. Patrick, General Ticket Agent.

In 1866 the Company bought out the Green Bay Transit Company, and placed two new boats on the bay to make connection between Green Bay and Escanaba.

The Union Pacific Railroad had, up to 15th May, 1865, completed 425 miles of their road. In 1866, the northern end of the present Kansas City, St. Joseph & Council Bluffs Railroad was completed from a point 45 miles south of Council Bluffs, and connections made with the Chicago & North-Western Railway at Council Bluffs. The Sioux City branch of Union Pacific—as the present Sioux City & Pacific Railroad was then called—was commenced this year. At the close of the eighth fiscal year of Chicago & North-Western Railway, it had under its control, by absolute ownership or perpetual lease, 1,152.4 miles.

In October, 1867, this Company bought of D. N. Barney & Co. their interest in the Winona and St. Peter Railway—a line being built westwardly from Winona, Minn., and of which 105 miles were built. It also bought of the same parties their interest in the La Crosse, Trempealeau & Prescott Railway—a line being built from Winona Junction, three miles east of La Crosse, Wis., to Winona, Minn. The Omaha & California line (Galena & Iowa Division), was opened to Missouri river, opposite Omaha, in April, 1867. The ninth fiscal year closed with the Company having 1,349.7 miles of iron.* The tenth fiscal year of the Company found J. C. Gault, General Freight Agent and Assistant General Superintendent, with H. P. Stanwood as General Ticket Agent. Henry Keep, Esq., the President of the Company, died August, 1869. Since the last report was printed (1868) the Pacific roads were completed, and the Chicago, Rock Island & Pacific Railway finished to Council Bluffs; the Sioux City & Pacific was also completed, and connection formed with it at St. John's (now Missouri Valley). Total length of road, 1,156 miles. Miles of iron, including side tracks, 1,367.7. With the 11th fiscal report, (May 31, 1870), we find J. F. Tracy, President; J. C. Gault, General Superintendent, and C. C. Wheeler, General Freight Agent. That year, (1869-70), the Burlington & Missouri River Railway of Iowa was finished to Council Bluffs, and the Winona & St. Peter was completed to Janesville, Minn., making 121 miles finished from Winona. The La Crosse, Trempealeau & Prescott Railroad was also finished this year. Total mileage of finished line, 1,186. With the 12th year, (May 31, 1871), we have J. H. Howe, General Manager, and J. C. Gault, General Superintendent. In this term the Company obtained control of the charter of the Baraboo Air Line Railroad—a line projected northward from Madison, Wis.; and after consolidating it with their Beloit & Madison R. R., and these both with the Chicago & North-Western Railway, which began the work, rapidly pushed the line from Madison towards Winona Junction, 126 miles. The bridge across the Mississippi river at Winona was commenced. The Winona and St. Peter line was completed to St. Peter, 140 miles from Winona; and a charter procured for the Winona, Mankato & New Ulm Railroad, under which the Winona & St. Peter Railroad Co. built a line into Mankato, 8½ miles. On the Galena Division, from Geneva, Ill., to St. Charles, Ill., the Chicago & North-Western Railway built a line, 2½ miles long. Some years before this, The Iowa Central Railroad Company was incorporated to build a line westward from Lyons, Iowa. The Iowa Midland Railway Company absorbed this line, and this year it was taken into the Chicago & North-Western Railway combination, with 85 miles of rail laid, and 75 miles of track graded. Many years before, a strap rail line had been operated north of, and in connection with, the Elgin & State Line Railway; a new charter was now procured, under which The State Line & Union Railway Co. was authorized to build a line from the Northern line of Illinois, 10 miles, to Lake Geneva, Wis. The line was finished, and operated from this year.

It will be remembered that at Green Bay the old Chicago & North-Western line terminated. This year it was arranged to build the Menomonee extension, and close the gap between Green Bay and Escanaba—some 120 miles—in the year. Fifty-two

* This included side track.

miles were put under contract and rapidly built. The new line from Madison north was opened to Lodi this year. Total mileage of road reported, 1,223.8. With the report of the 13th fiscal year, (May 31, 1872), we have Albert Keep, President; Marvin Hughitt, General Superintendent; and W. A. Thrall, General Ticket Agent. During this year the Winona & St. Peter line was finished, and (in February, 1872,) opened to New Ulm, Minn. The Iowa Midland was finished to Anamosa in October, 1871. The Madison Division was opened to Reedsburg. According to the report of the 14th fiscal year, W. H. Stennett was General Passenger Agent; and this year 64.6 miles of line between Menomonee and Escanaba; 43.6 miles of Madison extension; 8¼ miles of Stanwood & Tipton Railroad (a side line from Stanwood, on Iowa Division, to Tipton); 3 miles Batavia, Ill., Branch, (from Geneva to Batavia); and 5 miles of track connecting the Wisconsin and Galena Divisions in Chicago, were built and operated. The line from Fort Howard (Green Bay) to Escanaba was opened in December, 1872. The steamers on Green Bay were disposed of, and through trains run from Chicago to Negaunee. February 25, 1871, a line from Milwaukee northerly to Fond du Lac was incorporated, under the name of The North-Western Union Railway Co. The road was commenced in 1872, and in 1873 completed, and operated by Chicago & North-Western Railway Co. The length of line is 63 miles; it connects the Milwaukee with the Wisconsin Division, and shortens the distance between Chicago and Fond du Lac some 29 miles.

The West Wisconsin Railroad—a line running from Elroy to Hudson, and thence to St. Paul—was completed, and arrangements made by which the Chicago & North-Western Railway were enabled to compete for business to St. Paul and beyond. This new through line is known as The Chicago, Madison & St. Paul Line. This year 240 acres of land, five miles west of Wells street depot in Chicago, were bought, for the purpose of building thereon the machine and car shops of the Company. Total mileage reported this year, 1,849. With the report of the 15th fiscal year (May, 1874), H. H. Porter is named as General Manager. The Madison extension was completed to Winona Junction, where it formed connection with the La Crosse, Trempealeau & Prescott Railroad, and perfected the line from Chicago to Winona. The Winona and St. Peter Railway was completed to Lake Kampeska, 623 miles from Chicago, and opened, with an excursion, on September 17, 1873. The North-Western Union line was finished between Milwaukee and Fond du Lac, and opened on September 7, 1873. Total miles reported in operation, 1,992. In Illinois, 489; Iowa, 434; Wisconsin, 566; Michigan, 171; Minnesota, 293, and Dakota, 39. The general office building, in size, 60 x 200 feet, on Kinzie, between Market and Franklin Streets, Chicago, was built this year, and the new shops at Chicago commenced. With the end of the 16th fiscal year (May 31, 1875), and the beginning of the 17th year, the Company had 369 locomotives, 178 passenger cars, 28 Pullman drawing room sleepers, 4 parlor chair day coaches, and 9,146 freight and other cars. In the year that had then closed, its passenger trains had run 2,491,956 miles, and its freight trains 6,542,550 miles.

We have thus brought the history of the line down to the present day, and have shown how it has grown to its present enormous proportions. Thus, then, we have answered the queries—"Where is it, and What is it?" The other questions are more difficult of solution, but solved they can be—What can it do for you?

THE OMAHA & CALIFORNIA LINE.

The portions of the Company's lines that are used in a trip from Chicago to Omaha, are the Galena & Iowa Divisions, the building of which we have before referred to. The cities, towns and villages along this line will be described hereafter. By glancing at our map it will be seen that this route passes through the counties of Cook, DuPage, Kane, DeKalb, Ogle, Lee and Whiteside, in Illinois, and Clinton, Cedar, Linn, Benton, Tama, Marshall, Story, Boone, Green, Carroll, Crawford, Shelby, Harrison and Pottawatomie, in Iowa—counties that for productiveness of soil and general fertility, cannot be surpassed *anywhere*. Following closely along the forty-second degree of latitude, this line is far enough south to escape the rigors of a real northern winter, with its accompanying deep snows, and is yet far enough north to escape the scorching and blistering suns of July and August, that burn and brown the counties further south. To the person seeking a home in the settled part of the West, these counties offer vast inducements, good land, good water, plenty of timber, and a health-giving climate. Except on the western end of this route, the land is mostly all settled, and is well improved, hence is held at rates much higher than is asked for the wild lands of the farther West. West of Boone county, Iowa, the Iowa Railroad Land Company own large bodies of very fine land that they sell at prices ranging from $5 to $15 per acre. The Chicago & North-Western Railway Co. has not any lands for sale in Illinois, nor in Iowa.

This line forms junctions with other railroads in Illinois as follows: At Junction, with branch of Chicago, Burlington & Quincy; at Cortland, with Cortland & Sycamore; at Rochelle, with Chicago & Iowa; at Dixon, with Illinois Central; at Sterling, with Rockford & St. Louis; and at Fulton, with Western Union. In Iowa the junctions are at Clinton, with Chicago, Clinton & Dubuque; at De Witt and Wheatland, with the Davenport & St. Paul; at Stanwood, with Stanwood & Tipton; at Cedar Rapids, with Dubuque Southwestern, and Burlington, Cedar Rapids & Minnesota; at Tama, with Toledo & North-Western; at Marshalltown, with Central Railroad of Iowa; at Ames, with Des Moines & Minnesota; at Grand Junction, with Des Moines & Fort Dodge; at Missouri Valley, with Sioux City & Pacific; at Council Bluffs, with Kansas City, St. Joe and Council Bluffs; and at Omaha, with the Union Pacific, the Burlington & Missouri River, and the Omaha & North-Western. These numerous connecting lines give to this great route facilities for reaching all parts of the country north, south and west of its own line. With all of these lines friendly relations exist, and over them we daily send and receive both passengers and freight. From our ticketing stations, and from all prominent ticket agencies in all parts of the country, through coupon tickets over our line and via the junctions above named, can be procured to nearly all the stations on the roads above named. It may not be unprofitable to say here that if you are going to Galena, Dubuque, Prairie du Chien, La Crosse, Waterloo, Austin, Mason City, Des Moines, Ackley, Fort Dodge, Sioux City, Yankton, Blair or Wisner, your interests will be best served by using this line of The Chicago & North-Western Railway. If Council Bluffs or Omaha is your destination, you should certainly choose this route, as it is the *shortest* and hence the quickest, and is by all odds the most pleasant, as far as the country it passes through, or as to its equipment of cars, coaches, Pullman Drawing-room Sleepers, (*and here we will say that this is the only line running Pullman Drawing-room cars in which ladies and children can be isolated and free from the annoyance of having other passengers in the same compartment between Chicago and Omaha.* This is an important fact to be remembered by those who desire drawing rooms in sleeping cars.) This line is of steel rail, was the first to reach Council Bluffs and Omaha from Chicago, and the first to contract passengers and freight from the Atlantic to the Pacific Ocean. Lincoln, Neb., Cheyenne, Wy., Denver, Col., Salt Lake City, Utah, Carson and Virginia City, Nev., Sacramento, The Yo Semite, The Geysers, The Big Tree Groves, San Francisco, Cal., Portland, Ore., and all points on the Pacific Coast, as well as the ports of the Pacific, such as Yokohama and Nagasaki, in Japan, Hong

Kong and Shanghai, in China, Melbourne, Adelaide and Sidney, in Australia, and Auckland, in New Zealand, are all reached by passing over this line, and in all these places this Company sustains some form of agency, at which the public can always get full and reliable information, by simply applying for it. No preconceived notions, the stories of pretended travelers, or the paid emissaries of hostile lines, should be allowed to divert your attention from this line if you propose to travel between the East and the West.

At our Pacific Coast Agency, 121 Montgomery Street, San Francisco, Cal., at all times can be found gentlemen in the employ of this Company who are fully competent and willing to render Trans-Continental travelers any assistance or information they may desire. At our General Eastern Agency, 415 Broadway, New York City, and at our New England Agency, 5 State Street, Boston, Mass., as well as at all the leading Ticket Agencies in the East and West, full and reliable information can be procured by simply asking for it.

ON THE ROUTE WESTWARD.

VIA THE GALENA DIVISION.

Leaving Chicago, from the Wells Street depot of The Chicago & North-Western Railway, and running through Cook and Du Page counties, and almost to the east line of Kane county, to Junction, (Turner Junction), you pass through a succession of towns and villages that are not improperly called suburban to Chicago, for the larger proportion of their citizens are engaged in business in Chicago, while having their homes at these stations. To all of them "Commutation" tickets are sold, and suburban trains are run almost hourly each day. Below will be found the rates of fare charged (April 15, 1876) to these points, and to a few points beyond that are also reached by suburban trains:

Distances from Chicago.	BETWEEN CHICAGO AND	Single Ticket.	10 Ride Ticket, unlimited.	50 Rides, Family Ticket, good for 3 Months.	100 Rides, Individual Ticket.	Number Months 100 Ride Tickets are good.	Annual Ticket.	First Half-Yearly Ticket.	Second Half-Yearly Ticket.
4.6	West 40th Street	.15	1.20	2.80	6.50	3	38.00	23.00	18.00
5.6	West 48th Street	.20	1.50	3.40	7.20	3	42.00	25.00	20.00
6.7	Austin	.25	1.80	4.00	7.20	3	48.00	29.00	22.00
7.7	Ridgeland	.28	2.05	4.60	9.30	3	55.00	33.00	25.00
8.6	Oak Park	.30	2.30	5.20	11.00	3	60.00	36.00	27.00
9.8	River Forest	.35	2.60	5.90	12.50	4	65.00	39.00	29.00
10.4	Maywood	.38	2.75	6.30	13.00	4	68.00	41.00	31.00
11.4	Melrose	.40	3.05	6.85	14.25	4	71.50	42.50	32.50
15.8	Elmhurst	.55	4.20	9.50	18.00	4	75.00	45.00	31.50
20.0	Lombard	.70	5.30	12.00	21.50	4	80.00	48.00	36.00
22.5	Prospect Park	.80	5.95	13.50	23.50	4	85.00	51.00	38.00
24.9	Wheaton	.85	6.60	15.00	24.80	4	90.00	54.00	41.00
27.5	Winfield	.95	7.30	16.50	27.50	4	95.00	57.00	43.00
30.0	Junction	1.05	7.95	18.00	30.00	4	100.00	60.00	45.00
35.5	Geneva	1.25	9.40	21.30	35.50	5	110.00	66.00	50.00
38.0	St. Charles	1.25	9.40	21.30	35.50	5	110.00	66.00	50.00
38.0	Batavia	1.30	9.40	21.30	35.30	5	110.00	66.00	50.00
35.3	Wayne	1.15	9.35	21.20	34.00	5			
39.2	Clintonville	1.20	9.80	21.50	34.50	5			
42.5	Elgin	1.25	9.85	21.60	35.00	6			
47.5	Dundee	1.45	11.75	25.50	42.50	6			
52.8	Algonquin	1.60	13.23	30.00	50.00	6			

In many of these points more or less manufacturing is carried on, but in the larger part of them very little business is done, and they may be called residence towns.

After leaving the last "city" station you reach

Austin, 7 miles from Chicago, pop. 1,500.

Ridgeland, 8 miles from Chicago, pop. 200.

Oak Park, 9 miles from Chicago, pop. 3.000.

River Forest, 8 miles from Chicago; a new "suburban" station.

Maywood, 10 miles from Chicago. A pleasant village of 1,000 people on the Desplaines river. The town is located on ground 30 feet above the river, and 70 feet above Lake Michigan. It was laid out in 1869, and now has over 300 residences in it. It has a good hotel, four public schools, five churches, and a fine public hall, in which are held the meetings of the Maywood Library Association. No spirituous liquors are allowed to be sold in or within one mile of the town. A fine rock road runs through the village and to Chicago.

Melrose, 11 miles from Chicago, is a new station.

Elmhurst, 16 miles from Chicago. This place was until recently called Cottage Hill, and in the old "stage days" was a station on the route to the Galena Lead Mines, and to the Mississippi river. It stands on high rolling prairie, 106 feet above Lake Michigan, and is one of the best and easiest drained towns near Chicago, thus having secured to it for all time one of the most important elements conducive of public health. It has several good public graded schools, and some well conducted and prosperous private schools. The Evangelical Lutheran Church has a college under the presidency of the Rev. P. F. Mensch located here. It has three churches. Its streets and avenues are well graded, and range in width from 80 to 100 feet. Population about 750. *Addison*, a town of 500 people, and the seat of a Lutheran College having 200 students, is 3 miles north, and is tributary to and reached by stage daily from Elmhurst.

Lombard, 20 miles from Chicago, is a pretty village of 500 people. It has one public school, one church, and a public hall that cost $2,000.

Prospect Park, 23 miles from Chicago, is eminently a suburban town. It has one public (High) school, and one hotel kept by John Groof, and at $1.50 per day or $4 per week, can accommodate 100 guests. Population about 500.

Wheaton, 24 miles from Chicago. A thriving village of 1,500 people, (county seat of Du Page county, county organized 1839, population 19,000) situated on high rolling prairie, surrounded by a fine farming and grazing country. It has 7 churches, a good graded school, and the court house and other county buildings. It is the seat of Wheaton College, which stands on elevated ground on the north side of the railroad, has 200 students, is in a flourishing condition, and amongst the educational institutions of the West, holds no second place.

Winfield, 28 miles from Chicago—formerly called Fredericksburg—is a thrifty suburban village of 400 people. It is growing, and is in every way a desirable home for the tired business man.

Junction, 30 miles from Chicago, and at the west end of the double track of the Galena Division. The corporate name of the village and the official name of the Post Office is *Turner*, named for J. B. Turner, who laid out the first town plat in 1856. It has a population of 1,500, four churches, one good public school, occupying a brick house that cost $25,000, and three hotels—The Junction House, The Turner House, and the Railroad House, charging $2 per day for very excellent accommodations. This line of railroad reached "The Junction" in 1849, and for months thereafter the farmers of this part of Du Page county were prophesying that the road must become bankrupt, for "it can never compete with Frink & Walker's line of stages. It will take but a few months to demonstrate that the scheme must fail." So they argued and so they believed.

From this point "The Freeport Line" and "The Fox River Branch" of the C. & N.-W. Ry. diverge northwardly, and from here is a short line of railroad that runs southwardly to Aurora. At Junction the C. & N.-W. Ry. Co. has a repair shop and a mill for re-rolling and repairing iron and steel rails.

Geneva, 36 miles from Chicago. We have now passed out of Du Page and into Kane county. This county was first settled by Col. N. Lyon, in June, 1833, while the Pottawatomie Indians still held possession of the land, (they were removed in 1835 by Capt. C. B. Dodson), and the Colonel is still a citizen of the county. The county was organized in 1836; the first church and Sunday school started, (at Batavia), and the first post office established (at Harrington's Ford, now La Fox) in 1835. The first court in this county was held in a log house (also used as church and school house for years) on the bank of Fox river, in the homestead of the Harrington family, who are still residing there, and are amongst the leading and most respected citizens of the county. The present population of the county is not far from 50,000. Geneva, the county seat, is built on terraces on both sides of Fox river, which is well stocked with black bass, pickerel, pike, sun, and other fish.* It has over 2,000 population, seven churches, a school house built of cut stone, costing $25,000, and accommodating 500 pupils; two flour mills, one machine shop, employing over 100 men; jute, cheese and butter factories, and some other manufacturing interests. Its best hotel is The Union House, which can accommodate 100 guests at $2 per day. Its public hall will seat 500 persons, and its court house, which is of brick, and was built in 1856, cost $60,000.

The surrounding country is rolling, and is about equally divided between "prairie" and "timber." The county affords fine shooting in season. Prairie chickens, quail, woodcock, partridge, and other game abound.* *Nelson's Lake, Johnson's Mound*, and *Harrington's Island* are popular resorts from 1 to 7 miles from the village.

St. Charles, 38 miles from Chicago. While *not* directly on the Omaha and California Line of this road, it is so near, and the branch line reaching it

---

*In giving the names of birds and fishes that are found along this line, we would explain that the names given are "local," and are not scientifically correct. For instance, the text may say "partridge," "pheasant," and "grouse," while the birds are really quail, ruffled and pinnated grouse. The "local" names are those given by our agents, or by hunters and fishermen of the vicinity.

is so short, that we give its description, as we do that of Batavia, which is similarly situated in connection with the route now under advisement. From Geneva two short lines of road are owned by this Company; the one runs from Geneva north 2¼ miles to St. Charles, and the other runs south 2 miles to Batavia. They are operated as the Batavia and St. Charles Branches. St. Charles, with a population of over 3,000, is situate on both sides of Fox river and is picturesquely located on the gently rising banks or bluffs of the stream. It has two good schools, with 200 students; six churches; a paper mill, manufacturing 1,500,000 lbs. yearly; a cheese factory, making 600,000 lbs. yearly; a foundry, employing 60 men, and several flour mills. The Malory House is kept by D. B. Malory, who charges $1.50 per day. The town was first settled in 1833, and the first newspaper published in Kane county (The Patriot), was started here in 1841. This is the home of Hon. John F. Farnsworth, one of Illinois' best known congressmen.

Batavia, 39 miles from Chicago. (See St. Charles for railroad connection.) This village has over 4,000 population; is located on both sides of Fox river, which is here spanned by several fine bridges. The bluffs or banks of the river are of limestone, and rise above the water from 30 to 50 feet; they furnish very excellent building stone, which is largely used, and in the quarrying of which from 300 to 400 men find constant employment. In the village are many good schools and ten churches. The Ellis House, by ——, and The Revere, by C. E. Smith, at $2 per day, furnish ample and good hotel accommodations. Here is located the United States Windmill Co., employing 100 men, and manufacturing Halladay's windmills and iron pumps, to the value of $250,000 yearly; the Challenge Mill Co., making Nicholls' windmills and 1 Burr's patent feed grinder; the Newton Wagon Co., employing 100 men, and making 1,400 farm and 300 road wagons yearly; the D. K. Sperry & Co. Manufacturing Co., employing 60 men, and making stoves, caldrons, feed boilers, etc., to the value of $100,000 yearly. Osgood & Shumway employ here 30 men in making mill castings and the iron work for school furniture.

La Fox, 41 miles from Chicago, a village of 150 people, is situated on a well-watered, productive, rolling prairie, and in the midst of a fine dairy county. It has a cheese factory, turning out 100,000 lbs. yearly. The cheese from this factory finds a market west of the Missouri river.

Blackberry, 44 miles from Chicago, is on Fox river, and has a population of 400. Is on ground so high, that Batavia, St. Charles, Geneva, and many other villages and a large expanse of country can be seen from its streets. This village is also in the "Dairy County" of the Fox river valley, and is noted for its cheese and butter. It has a good hotel, The Hurd House, by J. O. Hurd, who can accommodate 40 guests, at $1.50 per day; one good graded public school, four churches, and one flour mill. *Kaneville*, 6 miles distant, is tributary to this station, and is reached daily by B. Cary's stage line. Fare, 50 cents.

Lodi, 51 miles from Chicago; has population of 500; has one school and four churches. The first justice of the peace in Kane county lived and still lives here.

Cortland, 55 miles from Chicago. This village is in De Kalb county, 4½ miles from Sycamore, the county seat, which is reached from Cortland by the Cortland & Sycamore Railway, a railway line owned by the enterprising citizens of Sycamore. (See Sycamore.) Cortland is on a high, rolling prairie, has 900 population, one graded school, one church, one flour mill, run by steam, and one hotel, kept by B. B. Parkhurst, who charges $2 per day.

Sycamore, 59½ miles from Chicago, is, by rail, reached only via Cortland. Sycamore is located upon an elevated prairie, near the Kishwaukee river, and is the county seat of De Kalb county, Illinois. Laid out and platted in 1839; chartered as a village in 1857; obtained a city charter from the Legislature in April, 1869. Population, 4,000. Distant from Chicago 59½ miles, and the northern terminus of the SYCAMORE, CORTLAND & CHICAGO RAILROAD. The streets are wide, laid out at right angles, and lined with forest and evergreen trees upon either side, giving the city an appearance of a forest. No pains have been spared to beautify the grounds and yards of private residences with evergreens and other ornamental shrubbery. The business portion of the city is compact. The city graded school house is one of the finest in the northern part of the State, capable of seating 800 scholars. The court house is located in the centre of the public park, containing about four acres, beautifully laid out and ornamented with forest maples and elms. The city is becoming quite a manufacturing centre—the Marsh harvester shop employing 300 workmen; the R. Ellwood Manufacturing Co. have just completed their shop, and are working 125 men, making the R. Ellwood combined riding and walking corn cultivator; its force will be greatly increased the coming season. A large and extensive planing mill, was erected the past season. In the city is a flax mill, making from two to three tons of tow per day; an extensive cheese factory; the Winn Hotel, (built the past season), a large, four-story brick building, complete in all its apartments; eight fine churches, four weekly newspapers, two monthly publications, one flour mill, one national and two private banks, one public hall, three grain elevators, and an improved system of water works, operated by steam. The surrounding country is a beautiful prairie, surpassed for richness of soil and adaptation to farming purposes by no section of the State, being upon an elevated ridge, midway between the Rock and Fox rivers. The city is noted for its steady growth and wealth, the energy of its business men, the vast amount of business done, and its general thrift and prosperity. The SYCAMORE, CORTLAND & CHICAGO RAILROAD has running arrangements in connection with the Chicago & North-Western Railway Co., connecting at Cortland Station.

De Kalb, 58 miles from Chicago, pop. 2,000, is located in the centre of a large prairie, and is an active, go-ahead town, enjoying a large trade with the surrounding country, which is settled by wealthy farmers. The town has cheese factories, two "Barbed Wire Fence" factories, employing over 200 men, (this barbed wire fence is "something new under the sun," and consists of wire twisted together and guarded by pointed wire prongs or "barbs" that serve as protection from injury by cattle), five churches, one public school, and two hotels—The Central House, by S. D. Burt, and The Eagle, by F. Scripton.

Malta, 64 miles from Chicago. It has a population of 600, one school house that cost $5,000, three churches, and The Scofield House, a very fair hotel, by William Scofield.

Creston, 70 miles from Chicago. We now pass into Ogle county. The village was formerly called *Dement,* after Col. John Dement, one of the oldest settlers of Northern Illinois. It has a school house that cost in 1869, $10,000, two churches, two grain elevators, one newspaper, The Times, edited by H. C. Robbins, and two hotels. The village was laid out in 1857, and was incorporated in 1867. The first settler in this part of the county was Thomas Smith, (Uncle Tommy), who for years was station agent, postmaster, justice of the peace, and hotel-keeper. The present station agent has held his place for 17 years. Population, 600.

Rochelle, 75 miles from Chicago. This town is in Ogle county, 15 miles from Oregon, its county seat, which is reached by the CHICAGO & IOWA R'Y, a line that runs from Rochelle to Forreston. Ogle county was organized in 1836; at its first election in 1837, only 190 votes were cast. The first wedding in the county was in 1833; the first birth in 1834; the first school opened and the first wheat grown in 1834; the first post office established in 1835, and the first mill built in 1836. Population, 28,000. Rochelle (formerly *Lane,* named after Dr. Lane of Rockford) was first settled in 1853. Population, about 2,000. It has wide, well graded and paved streets, many fine business blocks, six churches, several good schools, one occupying a building that cost $40,000, and that accommodates 300 pupils. Considerable manufacturing is carried on. Coal is plenty and cheap. Its hotels are The Rochelle House, by D. J. Davis, and The Simpson, by A. Simpson. The CHICAGO & IOWA R'Y runs nearly northwest from Rochelle, and offers its merchants facilities for controlling the business of the county east of the ILLINOIS CENTRAL LINE. It is probably needless to say that to reach Rochelle you should travel via the Chicago & North-Western Railway.

Flagg, 79 miles from Chicago, is an unimportant station ¼ of a mile from Kite river, that offers fair fishing. On its banks quail and prairie chicken are found in large numbers. Flagg has one grain elevator.

Ashton, 84 miles from Chicago. Crossing the county line we find this station in Lee county. This part of the county was the scene of many thrilling and interesting incidents connected with the "Black Hawk War," and here *Nada-chusa-sed,* as the Winnebago Indians called Col. John Dixon, acted the part of the friend and protector to Indian and white man many years before the city that now bears his name was thought of. In this vicinity are six large stone quarries, from which much fine building stone is being constantly shipped. The village has a population of 900, and has one good school, three churches, thirty-six business houses, and two hotels—The American House, kept by W. B. Welton, and The Ashton House, by E. H. Stoddart, each accommodating 75 guests at $1.50 per day.

Franklin, 88 miles from Chicago. This station is located in one of the most fertile portions of Lee county. Originally a naked prairie, it is now dotted all over with groves and belts of timber so that hardly a farm can be found that is not well supplied with wood grown on the ground. When first settled the only timber near was the grove from which the station takes its name. The village has 900 people, one school with four teachers, three churches, one flour mill, and a manufactory of agricultural implements making a specialty of Emmert's seed drills. A. R. Whitney's mammoth fruit tree nursery and cider wine manufactory adjoin the village. The hotels are The Hughes House, by J. Hughes, 30 rooms, and The Franklin House, by Gideon Williams, 18 rooms, at $1 per day. *Lee Center,* 6 miles south, and *Taylor,* 6 miles north, are villages tributary to Franklin.

Nachusa, 93 miles from Chicago. This village was named after one of the Indian names used to designate Col. John Dixon, (the word Nachusa meaning "White Head"), who was the first white settler in the county. The population of this village numbers about 300. Grape vines are largely cultivated in this vicinity. Col. Dysart (late of the 34th Illinois Infantry of the "War of the Rebellion") cultivates over 60 acres within half a mile of the station. *White Rock,* a popular picnic and fishing resort, is 4 miles north, and is much frequented by parties from all portions of the State. The rock is a noted landmark, rising as it does 60 feet above the surface of the water of Rock river, and above the surrounding prairie.

Dixon, 98 miles from Chicago. Dixon is the county seat of Lee county. This county was organized in 1839, has 22 townships, and a population of over 32,000 souls. Col. John Dixon, who yet lives (aged 91 years) in the suburbs of the city that was named after him, was the first white settler, coming here in 1830, when the Indians held all this fertile valley. Col. Dixon found Ogee, a half-breed, occupying a log cabin on the river's bank at a point afterwards known as Dixon's Ferry, and now known as the city of Dixon. Buying this cabin, Col. Dixon made it his home, and here he brought his wife in 1831. She was the first white woman who saw the Rock River Valley. The first house in the county was built in 1832. In 1835 a town was surveyed at Dixon's Ferry. In 1837 the county contained 18 families. In 1845 the river was dammed, and active milling operations began. Since that time the city of Dixon, with its 6,000 people, and the county adjoining, shows what changes have taken place. Of all the counties in Illinois, few equal Lee in productiveness of soil, and none surpass it in beauty of surface and healthfulness of climate. This western Eden, in the northern portion of the Rock River Valley, has lost none of those attractions which famous writers have so beautifully delineated in both prose and poetry. Forty years, it is true, have worked wonderful changes. Then it had been said that the country bore the character of one that had been inhabited by a people skilled in all the ornamental arts of landscape gardening. Villages, castles, and inclosures only were wanting; everywhere were lawns, flowers and gardens, and stately parks, as if they had been scattered by the hand of art at equal intervals, with frequent deer and peaceful cattle, yet all more suggestive of man than of nature. These lovely features still remain, and the herd have multiplied a thousand-fold. The villages have sprung up as it were in a day. The inclosures have been built, the stately thickets have grown to luxuriant forests, and what was then a paradise to the eye has become the fruitful garden of the world. Only a few years have passed since "Black Hawk" made these beautiful regions romantic with memories of Indian warfare, and gave to the "Rock River Valley" associations like those of "the dark and bloody ground" of Kentucky. But these events have almost passed out of recollection, and the traveler as he whirls over the country in a palatial car, is no longer pointed to the spot where the red man last struggled against the white usurper for the home of his fathers.

The city of Dixon is built on both sides of Rock river, which is here crossed by two handsome bridges. Its fine water power is utilized by many large manufacturing interests, amongst which may be named a sash, blind and door factory employing 12 men, Dixon city mills with 4 men, foundry and machine shops with 16 men, Bennett, Thompson & Funk's mill with 12 men, Baker & Underwood 42 men, a flax and bagging factory 80 men, The Grand De Tour Plow Works 70 men, Vann & Mean's carriage factory, 15 men, Adams & Davis 20 men, a woolen mill 10 men, a wind mill and pump shop 12 men, and Orvis & Co. plow works 75 men. Over $600,000 are here invested in manufacturing establishments, operating over 500 men, and paying out in wages over $20,000 monthly. Yet with all of these factories in active operation, less than one-sixth of the water power is used. Large quantities of lime of a superior quality is made here. The city is well supplied with hotels, of which the following are the best—The Nachusa House, by Major Cheney, for 150 guests; The Railroad House, by Person Cheney, with rooms for 100 guests, and a dining room that can seat 300 passengers at the dining tables that are so largely patronized by the through passengers of the great California route, at least two through trains dining here daily; The City Hotel, by Ludwig Baker; The Washington, by M. Remers; and The Revere by Mr. Huntley. In the city are seven churches, two national banks, three public halls, the city and county building, ample gas works, an active and efficient fire department, three newspapers, three large and fine school buildings and several smaller ones, and the Rock River University, a popular and growing college, with a full corps of thoroughly educated professors. The business portion of the city is built on the sides of hills sloping towards the river, with the residence portion on the higher hills beyond. It is one of the most sightly and enterprising cities in the West, and bids fair to attain very large proportions. Col. John Dement, who made a national reputation in the "Black Hawk War," still has his home here.

In the vicinity of Dixon are many attractive resorts and much picturesque scenery, a portion of which we illustrate. A small steamer runs between Dixon and *Grand De Tour*, 12 miles, and passes *en route* many islands and picturesque points of interest. Visitors to Dixon will be amply paid by taking a trip on the river and spending several days in its vicinity. The river provides ample fishing grounds, and the fisherman will be abundantly repaid by angling in its waters. Game abounds, the golden plover, upland plover, the

Dixon, Ill.—On the Rock River.

English, or jack snipe and woodcock being especially plentiful.

At Dixon we cross the Northern Division of the ILLINOIS CENTRAL RAILROAD, and by this road passengers can reach *Polo, Forreston, Lena, Nora, Warren, Galena* and *Dubuque* and *Mineral Point, Calamine* and *Plattville* north, as well as *Amboy, La Salle, Wenona, Minonk, El Paso, Normal, Bloomington*, and other points south. For other connections, via ILLINOIS CENTRAL RAILROAD, see "Freeport."

Nelson, 104 miles from Chicago. This station was opened in 1857, and is located one mile south of Rock River, on a rolling prairie. It has six schools, occupying school houses that cost $1,300 each; one church, but no saloons or liquor stores, as liquor is not allowed to be sold within one mile of the corporation limits. The population number over 600, and draw their business and support from the rich farmers of the surrounding country.

Sterling, 110 miles from Chicago, is a flourishing city of 6,000 people, situate on the north bank of Rock river. The city is lighted with gas, has water works. obtaining its supply from an artesian well, 1,655 feet deep, from which the water is thrown to a height of 14 feet, and in quantity large enough to supply the entire city; many fine school houses, twelve churches, two banks, two newspapers, two reading rooms, one large public hall, an opera house, and many large manufacturing establishments. It has ample hotel accommodations. Five miles west of this station the ROCKFORD, ROCK ISLAND & ST. LOUIS RAILROAD forms junction with the Chicago & North-Western Railway, and over our tracks runs its trains to our depot at Sterling. By this connection, *Lyndon, Moline, Rock Island,* and *Davenport* can be reached, as well as many towns south of Rock Island.

Galt, 113 miles from Chicago. Population about 100. It has one school, with public hall in its upper story. *Como,* one mile south, on Elkhorn creek, population 300, and celebrated in "stage days" as location of best hotel in the State; *Empire,* one mile north; *Milledgeville,* 18 miles north; *Coleta,* 12 miles north, are tributary to this station, and are reached by tri-weekly stage lines. Fare to Coleta 50 cts., and to Milledgeville 75 cts. The country surrounding Galt is prairie—rich, productive, and all thickly settled.

Rock Island Junction, 115 miles from Chicago. At this point the ROCKFORD, ROCK ISLAND & ST. LOUIS RAILWAY branches off, and runs southwardly. (See Sterling.) *Empire* is 2½ miles distant on Elkhorn creek; it has flour mills, a woolen factory, and one church.

Round Grove, 119 miles from Chicago, is built on the prairie, 3½ miles from Rock river, and has one school, one church, and one co-operative butter factory. At this point was erected the first saw-mill built in Whiteside county.

Morrison, 119 miles from Chicago. This is the county seat of Whiteside county, which was organized in 1839, and now has a population of over 35,000 souls. The county court house is a fine building, and cost $250,000 in 1864. The city has a population of 3,000. It was named after a Charles Morrison, of New York city; was laid out in 1855, incorporated as a village in 1856, and as a city in 1869. It has a graded school, with eight teachers and 1,000 scholars, in a building that cost $25,000; seven first-class churches, several agricultural implement and carriage factories, four flour mills, and a public hall, fitted up with stage and scenery, costing $15,000, and capable of seating 800 persons. The city is supplied with water works, drawing full supply from artesian wells. Rock creek is three-quarters of a mile distant, and has good water power on it. B. C. Bailey & Sons keep The Revere House; can accommodate 100 guests, and charge $2 per day. Three other hotels also offer accommodations, at about $1 per day. *Lyndon,* 9 miles; *Prophetstown,* 11 miles; and *Spring Hill,* 18 miles distant, are reached by daily stage lines.

Union Grove, 138 miles from Chicago, is the next station reached. It is eight miles from the Mississippi river, has a population of 100, and ships large quantity of grain, from a steam elevator, operated, at the depot, by E. O. Sherwin.

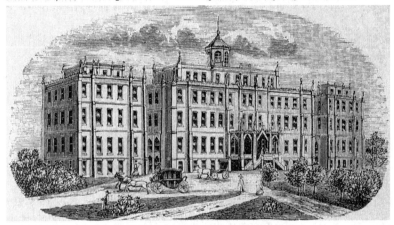

Rock River University, Dixon, Ill.—page 13.

Fulton Junction, 135 miles from Chicago. At this point we reach and cross the WESTERN UNION RAILROAD. By this connection we can reach *Albany, Cordova, Port Byron, Hampton, Moline* and *Rock Island,* south, and *Savanna, Mount Carroll, Lanark,* and *Shannon,* north. *All trains make close connections here at a union depot.*

Fulton, 136 miles from Chicago. This city, with a population of 2,500, is on the east bank of the Mississippi river. It is the seat of the Northern Illinois College, occupying buildings that cost $100,000, and having 125 students. The city is well built, on a commanding position on the bluffs; has fine schools, with an average attendance of 500 scholars; five churches; and two saw-mills, making each 3,000,000 feet of lumber, and employing 60 men, yearly. The Junction House, by Mrs. R. S. Sayre, has rooms for 75 guests; The Union House, by F. Marcellus, accommodates 40, and The Revere, by J. C. Kilgore, 65 persons, at $2 per diem.

ACROSS THE MISSISSIPPI.

One hundred and thirty-seven miles west of Chicago, we reach the Mississippi river, and cross it on a magnificent iron bridge, owned and used exclusively by this railway company. This was the second bridge that was completed across this river, and to-day stands unsurpassed for beauty, strength and permanency. Its length is 4,219 feet, and it has nine iron spans over west channel, and three iron spans and a "draw" over main channel. The original bridge was of wood, was built in 1865, and has since been rebuilt of iron, the American Bridge Co. building three spans and the draw, and the Detroit, Keystone and Phœnixville Bridge Companies each building two spans.

Clinton, Iowa—From the Bluffs.

Clinton, 138 miles from Chicago. This city, with its 11,000 people, is located on the west bank of the Mississippi river, at the west end of the bridge. The Iowa Railroad Land Company owned the ground on which the city is built, and desiring to have a town built at the most easterly point of their possessions, in 1855 laid out the present city of Clinton. The company built a church, a school house, and a "tavern," and since then the entire city has grown up around that nucleus. No city in the country is more indebted to railroads than Clinton. It has been built up by the influence of this railway, and by the facilities it offered to trade. Few cities anywhere, and certainly none in Iowa, control as large influence in the State as is done by this city. Its trade is immense, and is fast increasing, lumber and agricultural implements being leading staples in the city's trade. Its manufacturing interests are large. It has four banks, ten hotels, twelve churches, five ward schools, a high school, a fine masonic hall, an odd fellows' hall, a driving park, two public city parks, gas and water works, efficient fire and police departments, a fine turner hall, county court house, etc. Its streets are wide, well paved as a rule, and shaded with ornamental trees. Within the city limits are fine stone quarries, giving excellent building stone. Its "Press" takes a leading position not only in the State but in adjoining Sta'es. Taken all in all, it will be difficult to find a more attractive, driving, thoroughly go-ahead city. The Chicago & North-Western Railway Co. have large repair and machine shops, and the office of the Superintendent of the Iowa Division here.

THE CHICAGO, DUBUQUE & LA CROSSE LINE.

It will be observed, by examining our maps, that we show a line to *Dubuque* and *La Crosse*, via Clinton. While the Chicago & North-Western Railway Co. does not own the line north of Clinton, yet we give to and receive from that line a large trade, and it forms the northern end of the line named above. It runs along the west bank of the Mississippi river, and within a stone's throw of it most of the way. A more pleasurable trip cannot be taken than one along this line in the summer season. Starting northward from Clinton it passes through Lyons, *Sabula*, a thriving village of

1,100 people; *Bellevue*, with 2,000 inhabitants; *Dubuque*, the northern "gate city" of Iowa, with its 22,000 people; *Specht's Ferry*, with 1,000 population; *Buena Vista*, population 500; (near here a branch line runs westward, and passes through *Elkport*, with 1,200 people; *Littleport*, with 200; and *Volga City*, with 1,500; and through several smaller villages); *Guttenberg*, with 1,500 inhabitants; *Clayton*, with 1,100; *McGregor* and *North McGregor*, with 5,000 inhabitants, (connected with *Prairie du Chien* by bridge and ferry); *Harper's Ferry*, with 500; *Lansing*, with 3,000 inhabitants; *Brownville*, with 700 people; and to *La Crosse* (*La Crescent*), where a junction is formed with

THE SOUTHERN MINNESOTA RAILROAD.

By this connection we have access to and from the towns along that line. Beside passing through smaller places, it runs through *Hokah*, with 950; *Houston*, with 1,000; *Rushford*, with 3,000; *Lanesboro*, with 1,500; *Spring Valley*, with 1,500; *Ramsey*, an important junction (the crossing of the MILWAUKEE & ST. PAUL RAILWAY); *Albert Lea*, with 3,000; *Alden*, 800; *Wells*, with 1,500; *Delavan*, 900; and to *Winnebago*, 170 miles west of La Crescent, with its 3,000 people. This line runs through the great wheat region of Minnesota, and transports nearly one-third of the entire wheat yield of the State.

STILL WESTWARD.

Returning to Clinton after our trip over the Chicago, Clinton & Dubuque, Chicago, Dubuque & Minnesota, and Southern Minnesota Railroads, or if we continued westward without having left the train at Clinton, we next reach

Camanche, 143 miles from Chicago. The city of same name is one mile from the station, is on the west bank of the Mississippi river, and opposite the mouth of the Meredosia river, of Illinois. This last named river has large meadows or dry marshes (if they may be so named) extending for many miles along either bank, and furnishing the best duck, geese, brant and crane shooting that can be found in the West. Thousands of these birds are shot here every season, and hundreds of sportsmen visit these grounds from all parts of the country. Camanche furnishes many of the "outfits" for these hunting parties. In this city of 1,000 people, are large steam saw mills, one flour mill, three churches, several good schools and The New Haven Hotel, kept by F. Anthony, who charges $2.00 per day. On the east bank of the Mississippi river are many Indian mounds.

Low Moor, 148 miles west of Chicago. This town, pop. 500, was laid out in 1858. It is 4 miles north of the Wapsipinicon river, a stream noted for its most excellent shooting. Ducks, geese, and brant abound on the river and in the bayous setting into it. Snipe, several varieties, woodcock, prairie chicken and quail are found in countless numbers along its banks. In the village is one wagon factory, one church, one school house, and one hotel, by J. E. Mudgett, who charges $1.50 per day. *Elvira*, a village of 300 people, having one hotel and two churches, is 4 miles north, and is reached by mail stage three times weekly.

Malone, 152 miles west of Chicago.

De Witt, 157 miles west of Chicago, has a population of 2,500. It is well built, on a prairie sloping towards the south, and surrounded by groves; has good graded schools, one occupying a building that cost $28,000, and that seats 600 pupils; a convent and school of the "Sisters of the Sacred Heart"; a town hall, costing $12,000; court house, costing $12,000; masonic and odd fellows' halls, costing $5,000 each; one good newspaper, and several large manufacturing concerns, amongst which those of T. F. Butterfield and A. B. Cummings employ 75 men each. The Gates House, by J. M. Gates, has 60 rooms, and charges $2 per day. Within two miles of this station are five hominy mills, manufacturing over 500 barrels of hominy per day. At this point we cross the Maquoketa branch of the DAVENPORT & ST. PAUL RAILWAY, which line gives us connections for *Long Grove*, *Eldridge* and *Davenport* in the south, and *Welton*, *Delmar* and *Maquoketa* in the north. At Wheatland we cross another branch of this road.

Grand Mound, 163 miles west of Chicago. This village, of 250 people, is built on a high mound (hence its name), from whence the surrounding prairie can be seen for many miles in every direction. It is in one of the best farming regions in the State. Wild land is selling for from $25 to $50 per acre. The village has one school, one church and two fair hotels. Large shipments of hogs and cattle are made from this station.

Calamus, 169 miles from Chicago. It has population of 500; was incorporated in 1875; has one church and one good school. The land surrounding the village is somewhat sandy, but is very prolific.

Wheatland, 173 miles west of Chicago. This station, with population of 1,500, is near the Wapsipinicon river, and many sportsmen come here to shoot ducks, geese, snipe and woodcock, and to fish for the many varieties of fish with which the river is stocked. It has a fair hotel, The Wheatland House, by E. M. Tucker, accommodating 50 guests, at $2 per day. At this point we make connections with the DAVENPORT & ST. PAUL RAILWAY, for *Toronto, Oxford Mills, Wyoming, Monticello, Hopkinton, Delhi, Delaware* and *Fayette* in the north, and for *Eldridge* and *Davenport* in the south. The passenger trains make close connections here.

Loudon, 178 miles from Chicago. We have now passed over into Cedar county, and are, by stage, 16 miles from *Tipton,* the county seat. (See Tipton.) Loudon has 900 inhabitants, and is one of the regular "dining stations" of this line. It is four miles from the "Wapsie" river, and is surrounded by fine stock and grain farms. It has two schools, three churches, one grain elevator, four public halls, and many good business houses. The Railroad House, by Raymond & Risley, is at the depot, and is very popular with the traveling public. The St. Cloud is a good hotel, by C. W. Hassett; charges, $1.50 per day. *Hock,* 10 miles south, and *Masillon* and *Toronto,* each five miles northwardly, are reached by stage.

Clarence, 185 miles from Chicago, has a population of 1,000 persons, most of whom are from New England. The town is built on ground somewhat elevated, and has wide, clean streets. It has one graded school, four churches, one flour mill, two hotels, several grain warehouses. Many fine horses are raised in the vicinity, and several Boston, Mass., horse buyers, make this their headquarters.

Stanwood, 190 miles from Chicago. This station was opened in 1869; the town laid out by Malley & Preston, and named after H. P. Stanwood, the then Superintendent of the Iowa Division of this road. The village has a population of 400, and is surrounded by most excellent farming and grazing land. It has a good school, four hotels—The Houghton House being the best; two churches, and a grain elevator. An artesian well, 112 feet deep, and throwing the water 60 feet in height, supplies the village with good pure water. Fine building stone is quarried a few miles off. At this point the STANWOOD & TIPTON RAILWAY (owned by this Company,) branches off the main road and runs eight miles south-east to Tipton. Passenger trains run between Stanwood and Tipton, and connect with all the passenger trains of the main road.

Walden, 194 miles from Chicago, is four miles south of Stanwood, on the Stanwood and Tipton branch. Is an unimportant stopping place.

Tipton, 198 miles from Chicago, is at the southern terminus of the Stanwood & Tipton Railroad, and is the county seat of Cedar county. Cedar county was organized in 1837, in what was then part of the territory of Wisconsin. The early settlers were from Ohio, Pennsylvania and New England, and the county yet bears many marks of the enterprise and intelligence of these pioneers. The county has over 25,000 people, and last year sold over 3,000,000 bushels of corn, 700,000 of wheat, 700,000 of oats, 200,000 of barley, and 60,000 hogs. The court house, that cost $45,000, was built in 1860. The city of Tipton was laid out in 1840, and incorporated in 1857. It has 2,000 population, a fine city hall, that cost, in 1873, $20,000; several good schools, a ladies' seminary, The Fleming Hotel, by Mrs. C. Fleming, with 30 rooms, at $1 per day, and The City Hotel, by — Miller, with 25 rooms, at $1 per day. W. H. Tuthill has in this town a private library containing over 5,000 volumes. *Wilton,* 15 miles south, and *Rochester,* 7 miles distant, are reached, daily, by stage. Several railroads have been projected and graded through Tipton, but excepting the Stanwood & Tipton Railway, none have been completed. The surface of Cedar county is rolling, and is about evenly divided between prairie and timber. The Cedar river and several small tributaries run through the county, giving the citizens fine water power, and together with the fine grasses native in the county, render it one of the best dairy and stock counties there is in the State of Iowa.

Mechanicsville, 195 miles from Chicago. Returning to the main road again, we find this pleasant village of 1,500 people, built on a long ridge of elevated ground parallel with the railroad; the main street, over one mile long, follows this ridge. Before the railroad was built, a village called Iroquois had been started here, and to-day many of the citizens "stick to" the old name. The fair grounds of the District Agricultural Society of Cedar, Jones, Linn and Johnston counties, are located here. The village has two schools, one occupying a house that cost $15,000, four churches, twelve stores, three grain elevators, "The Pioneer" holding 30,000 bushels. The City Hotel, by H. T. Williams, has 30 rooms, and charges $2 per day. *Cedar Bluffs,* 10 miles south, and *Gower's Ferry,* 7 miles north, are post villages tributary to and reached by stage from this station. A semi-weekly stage also runs to Iowa City.

Lisbon, 202 miles west of Chicago, is a village in Linn county, of 900 people, built in the centre of a rich and thickly settled prairie, where land is selling from $40 to $75 per acre. The village is half a mile from station, which is reached by plank road and wooden sidewalks. It has one school, with five teachers, five churches, one public hall, several brick blocks, one of which is owned and occupied by the First National bank, and which would be called a fine building even in Chicago, and an agricultural implement factory, making Kynes' Corn Planter a specialty. The City, Clifton and Railroad are the principal hotels. At this station the railroad company have constantly stored about 10,000 tons of coal.

Mount Vernon, 203 miles from Chicago. This village has a resident population of 1,200 people. It is built on ground elevated above the railway some 80 feet, and being in the best wooded portion of Iowa, enjoys immunity from the bleak winds and storms that afflict many other neighborhoods. It has two churches, a large woolen factory, and several good schools, but the "lion" and pride of the town and vicinity is "The Cornell College," (see cut), which was named after W. W. Cornell, of New York City. The college buildings are built in the centre of a tract of 30 acres, of which one-fourth is forest; from the roof of the buildings the adjoining country for 30 or 40 miles around can be seen with its towns and villages. The college has 20 professors and over 500 students; the buildings are being enlarged to accommodate 1,000 pupils. It has a military department, presided over by a regular army officer, detailed by the War Department for this purpose. The United States has furnished arms for the students, and a battery of artillery for drill. The chapel was built by the Iowa Methodist Conference when the institution was called "The Iowa Conference Seminary."

Bertram, 210 miles from Chicago, is a village of 200 people; it is built on nearly level prairie, but is surrounded by high and somewhat broken ground. It has one school, one church, and a saw and flour mill. It needs a grain buyer. The American House, by H. A. Berry, with 10 rooms, at $1 per day, accommodates the transient guests.

Linn County. We have, since we passed Lis-

The Chapel, Cornell College, Mt. Vernon, Iowa.

PAGE 17.

bon, been in Linn county. It was organized in 1837, when Iowa was yet a portion of Wisconsin Territory, and was named after U. S. Senator Lewis Linn, of Missouri. The county seat is at *Marion*, 5 miles northwest of Cedar Rapids. Population in 1875, 37,000. The county contains 460,000 acres of land, of which 195,000 acres were covered with heavy oak, walnut, maple, and other hard timber. 240,000 acres in the county are cultivated, and last year produced 5,250,000 bushels of grain. Linn county was celebrated in "Indian days," and many legends are told about it. Of these one in regard to the Rapids, now Cedar Rapids City, has been preserved in verse as follows:

LEGEND OF THE CEDAR RAPIDS.

There's a legend from of old,
  Indian prophesy 'tis called—
Whence it came or where 'twas told,
  Age or race does not unfold.
Born upon the pregnant breeze,
  Growing in the blissful air,
Breathed in every breath with ease,
  Mortals thus inhaled it there.
"In the fulness of time with wings shall come,
"An angel race from the rising sun:
"Myriad in number, like light in their thought,
"Time shall not end till their destiny's wrought,
"And peace and prosperity with them shall reign."
This sachems, chiefs, their peoples taught,
  As yearly to this quiet ford,
Each annual pilgrimage, they brought
  Their tribes, to spend their festival.
A joyous thought to every will,
  To mark the spot, the link to hold,
From the pure stream each took a shell,
  As on the shore their mound will tell.

The county is well watered, having many streams running through it.

Cedar Rapids, 219 miles west of Chicago. This city, one of the most important in the State, is built on both sides of Cedar river, and bids fair to become the great manufacturing city of the State. The city is the most extensive railroad centre in the State. The adjoining county is fertile and well settled. The town site was located at the head of the rapids on the Cedar river in 1838; a town laid out in 1842; incorporated as a city in 1856, (in those days it was the head of steamboat navigation on the Cedar, and then steamboats ran up as far as Cedar Falls, 65 miles north). In 1869 a permanent water power, with first-class dam, was completed, at an expense of $50,000. The power is equal to 1,200 horse power, of which only 300 horse power is used. This town has had a rapid growth since 1869; the census in 1873 gave 4,059; in 1875, 7,480; and to-day it is over 8,000. It is essentially a manufacturing town. Many establishments are already in successful operation, the leading ones being pork packing houses, wagon factories, oat-meal mills, linseed oil mills, steam cracker factory, agricultural implement manufactories, woolen and knitting mills, flour mills, organ factory, breweries, and one railroad (Burlington, Cedar Rapids & Minesota) machine shop, which is permanently located here, and for which the city donated $60,000. It has four grain elevators, two manufacturing printing houses, and many smaller manufactories. Its wholesale business is so extensive that eighty traveling agents are constantly employed in looking after its interest. The following corporations have their headquarters here: Iowa Railroad Land Company, has 1,200,000 acres of land for sale in Iowa, much of it on the line of this railway; The Blair Town Lot and Land Co., The Cedar Rapids & Missouri River R. R. Co., Iowa Falls & Sioux City R. R. Co., Sioux City & Pacific R'y, Fremont, Elkhorn & Missouri Valley R. R. Co., Sioux City and Iowa Falls Land and Town Lot Co., Elkhorn Land and Town Lot Co., Moingona Coal Co., and The Burlington, Cedar Rapids & Minnesota R'y Co. Of banking and insurance companies, there are The First National Bank, with $100,000 capital; The City National Bank, $100,000; The Union Bank, with $325,000; and The Farmers' Insurance Co., with $125,000. There are twelve churches, with buildings that cost $189,000, and colleges and schools, with buildings costing $180,000. It has gas works, costing $50,000; water works, costing $75,000; three iron bridges across Cedar river, that runs through the city, costing $103,000; post office, built in 1874, costing $20,000; city hall and engine house, costing, in 1869, $15,000; an opera house, costing $20,000; and fire department apparatus, consisting in part of one steam, one Babcock and two hand fire engines, etc., costing $15,000. The total debt of the city is only $37,000. In hotels, the city is represented by The Pullman House, Brown's Hotel, The Centennial House and The Valley House; their charges range from $1.50 to $2.50 per diem. The city is well built, has fine brick blocks, wide, well-paved streets, fine residences, a public library, masonic and odd fellows' halls, and a daily and four weekly newspapers. We form a junction here with the DUBUQUE SOUTH-WESTERN RAILWAY, which runs northeast to Farley, on the Iowa Division of the Illinois Central. By this connection we are enabled to reach *Marion, Springville, Viola, Monticello, Farley* and *Dubuque*, and to this point passengers from the *West* should come when going into Northern Iowa and Southern Central Minnesota. Here, also, we cross the line of the BURLINGTON, CEDAR RAPIDS & MINNESOTA RAILWAY, over which route our passengers and freight for *Shellsburg, Vinton, La Porte, Waterloo, Cedar Falls, Shell Rock, Clarksville, Rockfield, Ia., Nora Junction*, and *Austin, Minn.*, find through trains and close connections. Traffic for *Linn, Independence, West Union, Clermont* and *Postville* is also sent over the Postville branch of this road.

West Rapids, is one mile west of Cedar Rapids. Passenger trains do not stop.

Fairfax, 228 miles from Chicago. The corporate name of the village, population 200, is *Vanderbilt*. It has one school and three churches.

Norway, 234 miles west of Chicago. Passing out of Linn we enter Benton county, and reach this station, which has a population of 400, and one flour mill, one school and three churches. The village was platted and named (after the native country of the founder,) in 1863. The surrounding county affords fine prairie chicken shooting.

Watkins, 239 miles west of Chicago, was named after the lamented John B. Watkins, who was killed while in the line of his duty as Superintendent of this "The Iowa Division" of the C. & N.-W. Ry. The village was laid out in 1873, has 100 population, two grain elevators, and a large trade with the surrounding country. Prairie creek runs past station.

Blairstown, 244 miles west of Chicago. This town of 1,500 people is in Benton county, which was organized in 1840, and now has over 40,000 population. The county is nearly evenly divided between prairie and timber, is well watered, and has a productive and rich soil. It is a fine grain and stock county, and is rapidly growing rich. The station was named after John I. Blair, of New Jersey, who was largely interested in building the railroad through this county. The village was incorporated in 1869, and has good schools, a female seminary, four steam grain elevators, one flour mill, four churches, and The State Blind Asylum. The Pennsylvania House, by H. & L. Gund, is the best hotel. *Vinton*, the county seat, is 20 miles distant. Small game is plentiful around Blairstown, and in Cedar river and in Prajrie creek pike and bass weighing 2 to 25 lbs. are caught.

Luzerne, 249 miles from Chicago.

Belle Plaine, 254 miles west of Chicago, is 25 miles by daily stage from *Vinton*, and 1½ miles from the Iowa river and from Salt creek, both streams being "full of fish." *Dysart*, 29 miles north, is reached via *Waltham* semi-weekly by stage, fare $1.50, and *Victor*, 12 miles south, is reached tri-weekly by stage, fare 50 cts. The town has a population of 2,100, and three schools, three churches, one public hall, a repair and other shops belonging to this railroad, a masonic hall, for meetings of lodge, chapter and commandery, an odd fellows' hall, two newspapers, flour mills, grain elevators, and many handsome business blocks. The hotels are The Sherman House, by J. F. Dunn, The Tremont, by —— White, The Union, by Mrs. Neagle, and The German, by F. Krabbenholft, with prices ranging from $1.00 to $2.00 per day. In the forests surrounding the village deer and wild turkeys are found, and on the prairie, chickens, quail, woodcock, snipe, and other game birds abound. Duck, geese and brant are found in all the streams, sloughs and bayous—in fact, this is the centre of the game region of Iowa. *Vinton*, though not a station on our line, yet is so plainly tributary to it that we feel that we should say that it is the county seat of Benton county, has 3,500 population, county court house, jail and other public buildings, several fine schools, churches, public halls, masonic lodges, chapter, commandery, and similar bodies of odd fellows, etc. This city is *best* reached via Cedar Rapids, from which point a line of railroad runs direct.

Chelsea, 260 miles from Chicago. We now come to Tama county, (see Toledo.) Chelsea has 300 population, one fair hotel, one grain elevator, F. A. Boomer & Co.'s manufactory of wooden measures, cheese boxes, etc., and two steam sawmills. It is 1 mile north of the Iowa river. Otter creek runs through the north part of the village. *Haven*, 6 miles southwest, and *Helena*, 5 miles south, are tributary to this station.

Tama, 270 miles from Chicago, is built on the north bank of the Iowa river. Fine building stone, plenty of timber, and good brick clay are found close to the town, thus giving facilities for building cheaply. The town has 2,000 people, one school occupying a house that cost $25,000, two churches, four banks, and several large business blocks. Three and a half miles from the city The Tama Hydraulic Co. have spent $100,000 in damming and otherwise utilizing the waters of Iowa river, and have developed what is said to be the best water power in the State. By canal and an expensive aqueduct the water is carried into the suburbs of Tama, where it is deposited in an artificial reservoir covering over 50 acres. A fall of 20 feet is thus secured, and produces over 1,200 horse power. Several manufacturing establishments, such as plow works, flour mills, furniture factories, pump factories, etc., are already in operation on this water power.

THE TOLEDO & NORTH-WESTERN RAILWAY

Starts from Tama, and runs three miles northwest to the county seat, TOLEDO, 273 miles from Chicago, which is reached only by this route. This road was built in 1871, by local aid mostly. W. F. Johnson, is Pres., L. Clark, Vice-Pres., C. C. Whitten, Gen. Agent, and D. D. Applegate, Treas. Tama county is well watered by Iowa river, Wolf creek, and other streams of pure spring water. It was organized in 1852, and now has 18,000 population. The county is underlaid with magnesian limestone and Oolite marble, that are worked to a considerable extent. The marble is susceptible of a high polish, and will be a source of wealth to the county in the future. Much of the land of the county is prairie, and has a deep, rich and lasting soil. In the northern part of the county is an Indian reservation, on which is a family of the Sac. and Fox tribe of Indians (here called Mas-qua-kees.) They number about 400 souls, and each receives annually $35 in money from the United States; a farmer is also employed by the Government. They and their farm and farmer are under the charge of T. S. Free. *Toledo* has a court house costing $30,000, jail, $10,000, six public schools, eight churches, three banks, two newspapers, and a goodly number of business houses. *Traer* is 20 miles distant, and can be reached tri-weekly by stage; fare $1.50. Returning again to the main line and passing westward, we reach

Montour, 278 miles from Chicago.

Le Grand, 280 miles from Chicago, is built on elevated prairie, 1½ miles west of the station, the station being in Tama county, and the village in Marshall county. The village has a population of 400 souls, many of whom are Friends (Quakers), and here they have a meeting house and a "Friends Academy." The Christian Church has also an educational institution at this point. Both occupy fine buildings, which are located on elevated and commanding ground.

Quarry, 283 miles west of Chicago. This village, with 800 people, is in Marshall county, and is noted for its fine building stone, that is here quarried constantly by over 100 men. In fact, the stone interest is about all there is here. The Quarry City Hotel. is kept by J. M. Jones. and entertains guests at $2 per day. *Spring Creek,* 13 miles north, finds its markets here.

Marshalltown, 289 miles from Chicago. This is the county seat, of Marshall county, which was organized in 1849, and has 21,000 population. The county is well watered by the Iowa, Linn, Timber, Minerva and Wolf rivers, and along all these streams are found large bodies of heavy timber. Coal is found in Bangor township, but as yet is not largely mined. The city is handsomely built, contains 5,500 people, is incorporated, has gas works, three large brick school houses, seven churches, two flour mills, a chair factory, a linseed oil mill, a steam printing office, and two banks. The Boardman, Williard, Bowler, City, Central, and American hotels together can accommodate 500 guests. Their rates vary from $1 to $2.50 per day. *Grundy Centre,* 21 miles north, and *Newton,* 30 miles south, can be reached, weekly, by stage; fare to the first, $1.50, and to the last, $2.00.

THE CENTRAL RAILROAD OF IOWA.

At this point we cross THE CENTRAL RAILROAD OF IOWA, and it gives us direct connections for *Liscomb, Union, Eldora, Steamboat Rock, Ackley, Hampton, Mason City* and *North Wood,* north of Marshalltown, and *Grinnell, New Sharon, Oskaloosa, Eddyville, Ottumwa, Albia,* etc., in the south. Passengers for any of the points here named should procure their tickets by the Chicago & North-Western Railway and the Central Railroad of Iowa, but failing to be able to procure through tickets, they should buy to Marshalltown, via C. & N.-W. Ry., and here they can buy tickets to their destinations.

La Moille, 296 miles from Chicago.

State Centre, 303 miles west of Chicago. A pleasant village of 1,000 people, built on the prairie. It has good schools, a growing trade with the surrounding county, and bids fair to be an important inland town. *Ellenville* is 7 miles distant, and reached by stage. All kinds of feathered game abound in this vicinity.

Colo, 311 miles from Chicago.

Nevada, 318 miles west of Chicago. This is the county seat of Story county, and has a population of 1,500 persons. Story county is in the geographical centre of the State; it was organized in 1853, and Nevada made the county seat in the same year. The first white settler located in 1848. The surface of county is undulating, the northern and central portions being prairie, and the southern heavily timbered. Coal is found in considerable beds, but is not much mined. Nevada has one bank with $75,000 capital, one flour mill, two grain elevators, a foundry, cheese factory, three churches, a school house that cost $17,000, and two newspapers. Three fair hotels accommodate transient guests—The Warring, Welton and Central, at $2 per day. *Iowa Centre*, 12 miles, *Cambridge*, 15 miles, *Story City*, 18 miles, and *Rolland*, 18 miles off, are reached by stages twice weekly.

Ames, 326 miles from Chicago, pop. 1,500. One mile distant, is the seat of the Iowa Agricultural College and Model Farm, situate in centre of 648 acres of land that were purchased for this purpose. It has a full corps of teachers, and is in a flourishing condition. Running south from Ames 37 miles, is

THE DES MOINES & MINNESOTA RAILROAD.

This is a narrow (3½ feet) gauge road, well built, and with first-class equipment. It runs through *Kelly*, pop. 250—*Sheldahl*, pop. 600—*Polk City*, pop. 800—*Ankeny*, pop. 200—*Saylor*, pop. 700, and other towns, to *Des Moines*, the capital of the State. The trains of this road make close connections at AMES with all of the passenger trains of the Chicago & North-Western Railway, giving us direct connections for Des Moines and the country beyond.

Ontario, 330 miles west of Chicago. This village of 200 people was originally owned by Col. I. B. Howe, of Clinton, and owing to various reasons, such as two fires, one in 1871 and a second in 1873, etc., has never advanced very rapidly. It is pleasantly located on elevated ground, and is surrounded by a fine farming country. Coal was discovered here in 1873, and there is now mined about 350 tons daily. No liquor is allowed to be sold in the village. It has two schools and two churches.

Midway, 335 miles west of Chicago. A station without a town.

Boone, 340 miles west of Chicago. This city, now having 3,500 people resident therein, is of barely ten years growth, it having been laid out by John I. Blair in 1866. It now has a high school, and two fine, brick, public school buildings, five churches, a city hall that cost $12,000, two steam flour mills, a woolen mill, furniture factory, a glove factory, foundry and machine shop, three banks, with an aggregate of capital amounting to $350,000, one (The Metropolitan) public hall, and four hotels, viz., The Lincoln, Eagle, St. James, and American Exchange, which entertain guests at from $1.50 to $2 per day. This railway company has a Round House holding twenty-nine engines, and a machine and repair shops here, in which are constantly employed a large force of skilled mechanics.

Booneboro, the county seat of Boone county, is one and a half miles west of Boone, and is connected by an hourly omnibus line. This city was settled before the railroad was built through the county, and has a fine court house, four churches, several good schools, two banks, three hotels, three potteries, and some considerable manufacturing establishments. *Swede Point*, pop. 300, is 15 miles south, and is reached by daily stage line. *Ridgeport* is 9 miles north, and is reached by tri-weekly stage line. *Boone County* is a good farming county, is well watered, and so liberally supplied with timber that firewood is "a drug in the markets" of Boone at $3.50 to $4 per cord. Immense beds of coal are found in many parts, and potters' clay, adapted for making stoneware and drain tile, is everywhere to be found below the deep rich black soil of the surface. Good building stone "crops out" along the water courses, and is largely quarried. The county was organized in 1851, and now has 19,000 population. The Des Moines river traverses the county from north to south, and secures perfect drainage for its entire surface.

Moingona, 346 miles from Chicago, is on the Des Moines river, and is the centre of the coal mining region of Central Iowa. The Moingona Coal Co., and the North-Western Coal Co., each have three shafts, and together "take out" over six hundred tons of coal daily. The population, of whom one-half are miners, number about one thousand persons. The village has one school, two churches, and two—The Moingona and The Yankee—hotels. Fare is furnished at $1.50 per day.

Ogden, 352 miles from Chicago, has population of about 400 persons.

Beaver, 357 miles from Chicago. An unimportant station.

Grand Junction, 363 miles from Chicago. Still running nearly due west, we pass into Green county. The village has 450 people, one school, two churches, and two—The Ashley, by J. P. Gullick, and The St. Lewis, by Jno. Allen—fair hotels, charging $2 per day. The village is built on rolling prairie. This station is of considerable importance, by reason of its being the point where we cross THE DES MOINES & FORT DODGE RAILROAD, that gives us close connections for *Des Moines*, south, and *Fort Dodge*, in the north. Passengers from the East or from the West should go to Grand Junction, if destined for Fort Dodge.

New Jefferson, 370 miles from Chicago. We are now at the county seat of Green county. The Raccoon river runs diagonally across the county from its northwest to its southeast corners, thus thoroughly supplying the entire county with unfailing water, as every few miles on either side of the main river are lateral streams that, fan shape, cover nearly every section of land in the county. Immediately adjoining New Jefferson are rich prairies. The village has 1,000 population, one public school occupying a building that cost $20,000, one select school or academy, four churches, two banks, a county court house that cost $40,000, and several coal mines. The Revere House, by —— Shercliff, and The Mansion, by C. T. Blake, furnish transient guests with good accommodations at $2 per day. *Panora*, 25 miles south, is reached weekly by stage.

Scranton, 379 miles west of Chicago, is three

miles south of Coon river, that furnishes most excellent fishing for pike, bass, pickerel, etc. The village has about 400 population, one school, in house that cost $5,000, and one hotel—The Hunter House, by F. Foster, who charges $2 per day. Prairie chickens abound here.

Glidden, 389 miles west of Chicago, has a population of 400, and is in the midst of one of the best shooting regions of Iowa. Two considerable rivers run within five miles, along the banks of which are large tracts of timber, that are "full" of deer, wild turkeys, and other forest game, while the contiguous prairies abound with prairie chickens, snipe, woodcock, quail, and small game, and the rivers, creeks, and bayous are full of ducks, geese and brant. It has been called the "sportsman's paradise," and if numbers of birds, and great variety constitute such a place, it is not badly named. The village has a good school, one church, a public hall that will seat 300 persons, and two hotels—The Glidden House, by N. D. Thurman, and The Dedrick, by J. C. Dedrick—both furnish excellent quarters, and abundant accommodations for the sportsmen who frequent the village.

Carroll, 396 miles west of Chicago. We have reached Carroll county, and find one of the fairest prairie counties that "the sun has shone on" in any State. Valleys and hills, covered with a dark, rich alluvial soil, produce grasses in unequaled quantities, and of unsurpassed nutritiousness. It is eminently a grazing and corn-growing county, and with its neighbor (Crawford) on the west, offers unusual inducements to the emigrant from Europe or the East. Being a new county, much of the land is still unreclaimed prairie, and can be bought at prices ranging from $5 to $10 per acre. The climate is salubrious and healthful. Being in the great middle belt of Iowa, it does not suffer from the extremes of winter or of summer. The Iowa Railroad Land Company, of which mention has been made elsewhere, owns large bodies of this productive land, in all parts of this and several counties west thereof. This company offers rare inducements to the settler, sells the land at low rates and on long time, and aids the purchaser in every way possible. No small inducement offered to the land buyer of this part of the State is the fact that he has a railroad at his door, double daily lines of palace cars to take him to Chicago, a daily mail, telegraph lines, and prompt and cheap carriage of his products to any market he may select.

The Head of the Boyer, near Dennison, Iowa—page 23.

(Engraved by J. H. Bond & Co., Chicago.)

East Side, 402 miles west of Chicago. An unimportant station, just east of the "Big Divide," or the elevated land dividing the waterflow between the Mississippi and Missouri rivers.

Arcadia, 406 miles from Chicago, has a population of 350, and is on the "Big Divide," before named. The surrounding country is a vast timberless prairie. *Wall Lake*, a curiously walled body of water, is 12 miles northeast. The lake is 14 miles in circumference, and is entirely surrounded with a wall of rock that appears as if placed there by human hands. Whence, why, when or how these rocks came, none know.

West Side, 409 miles from Chicago. Here we find the streams run west, and find an outlet in the Missouri river. The county is well watered with many "spring" creeks, having dry banks and gravelly beds. Sloughs or bayous are not found in this vicinity. The farmer can plow close to the water's edge. West Side has 450 people, is on the east branch of the Boyer river, and has one school, two grain elevators, one flour mill and one hotel, with 36 rooms. The land in this vicinity is being rapidly purchased by actual settlers.

Vail, 415 miles from Chicago. This station is in Crawford county, on a branch of the Boyer river, and has a population of 350 persons. The surrounding country is elevated, rolling prairie, and, unlike much table land, is productive to the highest points of its hills. The celebrated and nutritious "blue stem, or joint grass," covers hill and valley alike, and is not unfrequently found growing to the height of four to six feet. *Deloit*, a village that was laid out 25 years ago, is 7 miles northwest, and is reached by stage.

Dennison, 424 miles west of Chicago. Rapidly descending the "Big Divide" we reach the beautiful valley of the main Boyer river, that has for 50 years been noted all over the Missouri Valley as being one of the most beautiful and productive valleys to be found in any country. Its black, rich soil is from four to sixteen feet deep, and is, apparently, inexhaustible in all the elements needed for the growth of all the grains and grasses. Dennison is the county seat of Crawford county, has about 2,000 people, is growing rapidly, and is destined at no distant day to be a large city. It draws its trade from many miles north and south, for in neither direction is there a railroad for fully 60 miles. It has one good hotel, The Commercial.

Dowville, 433 miles from Chicago. At Dennison the road curves southward, and from there to the Missouri river opposite Omaha, follows nearly a southwest course. The village of Dowville is new, and has about 200 inhabitants. It has a good school, with four religious sects worshiping in it on alternate Sundays, one flour mill, one grain elevator and two hotels—The Dowville House, by John Rounds, and The Wiggins House, by M. G. Wiggins; they charge $1.25 per day for meals and lodging. The village is on the main Boyer river, and above all danger from overflow. Here the soil is of unusual fertility; seventy bushels of corn to the acre being a not uncommon crop. On the farm of S. E. Dow, which adjoins the village, in the fall of 1875, 30,000 bushels of corn were harvested from 400 acres.

Dunlap, 441 miles from Chicago. This town, of 800 people, is in Harrison county, which was organized in 1854, and has now about 13,000 population.

The village was laid out in 1869, and named after George L. Dunlap, the then General Superintendent of the Chicago & North-Western R'y. The Boyer river is half a mile west of the village. A most excellent eating house is kept by Mrs. Pierce at the station. This house has become celebrated for its excellent meals all over the Great West, and not a few through passengers are attracted to this line by the fame of this dining station. *Castana* is a post village, 13 miles west, reached by stage.

Woodbine, 451 miles from Chicago, is a village of 300 people situate on the edge of the great "Missouri Bottoms," as the wide valley of the Missouri river is familiarly called.

Sioux Falls, near Sioux Falls City, Dakota—page 24.

Logan, 459 miles from Chicago, is a flourishing village of 400 people, surrounded by rich valley prairie land.

Missouri Valley Junction, 467 miles from Chicago. The place was formerly known as St. Johns, and was for a season the terminus of the road. It is of considerable importance by reason of its being the southeastern terminus of the Sioux City & Pacific Railroad.

THE SIOUX CITY & PACIFIC RAILROAD.

This railway starts from Missouri Valley Junction, and runs north to Sioux City, 75 miles, and has a branch from California Junction to Fremont, on the Union Pacific Railroad, 47 miles west of Omaha, and another branch running from Fremont northwest to Wisner. This line of railway forms the western link in our SIOUX CITY & YANKTON LINE. Over this line *Mondamin, River Sioux, Onawa, Sloan, Sargent's Bluffs,* and *Sioux City,* in Iowa; *Blair, Fremont, West Point, Wisner,* and other points in Nebraska, and, by its connection with the DAKOTA SOUTHERN RAILROAD, *Elk Point, Vermillion* and *Yankton,* are reached direct.

California Junction, 6 miles from Missouri Valley. A village of 200 people, surrounded by a fine farming country.

Modale, 11 miles from Missouri Valley, pop. 100. Has one hotel, one school house, and one church.

Mondamin, 17 miles from Missouri Valley, has a population of 200, one school, one hotel, one church, and several good business houses.

River Sioux, 24 miles from Missouri Valley. The village *Little Sioux* is 1½ miles from the station, and has a population of 300. *Tekamah* and *Argona* are on the opposite side of the river, and distant 3 miles by ferry and stage. Game abounds in this vicinity, deer being especially plentiful. This station was the first one opened (Oct. 1, 1867) on the Sioux City & Pacific R. R.

Blencoe, 32 miles from Missouri Valley, is a non-important station.

Onawa, 39 miles from Missouri Valley, is the county seat of Monona county, which was organized in 1854, and has a population of 6,000. A large proportion of the county is valley land, upwards of 165,000 acres being in the valley of the Missouri river. The eastern portion of the county, a high rolling prairie, is well watered and drained by the Maple and Soldier rivers, and by Willow creek, which are bordered by large bodies of timber. Onawa has a population of 900, and has one good school occupying a brick building which cost $25,000, three churches, two newspapers, and two hotels— The Western, by T. C. Walton, and The Onawa, by D. J. Rockwell—charges $2 per day. A stage leaves daily for *Decatur, Neb.,* distant 12 miles, fare $1.50; and tri-weekly for *Castana, Mapleton, Smithland,* and *Ida Grove, Iowa.*

Whiting, 47 miles from Missouri Valley. This is an unimportant station, and was named after S. C. Whiting, the first settler in this county.

Sloan, 55 miles from Missouri Valley, is in Woodbury county, one mile south of the county line; population 100; it has one school house and one hotel. The surrounding country is valley land, with an unusually deep and productive soil. Game is plentiful; prairie chickens, ducks, geese and quail are found at all seasons of the year. Deer are also found in considerable numbers. *Smithland* is on the Little Sioux river, 16 miles east. *Oto* is 20 miles east. Farming lands in this vicinity can be purchased from $5 to $12 per acre. The reservations of the Omaha and Winnebago Indians are in Nebraska, opposite Sloan. The Indians at these reservations number about 3,500.

Salix, 61 miles from Missouri Valley, is an unimportant station, established in 1865.

Sargent's Bluffs, 68 miles from Missouri Valley, is 1¼ miles from Missouri river; population, 300; it has two brick school houses, two churches and one hotel—The City, by J. A. Risley. The village is located on a bluff, and overlooks the surrounding country from 30 to 50 miles.

Sioux City, 75 miles from Missouri Valley, is the county seat of Woodbury county, which was organized in 1851 under the name of Wahkaw, which was changed to Woodbury in 1853. Population is 9,000. This county is well watered and drained by the Missouri, Big Sioux, Floyd, Little Sioux and Maple rivers. The streams abound with fish; and deer, turkeys, geese, ducks, quail and prairie chickens are abundant. The Iona volcano, in Dixon county, Neb., is 25 miles distant, and is reached by stage. *Sioux Falls,* on the Big Sioux river, 80 miles north of Sioux City, and the famous pipestone quarries, are well worthy of a visit. Sioux City, with a population of 6,500, is pleasantly situated on the Missouri river, immediately above the mouth of the Floyd, and two miles below the mouth of the Big Sioux. There are ten organized churches, two school buildings, costing $60,000, and three less expensive buildings, in which are employed upwards of 20 teachers. Its hotels are The Hubbard, St. Elmo and Depot, which can accommodate 300 guests, at $2 per day. The Academy of Music, a fine brick building, will seat 1,000 persons, and cost $45,000. Three newspapers are published here, and from this point stage lines are run daily through *Covington, Dakota City,* the Winnebago and Omaha Indian agencies, *Decatur, Tekamah,* to *Herman, Neb.,* and semi-weekly for *Correctionville, Portlandville,* and *Sioux Falls City.*

THE DAKOTA SOUTHERN RAILROAD.

The Dakota Southern Railroad starts from Sioux City, Iowa, and enters the Territory of Dakota at the extreme southeast corner, and runs through the flourishing counties of Union, Clay and Yankton to the city of Yankton, the capital of Dakota, where it connects with the Missouri River Transportation Co.'s line of steamers for the Upper Missouri. The Dakota Southern, in connection with this line of steamers, runs nearly diagonally through the territory to Fort Benton, Montana, and has opened to settlement a large part of the best country both in Dakota and Northern Nebraska. This steamboat line furnishes an outlet to the Yellowstone and Upper Missouri. One of the shortest and best routes to the New Gold Fields of the Black Hills is by the

Dakota Southern Railroad to Yankton, the present terminus; thence by steamer up the Missouri river. *Elk Point* is 21 miles from Sioux City, is the county seat of Union county, and has 1,500 population. *Vermillion* is 34 miles from Sioux City, is the county seat of Clay county, has 1,600 population, and is an important stage point.

Yankton, the capital of this Territory and its largest town, is commandingly situated on the east bank of the Missouri river at the western terminus of the Dakota Southern R. R., and the starting point of all steamers for the Upper Missouri, Yellowstone and Black Hills. It is now the chief commercial center for Dakota, and is destined to be the chief commercial and railroad center for the whole vast region of Northern Nebraska, Dakota, and the rich mineral district of the Black Hills. It already ships 1,500,000 bushels of wheat, which is increasing fifty per cent. annually. It has an immense stretch of country tributary to it north, south and west, and owing to its rapid settlement, nearly all the immigration first coming to Yankton thence radiating from it in all directions, it offers superior inducements to all kinds of business. Population, 3,700.

Passengers destined for any of these points should buy their tickets to Sioux City by the Chicago & North-Western Railway. At Sioux City they can buy tickets to Sioux Falls City, Elk Point, Vermillion, Yankton, or the country tributary.

THE SIOUX CITY & PEMBINA RAILROAD.

From *Davis Junction*, a few miles west of Sioux City, and on the Dakota Southern Railway, a line of railroad is being built northward. It is now finished to *Portlandville*, 30 miles northwest of Sioux City and on the west side of the Big Sioux river, and is being pushed towards Pembina, in the northeastern corner of the Territory. It will run through Sioux Falls City and the Mennonite settlements up the river. A daily line of stages, owned by C. H. Howard, runs from Portlandville to Sioux Falls City. The Chicago and North-Western Railway, in its Chicago offices, sells through tickets to Portlandville and Sioux Falls City by this route.

The Sioux Falls are beautifully situated on the Big Sioux river, dividing Iowa and Dakota Territory, and are celebrated for their romantic scenery, peculiar rocky formation, and furnishing as well one of the finest water powers in the country, having a fall of 100 feet.

Sioux Falls City is located at the Falls, and is the centre of one of the finest agricultural districts in the West, the crop of 1875 being absolutely unequaled in any part of the United States, and it caused the projection of the Sioux City & Pembina Railroad named above, (leased by the Dakota Southern Railway,) which runs into the very heart of this vast grain producing country, and is found to be a very valuable feeder. It is the favorite summer resort in this part of the country, the river affording excellent fishing and the surrounding country fine shooting, besides magnificent scenery. Here is found the celebrated red pipestone quarry, held in almost religious veneration by the Indians. Indians of all tribes and from all quarters of the continent here congregate on what is considered neutral ground, and procure material for carving out their truly artistic pipes; the marble is bright red, and is capable of a high degree of polish. There are good hotels in Sioux Falls City, also two newspapers, churches, public schools, and all the advantages that can be desired for absolute settlers or visitors on business or pleasure.

DAKOTA.

The Territory of Dakota lies between the 42d and 49th degrees of north latitude, and between the 19th and 27th degrees west from Washington, extending 400 miles in length from Nebraska, on the south, to British Columbia, on the north; and stretches from east to west nearly 700 miles from the western borders of Minnesota and Iowa on the east, to Wyoming and Montana territories on the west. It embraces an area of 150,000 square miles or 90,000,000 acres. It is as large as the empire of France, and twice as large as England, Ireland, Scotland and Wales combined. Of this vast territory only the southeastern border is now occupied. A population of 30,000 white inhabitants occupy scarcely two per cent. of its acres; and under the wise provision of the Government, which secures for the head of every household a free farm of 160 acres, there are yet remaining homes for nearly a million families. Dakota possesses some of the grandest natural scenery upon the American Continent.

The Missouri river crosses the territory from east to west diagonally; the Big Sioux, the Vermillion, the James, the Yellowstone and Red River of the North flow within its borders, while along their banks grow majestic forests, which add health, wealth and beauty to the land. The Black Hills loom up gigantically to the westward of the Missouri, bearing on their slopes and summits immense forests of pine and cedar, and in their bowels inexhaustible quantities of the useful and precious minerals; while the Yellowstone region abounds in natural scenery which combines the grandeur of the Alps with the quiet, fairy-like scenery of Killarney.

Table Rock, Sioux Falls, Dakota—page 25.

But Dakota possesses something more of which her people are prouder than of all that has been enumerated; she has boundless prairies awaiting the hand of the immigrant, a soil rich and productive, and a climate unrivaled by that of any Northern State. To these, reader, you are invited to come.

Dakota, with its vast and various undeveloped resources, presents as promising fields for the investment of capital as any country in the world. Its clear and rapid streams seem expressly calculated by nature for the operations of milling, mining and manufacturing. Its boundless prairies promise a remarkable return to the stock-raiser and farmer. Its rich soil yields an abundant harvest to the husbandman, and its gay and growing towns and villages afford a good trade to merchants, and profitable employment to mechanics.

Here we give a list of the principal towns in Southern Dakota:

Sioux Falls, Minnehaha county, pop. 1,000, location Big Sioux Valley; Yankton, Yankton county, pop. 3,700, location Terminus D. S. R. R.; Vermillion, Clay county, pop. 2,000, location D. S. R. R.; Elk Point, Union county, pop. 1,600, location D. S. R. R.; Meckling, Union county, pop. 300, location D. S. R. R.; Gayville, Yankton county, pop. 500, location D. S. R. R.; Springfield, Bonhomme county, pop. 600, location Missouri Valley; Canton, Lincoln county, pop. 400, location Big Sioux Valley.

In addition to these, there are a score of new villages, whose populations range from 50 to 300 inhabitants. Among the latter is Rockport, on the James (or Dakota) river, lately established by the Army and Navy Colony of Chicago, which is progressing finely.

DAKOTA'S AGRICULTURAL WEALTH.

Statistical information is yet so imperfect concerning the agricultural productions of Dakota, that we are forced to select a few of the oldest settled counties for example, and as a basis of calculation, in figuring on the territory's agricultural wealth. We take, therefore, for example, the counties of Union, Clay and Yankton, through which the Dakota Southern Railroad runs. Union county, which is the most southerly in the territory, contains 540 square miles of land. one-half of which is bottom land lying in the valleys of the Missouri and Sioux rivers. In this county the soil is a dark loam, and varies in depth from two to seven feet. It is pre-eminently the great corn raising county of the territory, contains a population of 4,500 inhabitants, and is bountifully supplied with water and timber. It is not uncommon to see corn grow from ten to twelve feet high, and to yield as much as eighty bushels per acre, in this county. Its total taxation for 1874, according to authority of the Register of Deeds, amounts to thirteen mills upon the dollar. Seven years ago many men located upon free lands in this county without a hundred dollars capital, whose farms with improvements to-day are worth $10,000. To every poor agriculturist in the East we offer the friendly advice, "Go thou and do likewise." The actual value of real and personal property in Union county is estimated at $2,500,000.

Clay county, which adjoins Union on the west, contains, according to official returns, a population of 4,402. It is the model wheat raising county of the territory, and at an average yield will produce more than a million bushels of wheat in 1876. Land which the Government gave to settlers three five years ago is now worth $20 an acre. It contains 396 square miles of land, and is bountifully watered and timbered. Taxation here amounts to one per cent.

Yankton county, which contains Yankton city, the capital of Dakota, the most important town of the territory, and the seat of government, is in the third tier of counties west from Iowa. Its soil, surface and agricultural productions are like those of Union and Clay counties. It is watered by the Missouri and James rivers, and many minor streams, along whose banks grow beautiful groves of cottonwood and hardwood timber. Within the last year its population and wealth have so increased that it now ranks as the foremost county of the territory in these particulars. Comparatively little of its land is cultivated, scarcely ten per cent., yet the Yankton Press estimates that it will produce a million bushels of wheat in 1876. Taxation in this county ranges from eleven to thirteen and a half mills upon the dollar.

These counties, as we have said, are cited as examples. Their soil, climate and natural advantages generally are no, better than those of other counties, and the Government offers, free, to those who desire to take it, farming land, within a short distance of the line of this road, as productive, and in every way as good as any lands in the West.

It is asserted without fear of successful contradiction that the best Government lands remaining unclaimed, land equal for soil, and in producing capacity to the richest valleys of New York or the choicest prairies of Illinois, lie in Dakota Territory, within easy distance of the Dakota Southern Railroad. Every variety of crop grown in any Northern State will yield abundantly here, and 160 acres of this land may be had for the taking of it.

HOW TO OBTAIN A FREE FARM IN DAKOTA.

Many good men, deeply anxious to better their condition by emigrating to a new country, and taking free farms on Government lands, are deterred from so doing through ignorance of the way in which a farm is secured. The occupation of Government land is simple and easy. For example, a resident of Illinois desires to obtain a farm of 160 acres in Dakota. Let him come to Sioux City, Iowa, via the Chicago & North-Western Railway, and then take the cars of the Dakota Southern Railroad for Yankton, the seat of the land office for the most southerly land district in the territory, and there he will be supplied with maps or plats, which will guide him to the unoccupied claims. After selecting the 160 acres most suitable to him, he returns to the land office, pays a fee of $14, and then returns for his family to the East, if, indeed his family is not along with him. The officers of the Government will cheerfully supply all desired information relative to the taking of free land. U. S. Land Offices are situated at three convenient points in the territory, and to gain any desired information it is only necessary to address these offices respectively as follows:—Hon. G. H. Hand, Register, U. S. Land Office, Yankton, D. T.; L. D. F. Poore, Register, U. S. Land Office, Springfield, D. T.; Col. B. F. Campbell, Register, U. S. Land Office, Sioux Falls, D. T.

THE MENNONITES.

In 1873, a class of immigrants hitherto unheard of in the United States, settled in Dakota in large numbers, and continue to come, from week to week, and from day to day. By the accident of birth they are nominally Russians, but in blood, spirit and religion they are Germans. These immigrants are composed of two classes, Russian protestants and Mennonites, the latter class forming a majority of the new comers. The Mennonites (so called from Simon Menno, a German, who founded their sect,) settled in Russia in the reign of Catherine II. To them was made a solemn and binding promise and agreement, that on condition of their settling upon Russian territory, they and their heirs should for all time enjoy absolute freedom in the exercise of their religious faith, and in accordance with the teachings of their religion and the dictates of their consciences, they were absolved from the duty of bearing arms for the state, and were granted certain municipal privileges not enjoyed by Russian citizens. During the reign of the Czar Nicholas, the Government kept the contract in good faith, and the Mennonites prospered and multiplied. But the son and successor of Nicholas, Alexander, the present monarch of Russia, violated the pledges made by his predecessors, and insisted that if these people were to live in Russia they would be bound to become Russians in law, and military service, and he forthwith submitted to them the alternative of naturalization or emigration. In the conflict of affections, conscience triumphed over interest, and they determined, as did the Puritan fathers, to abandon the homes of themselves and their fathers, that they might live in a land where every man is a king, and where religion is not prescribed by statutory enactments.

They determined to leave the old homes in Russia and seek new homes in Dakota. Thus has Russia's tyranny proved Dakota's gain; and as religious intolerance in France gave the Huguenots to Carolina, as British persecution swelled the ranks of the American Revolutionary army with Irish Catholics; and as religious bigotry sowed the seed from which sprung this mighty Republic, so Russian despotism bids fair to furnish bone and muscle for an American State of Dakota. Already have 1000 families of these industrious immigrants made their homes on the rolling prairies of Dakota, north of Yankton City and westward from the valley of the James river. Though their earliest settlement is little over a year old, they will add liberally to the grain product of Dakota in 1876, some of them having already planted not less than 100 acres of wheat. They come not as a majority of foreign immigrants come, with mind and muscle alone as their capital. They bring with them, in gold and greenbacks, the accumulated savings of generations, and a knowledge of agriculture and arts, acquired by themselves, or transmitted to them by preceding generations.

Their knowledge they are applying to the development of Dakota's natural resources, and their capital is being liberally invested in building up the city of Yankton, or in promoting its trade and industry.

Their poorest family owns $500 at least, while many of them own amounts of money ranging from $1,000 to $50,000. Sheep raising with them is a favorite and lucrative industry, and as the grassy prairies of Dakota are admirably suited to this purpose, they propose to enter largely into sheep raising here.

One of their wealthiest men, whose capital is estimated at the enormous sum of $200,000, proposes to ship 400 Russian sheep, of an extra fine breed, all the way from Russia to Dakota, during the coming year.

Almost all of these people reached the territory by passing over the Chicago & North-Western Railway, and all of them advise their friends to seek this line.

DAKOTA'S INVOCATION.

Reader, if you are in quest of pleasure—that pure and unalloyed pleasure found in observing and contemplating the beautiful and wonderful works of God—let us call your attention to Dakota.

Have you ever seen that curious, beautiful and magnificent freak of nature, Big Sioux Falls ?

Have you ever stood upon the prairies of Dakota, and breathed the air which cures consumption ?

Did you ever travel over the Dakota Southern Railroad, which passes along the wooded margin of the "mighty Missouri," and across the Missouri Valley, the largest and most fertile valley of North America ?

Did you ever stand upon the deck of an Upper Missouri river steamboat and gaze upon the enchanting scenery along the serpentine windings of the mighty stream ?

Have you seen the Yellowstone Park, with its natural fountains, geysers and lakes, and its endless miles of walks and drives, macadamized by the hand of nature ?

If you have never beheld any of these scenes, visit Dakota before visiting Switzerland, and be convinced that in America there is scenery, which in point of curiosity and grandeur, is unrivaled by anything in the world. To anglers, hunters, or fowlers, Dakota offers great inducements, being perfectly alive with game of all kinds, from the mighty elk and buffalo to the lively little squirrel of the woods; from the king of birds, the soaring eagle, to the smallest quail or snipe; or from a hundred-pound catfish to that delicious morsel, a speckled trout of the stream; in short, sportsmen have universally proclaimed Dakota the happy hunting grounds of the West. Botanists, geologists, and scientists find here a new field for their researches, and are daily adding specimens of something new from the wonderful works of the great Creator of the Universe. We may mention here, for the benefit of botanists, that cacti of many kinds abound, and that curious shrub, the sensitive plant, here flourishes in a wild state.

Antiquarians in search of fossil remains of extinct animals and petrifactions, moss-agates, and other curiosities and trophies, both ancient and modern, will have every reason to be pleased should they visit this part of the world, for Dakota is particularly rich in the above specimens. One petrifaction was lately sold for $2,000, and went East, being quite a success as an exhibition.

Last, but by no means least, the Indian may be seen in all his native simplicity, and this without any danger whatever, the country having military forts surrounding them on all sides, and the sportsman can join with the genuine Indians in their wild and exciting sports. The Crown Prince of Russia and suite, on their late visit to this country, enjoyed the buffalo hunt more than anything else. In fact, we can guarantee more variety of amusement to the Tourist than any other part of the United States.

We will only add that the hotels through the country are good, well kept, and charges reasonable.

We have given this much of our space to this new territory, not alone on account of our controlling the line of railway into its southern border, but because, as will be seen elsewhere in this book, one of our own lines penetrates and runs some miles into the State from its eastern border.

ON THE WESTERN LINES OF THE SIOUX CITY & PACIFIC R. R.

After our hasty view of Dakota and its railways, we will return to Missouri Valley Junction, and take a hasty glance at the western branches of the Sioux City

& Pacific Railroad. We leave Missouri Valley Junction, and follow the main (or Sioux City) line to California Junction, cross the Missouri river by a steam ferry, and reach

Blair, 13 miles from Missouri Valley. This is the county seat of Washington county, Neb., which was organized in 1855, and has a population of 8,000. The surface of the country is rolling prairie, is well watered, and has abundance of timber. Blair has a population of 2,000, one bank, two schools, one occupying a building costing $15,000; three churches, one flouring mill, two grain elevators, with a capacity each of 30,000 bushels, and three hotels—The Blair House, by E. E. Kelly; The Germaine, by H. Teirs; and The Farmers', by Robt. Schetchley. A stage line runs to *Herman*, fare 50c.; *Tekamah*, $1.25; *Decatur*, $2.50; and *Dakota City*, $5.50.

Kannard, 25 miles from Missouri Valley.

Bell Creek, 29 miles from Missouri Valley, was laid out in 1869; has a population of 200, is located on an elevated plateau between Bell creek and the Elkhorn river; has one hotel, The Eagle House, by S. Masters; one grain elevator and one flour mill.

Fremont, 37 miles from Missouri Valley, is the county seat of Dodge county, and is, via the Union Pacific Railroad, 46 miles west of Omaha, and is at the junction of that line and the Sioux City & Pacific Railroad. The country surrounding Fremont is not surpassed by any in the West for productiveness of soil. Fremont has a population of 3,000, a fine opera house, two newspapers, seven grain elevators, and several hotels, of which The Occidental, by C. G. Pascall, is the best. From this station in 1875 one million bushels of grain were shipped.

Nickerson, 45 miles from Missouri Valley. This town is situated on the Elkhorn river, near the mouth of the Maple, and is surrounded by some of the best lands that are to be found in Nebraska. Population of the village is 200. It has one hotel, The Bassler House, $1.50 per day. *Fontenelle* is one mile east, and has a population of 200. It has one school, three churches, and several business houses. *Calhoun* and *Jamestown* are tributary to Nickerson.

Hooper, 53 miles from Missouri Valley. This village is less than two years old, and has a population of 300. It has two grain elevators, with a capacity of 20,000 bushels; three hotels, a spacious town hall, and two flour mills. Stages run tri-weekly to *Logan*, 2 miles; *Oakland*, 17 miles; *Lyons*, 22 miles, and *Decatur*, 45 miles; and semi-weekly for *Maple*, 7 miles, and *Everett*, 14 miles distant. To the farmer seeking a home in the West, this portion of Nebraska offers unusual advantages.

Scribner, 60 miles from Missouri Valley. This village, only two years old, and having a population of 300, is situated in the valley of the Elkhorn river. It has two flour mills, one grain elevator, and two hotels—The Culver House, at $2 per day, and The Farmers', at $1.50.

Crowell, 65 miles from Missouri Valley, is a small village, in the midst of a fine agricultural country.

West Point, 73 miles from Missouri Valley, is the county seat of Cumming county, Neb., which was organized in 1857, and has a population of 7,000.

Agnes Park, near Hill City, in the Black Hills, Dakota.

West Point has a population of 1,200, and has one flour mill, two banks, one grain elevator, one newspaper, county court house, which cost $40,000; one brick hotel—The Neligh House—that cost $15,000; one public hall, and about twenty stores. Population consists largely of Germans, Bohemians and Swedes. It has a good public school, with three departments; three churches, a masonic and an odd fellows' hall, and two fire companies.

Wisner, 88 miles from Missouri Valley. This village was laid out in 1871, and has a population of about 600; it controls a large trade with the surrounding country, and from 100 to 150 miles up the Elkhorn valley. The valley of the Elkhorn is one of the most beautiful and productive in the world; about 5 miles in width and about 150 miles in length. Much of its land is still sparsely settled, and can be purchased from $4 to $10 per acre. Horse-shoe, Deer, Swan, Goose, Pickerel, Beaver and Bull-head lakes are from one to four miles from Wisner, and are full of fish. Wild game is also very plentiful, amongst which are the antelope, deer, geese, ducks, prairie chicken and quail. The hotels are—The Elkhorn Valley and The Wisner. *La Porte*, population, 200, 15 miles; *Stanton*, population, 200, distant 18 miles northwest; *Norfolk*, population, 500, 33 miles west; *Madison*, 30 miles west; *Battle Creek, Oakdale, Neligh City* and *O'Neill City*, are all tributary to and are reached from Wisner by stage lines. Wisner is an important outfitting post for persons destined for the Black Hills of Dakota, and offers many facilities in this respect that cannot be presented by any other point. A popular route to Custer City, in Custer's Park, 375 miles distant, is that along the Elkhorn valley to a point 40 miles beyond O'Neill City, and thence via the Niobrara into the Hills.

ON THE CALIFORNIA LINE AGAIN.

We now return to the California line again, and will proceed on our trans-continental trip.

Custer's Park, near Custer City, in the Black Hills of Dakota.

Missouri Valley Junction has a resident population of about 1,600. Its site was purchased from the Sioux City & Pacific Railroad Company, in October, 1866, and it was incorporated in 1867. The machine shops of the S. C. & P. Ry. are located here, and give constant employment to about 250 mechanics. The village has excellent schools, (one of its public school buildings cost over $12,000, which speaks volumes for the enterprise of this "frontier" town.) It has a town hall that cost $4,000, a large hall fitted up with stage and scenery, one newspaper, two churches, and three hotels. It is built on elevated ground, from which can be seen the "Highlands of Nebraska," and the surrounding county for many miles. Corn, hogs, cattle and wheat form the principal freight shipments from this station. The surrounding county is full of game. Geese, ducks, brant, ruffled grouse, prairie chickens, quail, snipe, plover and woodcock are especially plentiful.

Honey Creek and Crescent are two small stations west of Missouri Valley Junction. Passing these we reach the city of

Council Bluffs, 488 miles from Chicago. Here we have a city of 10,000 people, and the western terminus of the Omaha & California line of our road, and of three other important railway lines. Council Bluffs is the county seat of Pottawatomie county which was organized in 1848, and which contains about 25,000 inhabitants. The site of the city was selected by the westward bound hosts of "The Church of the Latter-Day Saints," (Mormons), when making their exodus. They here erected their tabernacle and built their city, and named it Kanesville. From this point they set out on their tiresome overland journey to the then sterile, sage brush-clad plains of the apparently inhospitable valley of the Great Salt Lake. With the exodus of the Mormons a new people came in, and a new town was built, and from the fact that its site had been the scene of many Indian councils the city was named Council Bluffs. The ancient banks of the Missouri river are about three miles from its present shores, the intervening distance being what is known as "bottom land." The city is built partly on this bottom land and partly in the bluffs, the principal portion being fully three miles from the river. Situate as it is in the gorges in the bluffs, the city does not make a fair showing to the passer-by, but if he will leave his train and visit the city, he will be pleased and surprised to find as finely built and as active a city as he has passed through since he left the Atlantic coast. It contains seven public schools, eight churches, two flour mills, and several large manufacturing establishments, amongst which may be named the works of the Council Bluffs Agricultural Implement Company, using a capital of $150,000, and yearly selling over $100,000 worth of its product; and the Council Bluffs Iron Works, a chartered company employing 20 men, and producing $80,000 worth a year of the various forms of machines, etc., for which the company is noted. The county court house, a fine building, together with the jail and county offices, are surrounded by a high wall. Dohany's hall will seat 600 persons, and is arranged for concerts, theatre, shows, etc. The hotels are: The Ogden, (recently rebuilt), having 125 rooms; Pacific, 75 rooms; Metropolitan, 25 rooms; Bryant, 20 rooms; Clifton, 25 rooms; and Farmers, 20 rooms; charges range from $1.50 to $3 per day. Since the bridge across the river here was built, an effort has been made by the people of Council Bluffs to have the trains of the Union Pacific Road cross the bridge, and make Council Bluffs the eastern terminus of that line, but owing to various complications their terminus was held at Omaha, on the opposite side of the river, and the trains of the Iowa lines made Council Bluffs their western terminus. The result was a double transfer, the passengers from the trains from the East debarking here, getting into a "transfer train" that crossed the bridge, and again debarking on the Omaha side, and there taking the west bound trains of the Union Pacific Road. Coming from the West similar transfers were made. A recent decision of the Supreme Court of the United States seems to have settled the question, and very soon a joint

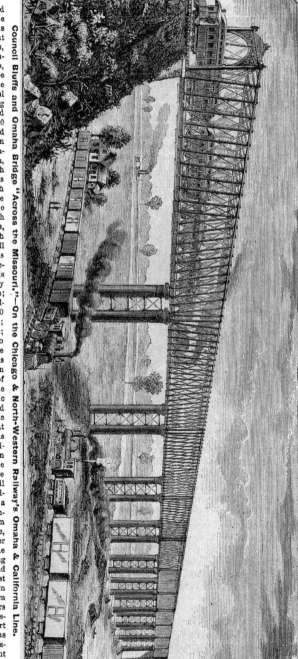

Council Bluffs and Omaha Bridge "Across the Missouri."—On the Chicago & North-Western Railway's Omaha & California Line.

depot is promised for the east bank of the river, and the usual double transfer will be avoided. At Council Bluffs we make close connections with the trains of THE KANSAS CITY, ST. JOSEPH & COUNCIL BLUFFS RAILROAD, which are taken by our passengers for *St. Joseph, Atchison, Leavenworth, Kansas City*, and other Western Missouri and Kansas towns.

OMAHA.

Hurriedly we have spanned the 492 miles that separate Chicago from Omaha, and crossing the beautiful railroad bridge (a view of which we give,) you are landed in that live, wide-awake city, whose name is Omaha. There you will find the Grand Central Hotel, with our ticket offices therein, many fine business houses, built along finely graded and paved streets, that are constantly crowded with the evidences of a large and rapidly growing trade. Besides the Grand Central, the city contains several other good hotels, an opera house, fine school houses, churches, public halls, large manufacturing establishments, the machine and car shops of the Union Pacific Railroad, and all other of the usual accompaniments of a great city. At the depot of the Union Pacific road you will find an excellent eating house, kept by that prince of caterers, Markel, and where, besides getting first-class meals, you can get your lunch baskets and well cooked lunches to take with you if going overland. If not going out on the Union Pacific, you can take the trains of the BURLINGTON & MISSOURI RIVER RAILROAD IN NEBRASKA, and by them reach *Ashton, Newton, Lincoln*, (the capital of Nebraska), *Crete, Beatrice*, or *Kearney Junction;* or you can take the trains of the OMAHA & NORTH-WESTERN RAILROAD for *Florence, Calhoun, De Soto, Blair*, or *Wisner*, and the country tributary.

Grand Central Hotel, Omaha, Neb.

Supposing you are going to Colorado, Wyoming, Utah, Montana, Idaho, Nevada, the Pacific Coast, or, perhaps, to China, Japan, Australia, New Zealand, or the Sandwich Islands, you will take the Chicago & North-Western Railway for Omaha, and there take the trains of the UNION PACIFIC RAILROAD, and pass through *Fremont, Columbus, Lone Tree, Grand Island, Kearney Junction, North Platte, Sidney*, and reach *Cheyenne*, 516 miles from Omaha, and 1,008 miles from Chicago. Here you leave the train if you are going to any point in Colorado. Passing south, by the DENVER PACIFIC RAILWAY, you cross apparently sterile plains, and run through *Greeley* and *Evans*, where you can study the vast system of irrigation that has made these plains bloom like a garden. You run along, with the snow-clad peaks of the main Rocky Mountain range in full view, and in six hours after leaving Cheyenne you reach DENVER.

COLORADO—THE FAR WESTERN SUMMER RESORT.

The Attractions for Invalids, Tourists and Idlers.

To the tourist and the invalid, Colorado has unexcelled and increasing attractions, and each recurring season offers new facilities for health and recreation. The preparations for this summer at all the watering places and towns whose vicinity affords scenic or sanitary advantages, are of a high order; and it is the object of this article, after pointing out the route of travel to Colorado, to give the tourist or traveler some idea, after he gets there, of what to see, and how to see it.

There is no end to the attractions of Colorado, and we advise those who can to make at least one trip out there, ere the country becomes more settled, as then the scenery will not appear half so attractive as at present, in its wild, romantic state. To those who intend going during the ensuing hot months, we offer the following suggestions: Leave Chicago via Chicago & North-Western Railway, for Omaha, thence via the Union Pacific to Cheyenne, and thence via the Denver Pacific Railway, to Denver.

At Denver, the principal hotels are the Grand Central, American, Inter-Ocean, (opened since last season,) Ford's, Sargent's and Charpiot's. The three first named are four-story buildings, and will accommodate from 100 to 150 guests each. The new Broadwell House is the largest in Colorado. The rate at all of them is $4 per day, and from $21 to $25 per week.

The principal watering places in Colorado are Manitou and Idaho Springs. Manitou is five miles from Colorado Springs station, on the Denver & Rio Grande Railway, and seventy-two miles south of Denver. The narrow-gauge cars, neat and comfortable, take the traveler along at the rate of 15 miles an hour, through Littleton, up over the Divide with its pineries, passing the lake at the summit surrounded with myriads of beautiful flowers, down the southern slope along the Monument, reaching Colorado Springs at noon. Taking time to see the notable improvements of the past few months in this stirring little city of 3,000 people, with its many handsome buildings, a carriage is taken to the Springs. Here the Manitou House, and the new Cliff House, and, two miles further on, the Tonic Springs Hotel—all having spacious walks, croquet grounds, drive ways, billiard halls, barber shops, and mineral baths—offer abundant comforts for guests. Saddle-horses and carriages can be obtained to visit all the points of interest; also guides and pack animals to the summit of Pike's Peak, where the new Government signal office is located, and whence weather reports are telegraphed over the country three times a day. Days and weeks can be profitably spent at Manitou and vicinity.

Idaho Springs lies in the valley of South Clear creek, 35 miles west of Denver. The tourist takes the Colorado Central, broad gauge, to Arapahoe Junction, below Golden, where he changes to the narrow gauge train, which whirls him through Clear Creek Canon to Floyd Hill, thence 5½ miles by Concord coach. The Beebe and Alvord houses furnish good hotel accommodations. The chief attractions of the place are the hot and soda springs, and the swimming baths. There is gorgeous scenery on every hand. Trips to Fall river, Chicago Lakes, and the mines can be made. The place has good liveries, boarding houses, daily mails, telegraph, and other accommodations.

Canon City, near which are some of the most notable springs, is surrounded by various attractions. At Georgetown, where the silver mines are to be seen, and from whence the brisk camps at Silver Flume, Empire, Bakerville, Argentine, the mills and furnaces of Stewart, Spanish Bar, Masonville, and the scenic attractions of Gray's Peak, Twin Lakes, Griffith Mountain, Chicago Lakes, and Middle Park, are to be reached, those spacious hotels, the Barton and American, have been renewed, and additions to liveries, boarding houses, and other improvements made. At Boulder, the Boulder and Colorado hotels have been repaired, daily stage lines to Gold Hill, Nederland and Caribou put on, liveries increased, and every advantage offered for trips up Boulder Canon and the falls, to Peabody Springs, Belmont Iron Works, Erie Coal Mines and Gold Hill; the place also has now the advantage of two railroads to Denver. At Longmont, a tri-weekly stage line has been arranged, from the St. Vrain Hotel to Estes Park, 40 miles, where the Evans Hotel, excellent fishing and hunting, saddle ponies and guides, and the climbing of Long's Peak, are the chief attractions. At Central City, the Teller House, and numerous smaller hotels and boarding-houses, and the fine liveries, are prepared to furnish every facility for visiting the gold mines, the great Sierra Madre tunnel, the stamp mills and reduction works, Black Hawk, Nevadaville, James' Peak, and Rollinsville.

The inducements offered by the Chicago & North-Western route, via Omaha, to Colorado are, the fine country it passes through between Chicago and Omaha, its splendid track and equipment, the comfort enjoyed while passing over the Union Pacific Road, the chances of seeing the plains, mountains, and other attractions not found on any other route; and the chance to visit Cheyenne, Greeley, Evans, etc., before you reach Denver. If you cannot at your homes buy tickets via this route through, you can buy to Chicago, and at our offices there get your through tickets. Better do that than miss the opportunity to go by this route.

Returning to Cheyenne from Denver, or if you have not broken your westward journey, you pass on to *Sherman*, at the summit of the Rocky Mountains, 8,242 feet above the sea; *Laramie*, with its *Fort Sanders*, and the rolling mills of the Union Pacific Railway; *Fort Fred Steel, Rawlings, Green River, Bryan, Evanston*, with its eating houses with Chinese waiters, near which are very extensive and valuable coal mines, and soon run down through those marvels of Utah—Echo and Weber canons—and at 1,032 miles from Omaha, reach OGDEN, an important Mormon city, and the junction of four railroads, viz: the UNION PACIFIC, over which you have come from the East; the CENTRAL PACIFIC, over which you will pass when going West; the UTAH NORTHERN, which you will take for *Logan* and points beyond (by stage) in Idaho or Montana; and the UTAH CENTRAL, over which you will pass with me in the contemplated trip to Salt Lake City, before we proceed further towards "sundown."

TO THE CITY OF THE SAINTS.

Then, bidding good-bye to our friends who have accompanied us from Chicago, and who fail to "take in" this pleasurable "side-show," we step into the cars of "Bishop Sharp's road," and start southward, with the Great Salt Lake on our right.

Stopping for a few moments at *Kaysville, Farmington, Centreville,* and one or two unimportant stations, we, in two hours' run from Ogden, are at SALT LAKE CITY, that marvel to the Mormons themselves, who have reared it or seen it grow, and that more than marvel to the gentile, who has had no part in its past and but little vital interest in its present; for in the past he was a rarely-seen stranger, and in its present is hardly at home, or willing to acknowledge that he has "come to stay." Without attempting to describe this wonderful city, or the blooming country around it, we yet must call your attention to the situation

ON THE CENTRAL PACIFIC RAILROAD.

We pass *Corinne,* a noted mountain stage depot, and at *Kelton* find a good point to take stages for all points in Idaho.

IDAHO.

In Idaho we reach by our connections *Boise City, Idaho City, Malade,* and *Silver City,* and the wonderful falls of the Snake river; these are, the American, 70 feet; the Salmon, 60 feet; and the Shoshone, over 200 feet perpendicular. These last vie with Niagara in beauty and grandeur. In Idaho the days are never sultry and the nights are always cool; on the plains and in the valleys snow does not lie

Walker House, Salt Lake City, Utah.

of the city itself, and ask you to note the glorious Wahsatch mountains to the left, and the Oquirrh range to the right, the lake at their feet, the silent Jordan at its foot, and not to overlook the ever-present evidences of the great work that has been wrought by these "peculiar people." Gentile, as we are, we freely and willingly join in repeating, as many have before, "No other people have before accomplished as much." For those who cannot see for themselves, we picture a feature or two of this visit that may be new and not uninteresting. From here you can reach by rail *Lehi* and *Provo,* and many other interesting points in the Territory. If you have time, fail not to take a trip over the AMERICAN FORK RAILROAD, and see the glories and beauties of the wonder canons it runs through. After dining at The Townsend or at The Walker, the leading "Mormon" and "Gentile" hotels, we hurry back to Ogden, and pursue our western journey.

on the ground; cattle feed out-doors the year round. The climate is much the same as that of Central Illinois and Southern Pennsylvania. Good hotels are found in all the towns; and daily newspapers, the telegraph, and other evidences of advanced civilization, are found on every hand. Stages run daily from various points on the Central Pacific Road to all the towns in Idaho, and no more attractive region can be found for a summer tour than is offered by the hill country of Idaho.

If we do not end our stage trip in Idaho, but continue it northward, we pass on to *Helena,* (pop. 4,000, and the capital,) *Virginia City, Deer Lodge, Argenta, Bannock,* and *Bozeman,* in Montana.

MONTANA.

Montana, with its mountains, lakes and rivers, will amply pay for a summer's sojourn there. The National Park on the Yellowstone, the geysers, and the mountains of the Bitter Root, Snow and other chains, are all accessible from Helena. The geysers of the Yellowstone and the Upper Missouri are the most wonderful in the world, those of Iceland and New Zealand not excepted. Here we have the Thud, Horn, Bath, Cavern, Beehive, Giant, Giantess, Old Faithful, Saw-mill, Grotto, Punch-bowl, Riverside, Soda, Fan, and other geysers within the Territory, bounded by latitude 43 and 47 north, and longitude 110 and 114 west. These geysers vary from the mere mud volcano to those throwing boiling water in columns six feet in diameter and 200 feet in height. The water in the various geysers varies from icy cold to boiling, and in color from the transparent to the inky black, through all the shades of blue, brown, red, yellow, green, etc. Some of the ejections occur at regular periods, varying from one hour to 32 hours apart, while others are always active. Not tarrying in Montana, we return to the Central Pacific Railroad, at Corinne or Kelton.

WESTWARD AGAIN.

Toano, Elko, Palisade, Battle Mountain, Winnemucca, Humboldt, (note its oasis) and *Wadsworth* are reached, and a stop is made at *Reno.* Here, after a good rest with friend Chamberlain in his pleasant hotel, we will take a fresh start, and run down the VIRGINIA & TRUCKEE RAILROAD to *Carson,* the capital of Nevada, and to *Virginia City, Gold Hill* and *Silver City,* in which are found the "Big Bonanza" and other mines, and especially notable those of the Comstock lode. Spending a day, week or months here with pleasure and profit, you return to *Reno,* and again taking the palace cars of the CENTRAL PACIFIC RAILROAD, are in the Sierra Nevadas; pass (if you do not go to Lake Tahoe) *Truckee, Colfax, Dutch Flat, Auburn, Sacramento, Stockton, Lathrop, Niles,* and, at 5.00 P. M., reach the "Golden Gate," with *San Francisco* to the south of it. From this wonderful city you can reach any part of the Pacific Coast, or the great East beyond. *Santa Cruz, Santa Barbara, Los Angeles* and *San Diego,* southward, are accessible by two daily lines of steamers; while *Portland, Tacoma, Victoria, Puget Sound* and *Vancouver's Island,* and all points in Oregon, Washington, and British Columbia, are accessible by steamers running up the coast. Inland, by rail, *Napa,* *St. Helena, Calistoga, Oroville, Marysville, Petaluma, Santa Rosa, Cloverdale, Santa Clara, San Jose, Hollister, Gilroy, Soledad, Salinas, Montery, Calienta,* and a hundred other towns are readily reached. To *Hong Kong,* in China, and *Yokohama,* in Japan, two lines of steamers furnish weekly departures; and to *Honolulu,* in the Sandwich Islands, *Melbourne* and *Sydney,* Australia, and *Auckland,* in New Zealand, one line of steamers are run regularly. In all this vast field, the Chicago & North-Western Railway is known and patronized. Even farther India lends her patronage and aids to swell the throng that constantly crowds its numerous passenger trains, and assists in loading its miles of freight cars. This, then, is one thing

City Aqueduct, Salt Lake City, Utah.

Reached by Omaha & California Line.

this great corporation can do for you. It opens wide the door to the great West and to the still greater East, and is the gateway for the millions who seek new homes, or desire to visit friends anywhere via THE GREAT TRANS-CONTINENTAL ROUTE.

IN CALIFORNIA AND THEREABOUTS.

The popular resorts of California reached by the Chicago & North-Western Railway and its connections are, "*The Yosemite,*" "*The Geysers,*" "*Mount Diablo,*" "*The Big Trees,*" "*Donner Lake,*" "*Lake Tahoe,*" "*Summit Soda Springs,*" "*Calistoga Sulphur Springs,*" Santa Barbara, Santa Cruz, and Los Angeles.

The fame of the Valley of Yosemite has now become world-wide. Its towering cliffs, waterfalls like cataracts from the clouds, and the gigantic vegetation surrounding it, have no comparison in the world. In sublimity of grandeur and enchanting beauty it surpasses expression, and must be viewed to be appreciated. Several eminent writers have attempted descriptions, but all have despaired in giving expression to the awe-inspiring feelings which fill the beholder of the mighty chasm. Bierstadt has painted it, and Watkins has photographed it, and these, as all writers say, give the nearest idea of the majesty of the scene to that of being present at the reality. As to the faithful, the admonition to "see Mecca and die," so to the traveler, "see Yosemite, the last of earth."

To reach the Yosemite Valley, the traveler goes to Lathrop, 82 miles east of San Francisco, and then, via the Visalia Division of the Central Pacific Railroad, from Lathrop to Merced; thence the tourist has choice of two routes — via Mariposa, Clarks (Mariposa Big Tree Grove), The Hermitage, and Inspiration or Glacier Points, or via the Coulterville Short Line, passing Snellings, Coulterville, Dudley's, Bower Cave, Pilot Peak,

The Tabernacle, Salt Lake City, Utah.
Reached by Omaha & California Line.

Merced Big Tree Grove, and the canons and cataracts of Merced river, (both "all wagon" roads).

TABLE OF ALTITUDES AT YOSEMITE VALLEY.

WATERFALLS.

INDIAN NAME.	SIGNIFICATION.	AMERICAN NAME.	HT. ABOVE VALLEY.
Po-ho-no	Spirit of the Evil Wind	Bridal Veil	940 feet.
Yosemite	Large Grizzly Bear		2,634 "
	First fall, 1,600 feet; Second fall, 434 feet; Third fall, 600 feet.		
Pi-wy-ack	Wide Water	Vernal	350 "
Yo-wi-ye		Nevada	700 "
To-lool-we-ack		South Fork	600 "
To-coy-œ	Shade to Indian Baby Basket	Royal Arch Falls	1,800 "
Loya		Sentinel Fall	3,200 "

MOUNTAINS.

Tis-sa-ack	Goddess of the Valley	South Dome	6,000 "
		Cloud's Rest	6,450 "
To-coy-œ	Shade to Indian Baby Basket	North Dome	3,725 "
Hunto	The Watching Eye	Round Tower	2,400 "
Mah-tu	Martyr Mountain	Cap of Liberty	4,600 "
		Mount Starr King	5,600 "

INDIAN NAME.	SIGNIFICATION.	AMERICAN NAME.	HT. ABOVE VALLEY.
Tu-tuck-a-nu-la	Great Chief of the Valley	The Captain	3,100 feet.
Wah-wah-le-na		Three Graces	3,750 "
Pom-pom-pa-sus	Falling Rocks	Three Brothers	4,300 "
Poo-see-nah Chack-ka	Large Acorn Cache	Cathedral Rock	2,400 "
		Sentinel Dome	4,500 "
Loya		Sentinel Rock	3,270 "

The Yosemite Valley is 4,060 feet above the sea. Its general course is northeasterly and southwesterly.

The "New Wagon Road" was completed early in April, 1875, between Clarks and The Hermitage, thence into the Valley. Visitors can leave Merced in the morning, stop over night at Clarks, the next forenoon visit the Big Tree Grove, six miles from Clarks, via Saddle Trail, and during the afternoon of the same day travel by Washburn, Chapman & Co.'s Passenger Wagons from Clarks to the Valley—making the trip, including the Big Trees, in two days from Merced; or, via the Coulterville all Wagon Route, passing Snellings and Coulterville; stopping over night at Dudley's Mills (45 miles from Merced); the next day passing Bower Cave, Pilot Peak, the "Merced Grove of Big Trees," the Cliffs and Canons of the Merced River, Bridal Veil and Yosemite Falls, arriving at the Hotels at 4.00 P. M., making but two days easy traveling, without change of vehicle, between Merced and Yosemite.

A third route for visitors to the Yo Semite and Calaveras Big Trees is to Stockton, via Central Pacific Railroad, and thence by rail to Milton, arriving at this railroad terminus at 1.45 P. M., where they will take dinner, and then proceed in easy riding carriages to Murphy's, where they will find splendid hotel accommodations and stop over night. The following morning they will drive to the Calaveras Big Tree Grove, where they will find equally good hotel accommodations and will spend most of the day there, returning in the evening to Murphy's. From Murphy's to the Valley the route is through an interesting Hydraulic and Placer Mining country, and over a good gravel road. Before reaching the brink of the Valley—at Crane's Flat—the traveler will find a small grove of the mammoth trees of California. Two of these, named the "Siamese Twins," growing from the same root, measure 114 feet in circumference, and with corresponding height. But he will hasten on to the rim of the mighty basin, and become transfixed in awe as he first beholds it from "The Stand-Point of Silence." Here he takes in the view in its awful majesty. None are so cold as to contemplate it without having awakened within them feelings beyond their power to express. From such feelings arose the name the point bears. From this summit to the valley below is a distance of three miles, by a horseback trail, descending four thousand feet, where Hutchings' stage will meet passengers and take them to Hutchings' Hotel, which is surrounded by the grandest scenery the eye ever rested on.

THE BIG TREE GROVE OF CALAVERAS COUNTY, CAL.

The Calaveras Group is the one known to the world as "The Big Trees of California," and the one chiefly visited by tourists. It comprises the Mammoth and South Park Groves. The Mammoth Grove contains ninety-three of these Giants of the Forest, among which are the Mother of the Forest, the bark from which was exhibited in the Crystal Palace, London; the Father of the Forest, through whose prostrate trunk thousands have ridden on horseback; and the Original Big Tree, the stump of which forms the floor of the famous Pavilion, 32 feet in diameter. The South Park Grove, distant six miles, is superior to the more famous Mammoth Grove, both in number and size of its Big Trees, of which 1,380 have been counted. It has only been recently opened up to tourists, and is readily reached with horses from the Mammoth Grove Hotel by a good bridge and trail. These two Groves comprise the Calaveras Group of Big Trees, surpassing all others in grandeur and beauty.

THE GEYSERS.

The geysers of California are in Sonoma county in a lateral gorge of the valley of Napa, called the Devil's Canon, near Pluton river. The canon is narrow and shut in by steep hills. Vapor fills the gorge, while springs hot, cold and great, gush out on all sides and lie within a few feet of each other. They differ in color, taste and smell. These waters are clear, white, black, red, blue; yellow and green, and are either pure to the taste, sulphurous, fetid, acid or alkaline. The most celebrated is "The Steampipe" which is an orifice in the hill side, eight inches in diameter, out of which is ejected continuously and with almost deafening roar, a volume of hot steam that is projected from 50 to 200 feet in height. "The Witches' Caldron" is a mass of black fetid mud that is ever bubbling and boiling with internal heat. These geysers are 1,700 feet above the sea level, and are reached from San Francisco by two routes:

Devil's Gate, Weber Canon, Utah.

On Omaha & California Line.

First, via the Vallejo Steamers and California Pacific Railroad through Napa Valley, connecting with Foss & Connelly's Line from Calistoga Springs; thence via Van Arnam & Kennedy's Line to Cloverdale, connecting with daily train of the San Francisco and North Pacific Railroad, running through Sonoma Valley.

Or Second, via Cloverdale and the San Francisco & Northern Pacific Railroad. Sailing up through one of the most spacious and beautiful bays in the world, surrounded with charming panoramic views; enjoying a ride of 56 miles in comfortable cars, through a level country; affording a wide view on each side of the fertile county of Sonoma, passing several thriving towns in the meantime. Arriving at Cloverdale, there connecting with Van Arnam & Kennedy's new stages, over a new road of easy grade, running through a section of country unsurpassed for grandeur of scenery and surroundings; only two hours staging.

No trip to California is complete unless including a visit to the great natural phenomena of the Pacific Coast.

LAKE TAHOE, VIA SUMMIT STATION AND DONNER LAKE.

The tourists' route between Summit Station, Donner Lake, Truckee, and Lake Tahoe, is via stage. Stages will leave Summit, daily, pass Truckee, arriving at Tahoe

City and return in the evening. Overland passengers going East, leave San Francisco in the morning, Sacramento about noon, arriving at Summit for supper. Remain over night at Cardwell's Hotel, and leave by next morning's stage, via the Donner Lake Route, for Lake Tahoe, and return during the evening of the same day to Truckee in time to connect with the eastward bound train. This route gives passengers an outside view of the wonderful snow sheds and galleries of the Central Pacific Railroad, not obtainable in any other way. Overland passengers going West, wishing to visit Donner Lake and Lake Tahoe, should leave the train at Truckee or Summit; returning from Tahoe City to Truckee or Summit to resume the journey westward on any subsequent day. The new passenger excursion (side-wheel) steamer Stanford, Captain Lapham, commanding, leaves Tahoe City after arrival of morning stage from Summit, and makes the complete circuit of the lake, touching at all points of interest en route, returning to Tahoe City same evening.

Better neglect visiting all the other "lions of California" than fail to visit this wonderful and beautiful lake. Many days can be spent with pleasure and with profit in this vicinity. Good hotels are found at convenient distances, and guides are always ready. Finer brook trout fishing cannot be found on this continent than may be enjoyed in this locality. The writer of this has seen trout taken that weighed, when dressed for the table, full ten pounds, real speckled beauties!

Santa Cruz is the California Cape May, and with Santa Barbara and Los Angeles can best be reached via San Francisco. The Summit Soda Springs are 240 miles east of San Francisco, and are reached by stage daily from Soda Springs Station on the Central Pacific Railroad. The White Sulphur Springs of Calistoga should be "taken in" on the trip to or from "The Geysers."

Mount Diablo,

The "Mount Washington" of California, the summit of which is nearly 4,000 feet above sea level, gives an unbounded view of the Alameda, San Joaquin, Sacramento and connecting valleys. The new wagon roads from Martinez and Haywards enable the tourist to reach the summit with only twenty miles travel in one of Kimball's passenger wagons, making close connections with trains and ferries. Leaving San Francisco any day (via Oakland), on the Central Pacific Railroad Overland Train, arrive at Haywards and connecting with Bennett's Line, you arrive at Mount Diablo at noon. Or leave San Francisco (from Broadway wharf) by the Sacramento river steamers "Amador" or "Julia;" arrive at Benicia at 6 P. M.; change to ferry boat for Martinez; remain there over night; and thence the next morning to Mount Diablo.

Returning—Stages leave Mount Diablo in the afternoon, in time to connect with train passing Haywards, for San Francisco. Or leave Mount Diablo in the afternoon to connect with ferry boat leaving Martinez at 5.00 P. M., connecting with steamers "Amador" or "Julia," passing Benicia daily (except Sundays), at 5.30 P. M., and arriving at San Francisco about 8.00 P. M.

OREGON, WASHINGTON AND BRITISH COLUMBIA.

Tourists and other travelers or emigrants from the East destined for the above named States have choice of two routes from the Central Pacific Railroad. Of course to reach that line you will buy your tickets via the Chicago & North-Western Railway, to Sacramento or San Francisco. The first route is via rail from Sacramento, up the Sacramento Valley to *Redding*, 180 miles; thence by stage, 280 miles, to *Roseburg;* thence by the Oregon & California Railroad, 200 miles, to Portland; while the other is to San Francisco, and thence by steamer up the coast to Portland. *Oregon City, Salem* (the capital), *Albany, Eugene City, Astoria, Jacksonville, Empire City, Dallas, Walla Walla* and *Umatilla,* in Oregon, may all be reached by these routes, while *Olympia, Steilacoom, Cascade City, Wallula, Port Townsend, Seattle,* points on Puget Sound and other points in Washington Territory, and *Victoria* and other points in *British Columbia,* are reached from San Francisco, or from Portland. Our agent in San Francisco will at all times be pleased to give prospective visitors to Oregon or beyond, all information about the country, routes, etc., that they may desire.

THE POPULAR ROUTE TO THE GREAT WEST.

Amphitheatre, Echo Canon, Utah.

On Omaha & California Line.

That the Chicago & North-Western Railway is *the* route of the masses is well known and acknowledged by all intelligent observers of railway travel. It is to-day, and always has been, the route selected by those eminent in this and other lands when making their trans-continental or round-the-world trips. As long ago as when the much-lamented Seward started on his over-land and over-seas trip, to the present day, when the thoroughly *posted* Dom Pedro, Emperor of Brazil, selected it as the route not only for his trip one way, but for the return trip as well, it has been recognized as the shortest, quickest, best. Reader, you cannot be wrong if you follow in the steps of your illustrious predecessors.

THE IOWA MIDLAND LINE.

Leaving California and its marvelous climate, we will take up another line of our road, and starting from the Mississippi river, take up a stitch we dropped, and try to unravel a little more of what we fear is, to many, a much-tangled skein.

At CLINTON we are on the west bank of the Mississippi river. Here we will strike northward for a short trip, and leaving the main line of the Iowa Division we will run over the IOWA MIDLAND RAILWAY, which is a branch line owned by the Chicago & North-Western Railway. Three miles above Clinton we reach

Lyons, 141 miles from Chicago. This city, with 4,500 population, is situate on the west bank of the Mississippi river, and was first settled in 1835. It has several important manufacturing establishments, amongst which we would mention a paper mill, employing 50 to 70 men; a sash, door and blind factory, with 30 hands; machine shops, agricultural implement manufactory, etc. Its educational facilities are good, having five large school buildings that cost from $20,000 to $30,000 each, and accommodating 1,200 pupils. "The Lyons Female College," and "The River Side," two "higher" schools, are also well patronized. Lyons has seven churches, two hotels—The Vandoran and The Sherman. Odeon Hall, seating 300, is a popular concert hall. The city has water works, and gas works will be erected during the present year.

Almont, 149 miles from Chicago, is a village of 200 people.

Bryant, 155 miles from Chicago, is a village of 200 people, and has a good public school, a public hall, two hotels—The Hass and The Western—charges $1.25 per day. *Elvira*, 8 miles southwest, and *Centre Grove*, 6 miles southeast, are tributary.

Goose Lake, 158 miles from Chicago, is surrounded by a fine farming country.

Charlotte, 163 miles from Chicago. The village has 300 inhabitants, and was named after Mrs. Charlotte Gilmore, the first white woman settling here. It is built on both sides of Deep river, the stores and business houses being in the valley along the river, while the residences, churches, school houses, etc., are on the higher bluffs. The poor farm and almshouse of Clinton county adjoin the village. The village has one school, three churches, two flour mills, and one hotel, The Sherman House, that can accommodate fifty guests. GOOSE LAKE, 3 miles southeast, is a great resort for sportsmen; geese, ducks and brant being very abundant. Deep river (well named, as it is over 15 feet deep) has recently been, by the State Fish Commissioner, stocked with young California salmon. Along the river, Indian mounds and the remains of ancient mining operations are found.

Delmar, 171 miles from Chicago, is at the junction of the Davenport & St. Paul R. R., and has about 600 inhabitants, one school, one church, (Methodist), a public hall and library, one newspaper, and two hotels—The Junction, and The Riggs. Maquoketa river is 4 miles, and large and valuable stone quarries 2½ miles distant.

Maquoketa, 176 miles from Chicago, is the county seat of Jackson county, which was organized in 1847, and now has 24,000 population. The city has 3,000 inhabitants, is built on both sides of the Maquoketa river, and on the edge of the largest body of timber there is in the State of Iowa (hence they call this the "timber city.") Before the railroad was built here, steamers ran from the Mississippi river to this point. The city is picturesquely located on high bluffs, and has fine, wide, well paved streets. Considerable manufacturing is carried on in the lines of furniture, agricultural implements, and other articles, in which wood is largely used. The city has one school house that cost $25,000, and several cheaper ones, six hotels, a fine county court house, four flour mills, two woolen mills, a tannery, three banks, four churches, and a large number of fine business houses. Two medicinal springs within the city limits have large local repute. Two miles off is an Indian burial ground. The business of this city for 1875 showed over thirty-three per cent. increase over 1874.

Nashville, 182 miles from Chicago. This village has 200 inhabitants, and is 1½ miles south of Maquoketa river. *Burt's Cave*, 6 miles north, is a pleasure resort.

Stephenson County Court House, Freeport, Ill.—page 44.

Baldwin, 185 miles from Chicago, is three miles from Maquoketa river; has 300 inhabitants, one school, and one hotel. Wild game of all kinds abound in the vicinity. *Mill Rock*, 1 mile, *Four Corners*, 4 miles, *Smithland*, 4 miles, *Canton*, 9 miles, *Crabbtown*, 8 miles, *Garriowen*, 18 miles, and *Zwingle*, 18 miles distant, are all tributary to this station.

Monmouth, 188 miles from Chicago, is a village of 500 inhabitants, with tri-weekly stages to *Canton*, 6 miles, and *Ozark*, 9 miles distant. The town is built on rolling prairie, at the head of the Maquoketa valley, and has one school, two churches, and two hotels.

Onslow, 195 miles from Chicago, has 100 inhabitants, a graded school, two churches, and is connected with *Wyoming*, pop. 1,500, 4 miles distant, by daily stage.

Centre Junction, and Blue Cut, respectively 199 and 202 miles from Chicago, are unimportant villages.

Anamosa, 210 miles from Chicago, is the county seat of Jones county, which was organized in 1839. Present population, 20,000. Much of the land is rolling prairie, but a portion is hilly and somewhat broken, especially along the course of the Wapsipinicon river, that runs through the county. The Iowa State Piscicultural establishment is located in this county, and from it many thousands of young fish are being sent out to stock the streams and lakes of the State. Much easily worked fine building and flagging stone is quarried in the county. Anamosa contains five churches, two good schools, extensive manufactures, a court house that cost $80,000, two public halls, one bank, two hotels—The Gillen House, by E. Gillen, accommodating 50 guests, and The Fisher, by K. Parker, for 100 guests; they charge $2 per diem. The Iowa Midland Railway reached the city in 1871. The streets of the city are shaded with handsome native trees, and in the summer season seem embowered in foliage. The city has water works, which supply from the Wapsipinicon river ample water for protection from fire, and for manufacturing and domestic uses. This ends our trip over this little line, and we can say that we have passed through as beautiful and as productive a portion of country as can be found within the borders of the State.

THE FREEPORT AND DUBUQUE LINE.

Leaving Chicago from the Wells Street Depot, and following the course of the Chicago and Omaha Line to Junction, 30 miles west of Chicago, we reach the "Freeport Branch," and will follow it to its junction with the Illinois Central Railway, which forms the northwestern portion of the "Dubuque Line." At 35 miles from Chicago we reach

Wayne, in Du Page county, and in the great dairy region of Northern Illinois. It was settled first in 1834, and now has 1,500 inhabitants. The land in the vicinity of the village sells for from $60 to $100 per acre. A weekly stage runs to *Wayne Centre*.

Clintonville, 39 miles from Chicago. This village of 800 inhabitants, is built on both sides of Fox river, and at one time was a place of considerable manufacturing importance, but fires swept away the largest, and they have not been rebuilt. It now has two flour mills, one paper and felt mill, one tannery, a foundry and machine shop manufacturing iron fixtures for school furniture and sewing machines, a fork factory producing 100 dozen forks daily, a large malt house, and one cheese and butter factory.

Whiting House—Lake Geneva, Wis.

PAGE 46.

Elgin, 43 miles from Chicago, divided by Fox river into West and East Elgin. We here have a beautiful city of some 9,000 persons. It is the headquarters of the dairy interest of the Fox River valley, and is the market for most of its dairy products. Elgin butter and cheese are noted the country over for their excellence. Within five miles of the city are cheese and butter factories that in 1875 produced over 2,000,000 lbs. of cheese, and 600,000 lbs. of butter. Besides manufacturing butter and cheese, the dairies ship large quantities of milk and cream to Chicago. The Illinois Milk Condensing Co., using the Gail Borden process, buys about $8,000 worth of milk monthly, and daily ships one car load of its product. The Fox River Woolen Manufactory employs 50 hands, and uses daily 500 lbs. of wool. The Elgin Packing Co. employs 100 men, and cans and packs corn and vegetables that cost at the factory, $40,000 yearly. One carriage factory employs 35 men; one foundry makes castings for sewing machines, and for machinery for dairies, its exclusive business. In the city are twelve churches, seven public schools, one academy, one catholic school with 200 students, a fine *free* public library having 5,000 volumes, three public halls, (Dubois seating 1,200), two national banks, four flour mills, two daily, three weekly and two monthly newspapers, and several hotels, best of which are The Waverly, by Lasher & Sons, with 60 rooms at $2 per day; The Western, at $1 per day; The City, by W. Shaw, at $2 per day, and The Chicago, at $1.50 per day. The court house is of brick, and connected with it is the jail and city offices. The city is lighted with gas, and has a paid fire department with steam fire engines. Wherever known Elgin is noted for its beauty, thrift and enterprise. The Northern Asylum for Insane is located in the centre of a tract of 480 acres of land, of which 160 acres were donated to the State by the city of Elgin. The buildings of the asylum are one mile southwest of the city, on the west bank of the river, and are in plain view from the cars as you pass along. The buildings and purchased grounds have cost the State some $900,000, and are said to be the most complete and best conducted of any in the West. The National Watch Company have their works here, and employ constantly from 600 to 1,000 operatives, of whom one-half are females. Since the works were started, they have made over 20,000 watches. The buildings and machinery cost about $600,000.

Gilberts, 50 miles from Chicago, is a village of 100 people. *Udina*, 4 miles, and *New Hampshire*, 8 miles distant, are tributary, and are reached from this station.

Huntley, 55 miles from Chicago, is in McHenry

county, and is a village of 600 persons. It has large dairy interests, two flour mills, one flax mill, three churches, one graded public school, and two hotels.

Union, 63 miles from Chicago, pop. 360. Has one grain elevator, one cheese factory, one good school, three churches, and one hotel. *Coral,* 2½ miles south, and *Franklinville,* 4½ miles north, are tributary.

Marengo, 66 miles from Chicago. This is an incorporated village with 2,000 inhabitants, built on the prairie, 1 mile south of the Kishwaukee river. It is surrounded by a stock growing and dairy country. The cheese and butter establishment of J. Boies & Son, use constantly the milk of 800 cows. In the village are one public school building of six rooms, six churches, "Lansign" and "Deitz" halls for public entertainments, and The Vermont House and The Marengo Hotel, to provide accommodations for transient guests.

county seat of Winnebago county, which was organized in 1836, has 55,000 inhabitants, and is one of the most densely settled counties of the State. At Rockford was held in 1845 the first meeting in the interest of railroad building west of Lake Michigan, and from the results of that meeting, and the aid then pledged, the great railroad we are now illustrating can be clearly traced. Rockford is essentially a manufacturing city. It is built on both sides of Rock river, which is here dammed, and supplies power for 135 manufacturing establishments which use its waters. Over 4,000 men are constantly employed in these establishments, and as can readily be imagined, they tend largely to make the city what it is. In the city are four flour mills, the manufacturing firms of Emerson & Co., Norman C. Thompson, F. H. Manny, J. P. Manny, W. A. Knowlton, Bertram & Sames, A. Haines & Co., Briggs & Enoch, Derwent & Sons, Gault, Hill & Co., and Jones & Yard, all making agricultural

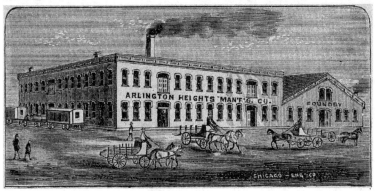

Arlington Heights (late Dunton), Ill.—page 50.

Belvidere, 78 miles from Chicago. This is the county seat of Boone county, which was organized in 1837, and has 15,000 inhabitants. Kishwaukee river runs through the city, and divides it into North and South Belvidere. South Belvidere is built on elevated prairie, and contains more than half of the 4,000 persons who comprise the population of this joint city. In the court house square is the grave of "Big Thunder," a noted Indian warrior, who was killed there during the "Blackhawk War." The city has two fine school houses, eleven churches, two public halls with seats for 2,000 persons, and two banks with capital of $150,000. Broom corn is largely grown in this vicinity, one person in 1875 having over 400 acres on his farm.

Cherry Valley, 84 miles from Chicago, is in Winnebago county, and has a population of 1,200. The camp meeting ground of the Northern Methodist Conference is located one-half mile west of this village. The village has one school house that cost $16,000, three churches and two hotels—The Valley House, by L. N. Doty, and The Union, by C. A. Dunwell. Around Cherry Valley are many "maple orchards," in which large quantities of maple sugar are made annually.

Rockford, 93 miles from Chicago. This is the

implements; several large iron works, glove factories, boot and shoe, pump and furniture factories, paper mills, oat meal mills, etc. A recent acquisition is the establishment of a watch company having a capital of $150,000, and although but one-fourth of the buildings are erected, they employ 200 operators. The city is lighted with gas, has water works, a fine public library with 6,000 volumes of bound books, an efficient fire department, several newspapers, and several iron and stone bridges crossing the river. The schools, of which there are eight, and the churches, of which there are sixteen, should not be forgotten. The population of Rockford is over 15,000, and is steadily increasing.

Winnebago, 100 miles from Chicago, is a village of 600 strictly *temperance* people, for they allow no liquor to be sold in the village, or within one mile of it. It has one school, four churches, one hotel, and one grain elevator. *Fountaindale* is tributary, and is reached twice weekly by stage.

Pecatonica, 107 miles from Chicago. Here we have another town of 2,000 people who do not allow liquors to be sold within its corporate limits. The town was chartered in 1855, and having fine water power utilizes it to run the machinery of a flour mill, a wagon factory, butter tub factory, saw mill, machine shop, and other minor shops. The town has one good school house, five churches, one newspaper, a masonic and an odd fellows' hall, three public halls, and one hotel, The Pecatonica House, by Jas. O'Brien, with 20 rooms for guests at $2 per day. The town is built on Pecatonica river, which is here crossed by a substantial iron bridge.

Ridott, 114 miles from Chicago. In Stephenson county is this village of 300 souls. It has one grain elevator, a cheese factory, a public hall that cost $7,000, three schools, one church, and one hotel. *Orangeville, Oneco,* and *Cedarville* are tributary, and are reached by stage.

Freeport, 121 miles from Chicago. This city, with its 11,000 inhabitants, is the county seat of Stephenson county. The county was organized in 1836-7, and was named for the Winnebago tribe of Indians, who had their homes in the vicinity until 1835, when they were moved beyond the borders of Illinois. Winnesheick, the head chief of the tribe, had in 1827 his village of 200 lodges on the ground where Freeport is now located, and the burial ground of his fathers is now covered by the freight houses of the C. & N.-W. Ry! In early days considerable lead was mined in Stephenson county, and in 1827 a war broke out between the miners (of the Galena district) and the Indians, and had it not been for Winnesheick's friendly warning, every white person in Northern Illinois would have been treacherously murdered. He was always friendly to the whites, and his memory is honored by the descendants of the early settlers of Stephenson county. The county contains fifteen townships, through each of which at least one stream runs, thus having ample water and drainage. The first white permanent settler was Oliver W. Kellogg, of New York State who came in 1826; the first mill in, and the jail for the county were built in 1837, by T. J. Turner, once President of The Galena & Chicago Union Railway, as noted in the history of that line; the first school was opened in 1839, and at the first county election held in 1838, eighty-four votes were cast.

Freeport is on Pecatonica river, 30 miles from its mouth; its first house was built in 1835, its first store in 1836, first tavern in 1837, first school in 1839, and was made the county seat in 1837. In 1845 it had a population of 500, in 1850, of 1,100, and has 11,000 now. The river is dammed here, and a water power, with a fall of seven feet secured thereby, which is utilized by many manufacturing establishments built along it. In the annals of this city we find, that on July 12, 1849, the mercury stood at 114 degrees in the shade, and on January 12, 1864, at 35 degrees *below*. In 1852 from twenty to thirty stages arrived and departed from this city daily, it being then the farthest limit that could be reached by any other public conveyance.

Public School, Arlington Heights, Ill.—page 50.

The first locomotive reached Freeport on August 25, 1853; the city was incorporated in 1855, and in 1856 it was lighted with gas. The telegraph reached it in 1861. It contains the following manufactories, viz: Champion corn cultivators, fanning mills, Stover wind mills, iron pumps, Pattison's reapers, Morgan & Co.'s plows, Emmert's churns, two flour mills, one woolen mill, four machine shops, a large beet-root sugar factory, and many minor establishments; a fine court house, that cost, in 1872, $140,000; a soldiers' monument, that cost $12,000; five banks, with capital of $480,000; two public halls, that will seat 1,800 persons; four school houses, that cost $46,000, and will seat 1,950 children; eleven churches; six masonic lodges, chapters, etc., occupying a fine masonic hall; four newspapers, and six hotels, viz., The Brewster, by J. S. Gates; The Pennsylvania, by J. S. Zartman; The Tremont, by Robey & Myer; The New York, by John Kerch; The French, by J. French, and The European, by H. E. Brown. *Orangeville, Oneco, Shucey Mills, Monroe, Wis., McConnell's Grove, Elizabeth, Waterman's Mills, Yellow Creek, Kent, Loran, Winters, Plum River, Willow,* and *Yankee Hollow,* are reached from Freeport by stages. At this point we reach the NORTHERN DIVISION OF THE ILLINOIS CENTRAL RAILROAD, and with it form the CHICAGO, FREEPORT & DUBUQUE LINE, over which the through distributing postal cars carrying the United States mails are run between Chicago and *Lena, Nora,* WARREN, *App'e River, Scales Mound, Council Hill,* GALENA, *Dunleith,* DUBUQUE, and all points west of that city. This forms the direct northern route to those points, and all passengers passing through Northern Illinois destined for any of them, should be certain to buy tickets to or via Freeport over the Chicago & North-Western Railway, and should not be induced to take less favorable routes.

At Freeport we form connections with the WESTERN UNION RAILROAD for *Shannon, Lanark, Mount Carroll, Savanna,* and points west. The position occupied by Freeport, and its railway facilities, give to it a commanding influence over the trade of a large district on all sides, and how well this is taken advantage of, its prosperous merchants and manufacturers plainly show.

THE CHICAGO AND LAKE GENEVA LINE.

Two routes owned by the Chicago & North-Western Railway Co. are open to the traveler from Chicago destined for Lake Geneva and the surrounding country. The one route takes him via the Wisconsin Division and Crystal Lake, and will be described elsewhere. The other route is the one we would now call your attention to. By it you leave Chicago from the Wells Street depot, follow the Galena double track, steel rail line to Junction, thence northwesterly to "FOX RIVER SWITCH," (44 miles from Chicago), over the FREEPORT BRANCH, and thence via the "FOX RIVER BRANCH," to

Dundee, 48 miles from Chicago. This pleasant city of 2,500 people is on Fox river, which divides it into East and West Dundee, which have separate municipal governments, and are really two corporations, but here must be treated as if one. The cities have one high school in a building that cost $30,000, several other public schools, a public hall that cost $5,000, six churches, a cheese factory using 2,500 gallons of milk daily, two hotels—The Bowman and The Dundee, and many large business establishments. The Dundee Brick Co. employs $25,000 capital, and makes 4,000,000 bricks yearly. From this station large quantities of milk are daily shipped to Chicago. It is claimed, and probably correctly, that from this station is daily shipped more milk than from any other station in the United States. The cheese and butter of this valley command a high price in the markets of Europe, and owing to the grasses and water consumed by the cows, is said to be of peculiarly good quality. *Carpenterville* is one mile from Dundee, and is an active manufacturing village with 500 people. It is connected with Dundee by a side track, and has one flour mill, one woolen factory with two sets machinery, and employing 25 to 50 men; an iron and bolt company, employing 100 men, and paying in wages $4,000 monthly; an agricultural implement factory, employing 80 men, and several smaller factories and mills. Fox river is here spanned by an iron bridge built by the American Bridge Co.

Algonquin, 53 miles from Chicago. The quiet village of Algonquin is delightfully situated in a little triangular valley at the junction of Crystal Lake outlet with Fox river. The bluffs, which at Elgin, ten miles below, are gradual slopes, here assume the character of steep hills of very considerable elevation, and in consequence the place has more the appearance of a New England village, than of a typical Western prairie village: nestled down here quietly, and necessarily from its situation quite compactly built, with the Fox river and clear waters of the lake outlet flowing through it, one hardly realizes that he is in a prairie country. The bluffs above and below the village are well wooded, and when clothed with their spring and summer foliage, give the place an attractive and captivating appearance. Taken altogether, Algonquin possesses a picturesqueness and beauty rarely found in the West, and should be better known, that it may be appreciated as it deserves. The village has had several names since its earlier days. For a time it was known as *Cornish's Ferry,* then as *Osceola,* and finally in 1856 it had permanently attached its present name. The railroad crosses Fox river at this point. Large quantities of milk are shipped from here to Chicago, and more is consumed in its cheese and butter factories, which together absorb daily the milk of 1,500 cows, which are owned on fifty-four farms near this station. Grazing land sells for from $50 to $100 per acre. Algonquin contains three flour mills, one milk can factory, two fine school houses, and several churches.

Ayer's Hotel, Harvard, Ill.—page 52.

Crystal Lake is 58 miles from Chicago by this route, and will be described when we reach the Wisconsin Division of the C. & N.-W. Ry.

McHenry, 66 miles from Chicago. This is a village of 2,000 people, built on high ground on the banks of Fox river, in McHenry county, Ill. It has three hotels, one school, several churches, and one newspaper. Five miles distant we come to a chain of small lakes that extend eastward some thirty miles. These lakes are full of fish, and along their shores game is found in abundance.

Ringwood, 70 miles from Chicago, is a village of 400 people, surrounded by a fine grazing and farm country, well settled and finely improved. In the village are two hotels, one school, two churches, and the usual supply of stores, shops, etc.

Richmond, 75 miles from Chicago. This village has 750 inhabitants, and is built on the banks of Neipersink river. It has one flour mill, one school, four churches, an agricultural implement manufactory, and one hotel. *Twin Lakes* are three miles from the station. Game abounds in the vicinity.

Genoa Junction, 77 miles from Chicago.

Passing out of McHenry county, and out of the State of Illinois, we here reach Walworth county, in Wisconsin, and here cross the KENOSHA & ROCKFORD RAILROAD, one of the lines owned by the C. & N.-W. Ry. Co. The village contains 300 people, and has one flour mill, one hotel, a planing mill, one school, and one church. Wooded hills surround the town, and add no small charm to the scenery of the vicinity.

LAKE GENEVA, WIS.

Lake Geneva, via Elgin, is 86 miles, and via Crystal Lake, 70 miles from Chicago. During the summer season through trains are run by both routes, but during the winter *through* trains are run only via Elgin, yet in the winter close connections are made by the Wisconsin Division trains at Crystal Lake, with the through trains that run by the Elgin route.

This delightful and thriving village is situated upon the north shore of Lake Geneva. No more lovely sheet of water can be found in the Northwest, and no town could be blessed with more charming scenery. It is fast becoming noted for its beauty, and many hundreds are making it their summer resort. Its growth and improvement for the past few years have been marked, and the extensive hotels now building upon its banks only await completion to be thronged with the tourist and traveler from every part. Two fine side-wheel steamers make regular trips from Geneva to Fontana and intermediate points of interest, affording the richest enjoyment to the seeker of pleasure. The waters are remarkably clear and cold, being supplied by springs, and in many places are known to be very deep. The lake was called by the Indians "Kish-wa-ke-ta," signifying "crystal water." In later times it was known as Big Foot

The Lake and the Oakwood Hotel, Green Lake, Wis.—page 58.

Lake, from its slight resemblance to the human leg and a monstrous foot. The lake as it is now known was named for Geneva Lake in New York, which in turn was named for Geneva Lake in Switzerland. Its shores are in places bold, at others undulating; here topped with grand old forests of oak, there opening out into a wide rolling stretch of country, dotted with fields of waving grass and grain, and beautiful farm houses. Mansions of great size and immense cost, displaying exquisite architecture, and surrounded by grassy terraces and rarest flower gardens, adorn the shores near the village, while the lands for some miles out have been purchased by capitalists, and at no distant day will be adorned with all that money and skill can do to make a rural home inviting and lovely. Springs of mineral properties, and it is hoped value, have been discovered at the head of the lake, where a large summer boarding house is to be erected. The fish of the lake are pickerel, rock and black bass, and perch; but most important of all is the celebrated "cisco," which comes to shore and is usually seen but once during the year, which is from June 10 to June 15, when a certain fly becomes unpleasantly abundant about the shore, and which becomes food for the cisco during this their spawning time. Cisco fishing is a sport relished by many, who travel ofttimes long distances to share it with the villagers and visitors, who generally turn out and make it a gala week. The village is well laid out, the site being a little elevated and quite level, with high rolling hills to the east, west and north. The outlet of the lake furnishes a valuable water power, which operates a large grist mill, woolen mill and saw mill. Geneva at present has about 2,500 inhabitants, the census of 1870 showing 2,042. The town has six churches, three hotels, one of which is valued at $50,000, a large and flourishing ladies' seminary, a fine public school building, the most valuable in the county, one bank, one newspaper, and the usual amount of store and other village property. Geneva was for many years the direct point from which most supplies of lumber, flour, feed, and other pioneer necessities were obtained. The prospects of this town we think unusually flattering; with a proportionate growth in manufacturing, with its watering attractions it must at no distant day rank among the best towns of the State.

The Sherwood Forest, Green Lake, Wis.—page 59.

TO THE NORTH & NORTHWEST.

The Chicago & North-Western Railway Company owns two lines that run from Chicago northwardly, and one of these lines, 62 miles beyond Chicago, divides, and thereafter two lines are formed that continually diverge until their northern and northwestern termini are many hundred miles apart. Examine our map. Note Harvard Junction as the point of bifurcation—Ishpeming in the north, close to Lake Superior, as the northern terminus of one line, and Lake Kampeska as the northwestern terminus of the other. Yet another peculiarity should be noted,—after the North-Western line has reached Elroy, 150 miles from Harvard Junction, and 212 miles from Chicago, another line starts off towards the north, and ends at St. Paul and Minneapolis. This will be treated of in its proper place as a portion of our CHICAGO, MADISON & ST. PAUL LINE.

Magone Falls, near Green Bay, Wis.—page 65.

We trust you will fix in your minds the locale of these three lines, and be enabled to follow us when we come to describe the various points along them. They will be mostly treated as independent lines, as they are to a large extent. The other line running northwardly from Chicago, referred to above, is the old Lake Shore, Chicago & Milwaukee Line, and is here mentioned for the reason that it, too, reaches at Fond du Lac, the Wisconsin Division, which forms a portion of the Green Bay & Lake Superior Line, which we propose to take up first. The Milwaukee Line, and its connection at Fond du Lac with the Wisconsin Division, will be discussed in its proper place. With this preface, we will attempt to produce for your use a faint picture of the noted

CHICAGO, GREEN BAY & LAKE SUPERIOR LINE.

This line is formed of the Wisconsin and Peninsula Divisions of the Chicago & North-Western Railway. The first runs from Chicago, via Harvard, Janesville, Watertown, Fond du Lac and Oshkosh, to Fort Howard (Green Bay); and the last from Green Bay, via Oconto, Menomonee, Escanaba and Negaunee, to Ishpeming, in the heart of the iron region of Lake Superior, and within 12 miles of the city of Marquette. Leaving Chicago from the Depot on the corner of West Kinzie and Canal streets, it runs through the northwest suburbs of the city, out of Cook and into and through Lake and McHenry counties, in Illinois; Walworth, Rock, Jefferson, Dodge, Fond du Lac,

Winnebago, Outagamie, Brown and Oconto counties, in Wisconsin; and Bleeker, Delta and Marquette counties in the northern peninsula of Michigan. This line is 421 miles long, without counting the many short branches that radiate from the main line near its northern terminus, and, with its connection to Marquette, gives us an all rail line, and the only one from Chicago to the shores of Lake Superior. It passes through as great a variety of scenery as can be found on any line. First, the old settled eastern part of Northern Illinois, with its suburban villages and cosy little towns; then through the grass and dairy region of Southeastern Wisconsin; then through as fine a farming and fruit region as the West or any other country produces, followed by the pine lands of the northeastern part of that State, and of the southern portion of the northern peninsula of Michigan; then the sand hill and cedar country,

First National Hotel, Green Bay Wis.—page 66.

along upper Green Bay and the Escanaba river, and, finally, in the ribbed and rocky iron country. All this can be passed through in a summer day's journey, and can be viewed and enjoyed from the luxurious seats of the Pullman Palace Coach, as it passes daily in its journey from Chicago to Marquette, or *vice versa*. Besides opening up the charming country along its own line, this road crosses and forms connections with a series of east and west roads, which together give entrance to all parts of the State of Wisconsin, and offer gateways to the summer resorts and fishing and shooting grounds that are becoming so well and favorably known, not only over our own land, but in "the lands beyond the sea."

We will now commence our trip up this line, and having seated ourselves in the elegant coaches of the line as they stand in the West Kinzie and Canal streets depot, we will first see what is offered for suburban patrons, and to do that, we show the commutation rates as follows:

Cook's Hotel, Green Bay, Wis.—page 66.

COMMUTATION RATES — WISCONSIN DIVISION.

Distances from Chicago.	BETWEEN CHICAGO AND	Single Ticket.	10 Ride Ticket, unlimited.	30 Rides, Family Ticket, good for 4 Months.	100 Rides, Individual Ticket.	Number Month, 100 Ride Tickets are good.	Annual Ticket.	First Half-Yearly Ticket.	Second Half-Yearly Ticket.
4.1	Maplewood	.15	1.10	2.50	6.50	3	38.00	23.00	18.00
6.7	Irving Park	.25	1.80	4.00	7.20	3	48.00	29.00	22.00
7.6	Montrose	.27	2.00	4.60	9.10	3	54.00	33.00	25.00
8.8	Plank Road	.30	2.35	5.80	11.00	3	60.00	36.00	27.00
10.4	Norwood	.35	2.75	6.30	13.00	4	68.00	41.00	31.00
12.1	Canfield	.40	3.20	7.30	15.00	4	72.00	43.00	33.00
13.1	Park Ridge	.45	3.50	7.50	15.75	4	72.50	43.50	33.50
16.6	Des Plaines	.60	4.40	10.00	18.50	4	77.00	47.00	35.00
19.9	Mount Prospect	.70	5.30	12.00	21.50	4	80.00	48.00	36.00
22.4	Arlington Heights	.80	5.95	13.50	23.50	4	85.00	51.00	38.00
26.1	Palatine	.90	6.90	15.70	26.10	4	95.00	57.00	43.00
31.6	Barrington	1.10	8.40	19.00	31.60	5	110.00	66.00	50.00
38.5	Cary	1.35	10.15	23.00	38.50	5	115.00	68.00	53.00
42.9	Crystal Lake	1.50 / 2.05	11.35	25.80	42.90	6	120.00	72.00	54.06
50.2	McHenry	1.75 / 2.30	13.30	30.15	50.20	6	.....	.....	.....
54.2	Ringwood	1.90 / 2.45	14.35	32.55	54.20	6	.....	.....	.....
59.7	Richmond	2.10 / 2.65	15.85	35.85	59.70	6	.....	.....	.....
61.5	Genoa Junction	2.15 / 2.70	16.30	36.90	61.50	6	.....	.....	.....
70.2	Lake Geneva	2.50 / 3.00	18.60 *17.00	42.00	70.00	6	.....	.....	.....
45.7	Ridgefield	1.60	12.10	27.50	45.70	6	125.00	75.00	56.00
51.3	Woodstock	1.80	13.60	30.80	51.00	6	150.00	90.00	67.00

* Family Tickets limited to Six Months.

All these points are amply provided with many fast trains daily to and from Chicago.

Passing out of the depot, and through the northern limits of the city of Chicago, we run past MAPLEWOOD, a bright little village, and IRVING PARK, of similar character, and eight miles out reach MONTROSE, a new station on a level prairie, where we cross a railway line, and make a halt of a few seconds only, as, beyond the artesian wells, there is nothing to detain us for description. One mile further on we reach PLANK ROAD, with a population of 800 and two hotels; then one mile beyond we have NORWOOD, and two miles further, CANFIELD; and 13 miles from Chicago, PARK RIDGE, with its 700 people, two churches, one school, one hotel, and an artesian well 1,600 feet deep, that cost $5,500, and flows water strongly medicinal, and having a local reputation as a powerful remedial agent. Pushing on, we get beyond the line of residence villages, and

Des Plaines, 17 miles from Chicago, is reached, and is found to be a thrifty growing village of 1,500 people, located on the banks of the Des Plaines river, which is here crossed by a fine bridge. Along the river are many pleasant groves, through which roads have been opened, giving facilities for pleasant drives. The Methodist camp meeting grounds are contiguous to the village; on these grounds are now over 100 houses. In the village is a large brick school house, four churches, and one hotel—The American, by H. & A. Ward, at $2 per day. *West* and *East Northfield, Wheeling, Half Day* and *Elk Grove*, are tributary villages, six to ten miles distant, and reached by stage lines.

Mount Prospect, 17 miles from Chicago, is a new station.

Arlington Heights, 22 miles from Chicago. This is the village that has for many years been known as Dunton. It is built on ground elevated 200 feet above Lake Michigan, and 75 feet above the railroad track, yet water is obtained in abundance in digging wells not more than 25 feet deep. The town was laid out in 1853, and now has 1,500 inhabitants. Considerable manufacturing is carried on—one concern employing 150 men, and another (a brass foundry) employs 100 men. In the town are five public parks, adorned with flowers and shrubs; one school, in a house that cost $10,000; three churches, a steam flour mill, two grain elevators and three hotels. Marl and peat beds are found in the vicinity, and are worked to some extent. *Lake Zurich*, a pleasant summer resort, seven miles northwest, *Elk Grove*, two miles south, and *Long Grove*, two miles north, are tributary.

Palatine, 26 miles from Chicago, This village, with its 1,500 inhabitants, is on the borders of the

"Lake Country" of Northern Illinois. *Lakes Zurich, Diamond, Grass, Honey* and *Bangs* are near the station, and furnish excellent fishing, boating and bathing facilities. Of these, Lake Zurich may be especially mentioned, as it is one of the most beautiful bodies of fresh water to be found anywhere. The village of the same name is on its shores, and has in it two good hotels, for 70 summer guests. Palatine contains two grain elevators, one public hall, two newspaper offices, one school and three churches.

Barrington, 32 miles from Chicago, pop. 1,200, is in the northern part of Cook county, and is surrounded by a fine agricultural country. It is a large milk shipping point, and has several butter and cheese factories within its limits. In the village are four churches, one school, two hotels, and many fine business houses. *Wauconda* is 9 miles north, and to it stages run daily, stopping at Lake Zurich en route. Fare to Lake Zurich 25 cents, and to Wauconda 50 cents.

LAKE ZURICH.

Unlike many less favored places, little has been said of the one named above. Last year a few of the lovers of quiet and the beautiful sought this place out—one of them, writing to the Chicago *Tribune*, says:

"It may be, and probably is, the fact, that many of your readers are not aware what a beautiful summer resort lies within an hour and a half's ride of Chicago. Many people who swelter through the hot season, and who cannot afford to take a vacation, or expend much money in pleasure-seeking, will undoubtedly be glad to know that within so short a distance, and which may be reached in so short a time, and at a comparatively nominal cost, there lies one of the most beautiful spots that can be found anywhere in the Western country. Lake Zurich is named after one of the most splendid lakes in Switzerland, and when once seen, and its scenery and loveliness enjoyed, no one would for a moment think that he who named it was guilty of any presumption in the christening. This place is situated on the edge of Lake county, four miles north by east from Barrington Station, on the Wisconsin Division of the Chicago & North-Western Railway. An omnibus is in waiting on the arrival of trains, to convey passengers to the Lake Zurich House. The short ride by stage is even more delightful than by rail. The road runs through a splendid farming country, teeming with all the exuberant richness of a bounteous soil, alternating with woodland and prairie, hills and valleys, fields of waving grain, and farm houses embowered in shrubbery—making one of the finest landscapes I have ever seen anywhere.

"This letter is written at the close of the celebration of our National Anniversary, which has been a glorious day here. Though writing from Lake Zurich, yet I do not live here, and have never been here before. I have, therefore, no ax to grind and nobody's horn to blow, but am actuated by a desire to let the people of our great city, who may long for the inexpensive luxury of a brief respite from the dust, and din, and heat of the restless, surging

Mineral Dock, Escanaba, Mich.—page 69.

multitude, know what a delightful rural retreat lies upon our very outskirts, where pleasure and rest are within the reach of all. I never till to-day so fully realized the force of the expression, 'Man made the city, but God made the country;' it was, perhaps, because the contrast was so great and so immediate—as the saying is, 'Out of Purgatory into Paradise.'

"Lake Zurich is belted all around with beautiful groves of timber, among the openings of which, grass-plats slope down to the pebbled beach, where the pure crystal waters lave the shore. The lake, as I am informed, abounds with fish of various kinds, the principal of which are pickerel and black bass, which may be taken with the spear by torchlight in the shallower parts of the lake, or with hook and line, and by trolling.

"I shall not soon forget my first visit to Lake Zurich; and, in conclusion, can only express the hope that hundreds of others, from our crowded and dusty city, may enjoy, in this quiet and secluded retreat, the delight which will not be excelled though they travel hundreds of miles to find it."

The above was written by a gentleman who has visited every celebrated watering place in this country and in Europe, and speaks from personal experience.

Cary, 38 miles from Chicago. This village of 100 people is one mile from Fox river, in which is most excellent fishing. The village has one good hotel, in which sportsmen always find a hearty welcome.

Crystal Lake, by this route 43 miles from Chicago. At this point we cross the Fox River Branch of the C. & N.-W. Ry, and can, via this route, reach Lake Geneva, as stated elsewhere. Crystal Lake has a population of 1,000, and is built 1½ miles from the lake of the same name, which was named from its purely clear waters. From this lake thousands of tons of ice are cut and yearly shipped to Chicago and more southern points. The village was laid out in 1855, and has good schools, four churches, and several manufactories, amongst which are pickling and canning establishments that alone occupy $400,000 of capital, and 200 to 300 men. Its hotels are The Hyett House, and Ashton's.

Ridgefield, 46 miles from Chicago. This station is built on the edge of a large tract of timber, has 500 inhabitants, a good school, one church, fine fishing and shooting in its vicinity, and is surrounded by as fine farming land as is to be found in the State.

Woodstock, 51 miles from Chicago. This is the county seat of McHenry county, which was organized in 1836, named after Col. Wm. McHenry, of Blackhawk War fame, has 26,000 inhabitants, and is one of the richest, most productive, and most thickly settled counties in the State. The land of the county is very evenly divided between prairie and timber. In the county are thirteen flour mills run by water, twenty-seven cheese factories, and twenty-three butter factories. What is now Woodstock was until 1844 known as Centreville, and as such had been the county seat for 7 years. The name was changed at request of the then County Clerk, and was named after Woodstock, Vermont. The city is built on a ridge running between Fox and Rock rivers, and has 2,500 inhabitants, a county court house, a theatre, four public halls, one hotel —The Waverly house, having 60 rooms, and several manufactories. The Woodstock Pickle Factory employs 50 men, and uses of cucumbers 34,000 bushels, cabbage 10,000 tons, cauliflower 1,000 tons, and equally large lots of other vegetables yearly; in 1875 it produced over $350,000 worth of pickles.

Teal Lake, Negaunee, Mich.—page 70.
From a painting by E. Schrottky, of Negaunee.

The northern portion of the C. & N.-W. Ry. was first projected by citizens of Woodstock, who lent their aid in its building, and all through its earlier trials.

Kishwaukee, 56 miles from Chicago, a station without an agent.

Harvard, 62 miles from Chicago. This city is built on the brow of a hill, which descends towards the south, and is crowned (in the back ground) by a forest of hard woods. Its situation is picturesque, and from its streets many charming views of the highly cultivated and beautiful surrounding country may be enjoyed. The Kenosha & Rockford Division of the Chicago & Northwestern Railway here crosses the line we are describing, and here also the Chicago, Madison & St. Paul Line diverges toward the northwest. When reading about this last-named line, please remember that it follows the Wisconsin Division, or the Green Bay & Lake Superior Line, to this point, but is an independent and distinctly different line beyond this station. Harvard is growing rapidly; 60 residences were erected in the town in 1874, and over 100 in 1875. It contains over 3,000 people, three grain elevators, flour mills, wagon and sash, door and blind factories, good schools, a fine public hall ("Ayer's"), that cost $15,000, and will seat 600 persons; four churches, two hotels—The Walker, with 20 rooms, and last, but not least, the well-known and admirably kept Ayer's Hotel, of which the proprietor, Judge Ayer, is known far and wide as eminently *the* hotel keeper of Northern Illinois. This house is a regular dining hall for this road, and on its tables, at all seasons of the year, are found not only the substantials, but all the delicacies of the table; game and fish are always to be had, and it is no stretch of truth to say, that its tables always "groan" with the good things of this life. At this point the railroad company has a repair and machine shop, with a brick round house for 18 engines.

Two malthouses are in constant operation, and produce over 100,000 bushels of malt yearly. *Ayer's Corners*, five miles north, is reached by stage daily for 50 cts. *Twin Lakes*, a popular fishing resort, is 20 miles distant. A line of stages runs to the shores of Lake Geneva, from whence passengers are taken by steamer to the village of Geneva, at the foot of the lake.

Lawrence, 65 miles from Chicago, is a village of 200 souls, built on Piskasaw Creek—the Big Foot Prairie—which was the home of a celebrated Indian chief, called "Big Foot." Passing out of the State of Illinois, we find the southern line of Wisconsin close to the next station.

WISCONSIN.

The "Badger State" is yearly becoming more widely and more favorably known to the summer tourist, and to the seeker after rural pleasures. While comparatively a new State, it is yet old in many respects. As long ago as the middle of the 17th century, it was visited by French missionaries and traders, who took home with them glowing accounts of the fertility of its soil; of the splendor of its scenery; of the freshness of its odorous pine-clad hills; of its flashing, dazzling, rapid running streams, full of many kinds of fish; of its clear, deep, cold, pure and beautiful lakes, of which the State has many hundreds; and of its delightful, balmy and invigorating summer climate. The stories of these advantages were not lost on the beauty-loving French, and soon colonies were formed for the settlement of this beautiful "Neekoospara," as they had learned to call from the Indians the country we now name Wisconsin. It may rightly then be inferred that the French were the first whites to make homes along the bays, lakes and rivers of this well favored land. Prairie du Chien, La Crosse, Fond du Lac, Green Bay, Menomonee, and many other now flourishing towns or cities, were founded by the French, and in many of them can yet be found the descendants of the early pioneers.

Iron Mine and Ore Train, near Negaunee, Mich.—page 70.

Objects of Interest to Tourists.

Scattered, if we may so speak, all over the State, can be found objects of interest to the lover of the picturesque, and not a few of interest to the antiquary. Scattered over her undulating plains are found earthworks, modeled after the forms of men and animals, that are evidently the work of a race different from those who possessed the country at the period of the arrival of the French. At Aztalan, in Jefferson county, is an ancient fortification, 1,700 feet long and 900 feet wide, with walls five to six feet high and more than 20 feet thick; this, with another near the Blue Mounds, near Madison, resembles a man in a recumbent position. Another, near Madison, in Dane county, resembles a turtle; one at the south end of "The Devil's Lake," in Sauk county, closely resembles an eagle; and one near Cassville, in Grant county, on the Mississippi river, resembles the extinct mastodon. The Blue Mounds, in Dane county, rise to 2,000 feet above the surrounding country, and are prominent landmarks in that prairie country. This State shares with Minnesota the beautiful Lake Pepin, an expansion of the Mississippi river, mostly walled in by precipitous shores which rise in places to 500 feet. Connected with almost every cliff or promontory along the shores of this beautiful lake, are legends of the Indians who formerly had homes here. Along the rivers of this State are found many beautiful falls, rivaling those of older States. In the St. Louis river are "The Dalles," which have a descent of 320 feet. The Dalles of the St. Croix are also well known. Quinnessec Falls, in Menomonee river, have a perpendicular pitch of over 50 feet, and a general descent of 150 feet in a mile and a half, besides many other rapids, where the river tosses and dashes through narrow and tortuous defiles. Chippewa Falls and Big Bull Falls might also be noted. Along the Wisconsin river are many grand and picturesque views; in Richland county the banks of the river rise to a height of 200 to 250 feet, and in Sauk county it passes through narrow gorges where the banks rise to 500 to 600 feet elevation. Grandfather Bull Falls. the greatest rapids of the Wisconsin river, are in north latitude 45, and are a series of cascades breaking through a ridge 150 feet perpendicular height, for a distance of nearly two miles; on the same river, near latitude 44, is Petenwell Peak, an oval mass of rock, 900 feet long by 300 wide and 200 high, and from which commanding views can be obtained. About 70 feet of the upper portion of this rock is cut and split into fantastic shapes, many of the fragments resembling castles, towers and turrets. A few miles from this rock is Fortification Rock, which rises perpendicularly several hundred feet. At The Dalles this river is compressed for five or six miles between red sandstone bluffs, averaging over 100 feet in height.

The principal lakes are Lake Winnebago, in the southeastern portion of the State—this lake is about 30 miles long and 10 miles wide, and communicates with Green Bay (an arm of Lake Michigan) through Fox or Neenah river—Horicon Lake, Devil's Lake, Lake Koshkonong, Lake Geneva, Lake Zurich, and the four lakes around Madison; these are the larger lakes of this lake-studded State. Along all the rivers of the State, and at their "heads," *hundreds* of little lakes are found, like gems glittering in the sunshine.

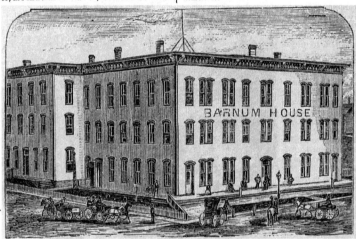

Ishpeming, Mich.—Its Hotel—page 71.

Sharon, 71 miles from Chicago. The first station we reach after crossing the State line is Sharon, a village of 2,000 people, in Walworth county. A local history says: "Sharon village and township are situated in the extreme southeast portion of the county, on the Chicago & North-Western Railway. The township contains two villages, Sharon and *Allen's Grove*, on the Western Union Railroad. The land is all valuable, there being no lakes or swamps. The business of Sharon village is in a thriving and healthful condition. The village has several churches and hotels, one newspaper, one academy, and one public school building. Its population in 1870 was 1,865. The first settler in this town was John Reeder, who came the latter part of 1836 or first of '37. He made a claim and broke the first ground. Soon after came Josiah Topping, and settled at Topping's Corners. Here he built the first frame house, and here was erected the first school house in the township. The village was named for Sharon, Schoharie county, N. Y. Allen's Grove has an academy building." Our notes show that Sharon now has two good graded public schools, a flour mill, a public hall, three churches, two hotels—The Corliss and The Wolcott, and the largest cheese factory in the State.

Walworth county is said to have been the first organized, in 1838, when the Territory of Wisconsin embraced the country now known as the States of Iowa, Minnesota, Wisconsin, and parts of Nebraska, and of the Territory of Dakota. In the county are 24 lakes, amongst which are Lakes Geneva, Crooked, Army, Potter's, Booth, Lulu, Como, Turtle, Whitewater, Bass, Holden's, Grove, Middle, Mill, Otter and Pleasant, ranging from one-half mile wide and one mile long, to 3 or 4 miles wide to 10 or 12 miles long. All are stocked with fish, and on several of them are various pleasure boats, including yachts and steamers, and on the shores of several are club houses and summer hotels. At *Delavan*, in this county, is located the State Deaf and Dumb Asylum, which is built on lands donated in 1857 by that well known philanthropist, F. K. Phoenix, of Bloomington, Ill. This asylum has a school connected with it, in which 347 children have been taught.

Clinton Junction, 78 miles from Chicago. We here cross the WESTERN UNION RAILROAD, which it will be remembered other branches of the C. & N.-W. Ry. have been shown to cross at Freeport and at Fulton. At this point we get connections for *Darien, Delavan, Elkhorn, Springfield,* and *Burlington* eastwardly, and for *Rockton, Durand, Davis,* etc., westwardly. The village is in Rock county, has 1,500 inhabitants, good schools, flour mills, three churches, *the largest carriage factory in the State*, (owned by F. P. Wallis & Co.), and several manufactories. Its hotels are The Taylor House, by Lots Taylor, and The Snyder, by J. Snyder. The surrounding country is mostly prairie, and furnishes fine chicken shooting in the fall.

Shopiere, 82 miles from Chicago. The village, with its 500 population, is on Turtle creek, 1¼ miles from the station. It has one flour mill and two churches.

Janesville, 91 miles from Chicago. This is the county seat of Rock county, which was organized in 1839, and now has over 30,000 population. Few counties in any State can show as beautiful and as diversified scenery, or as highly cultivated farms, as Rock county. Its earlier settlers, who were mostly from the State of Maine, brought with them the habits and industry of that far eastern State, and the county is to-day enjoying the fruits of those industrious, intelligent pioneers. Janesville is noted for the beauty of its location, for its wide, clean streets, for its many thriving manufactories, for its fine business houses and residences, and for the thrift and "drive" of its enterprising people. It is often called the Chicago of Wisconsin. It is built on high ground, on both sides of Rock river, which furnishes the power for its many factories. Around the city are many groves of fine timber, and in its streets are many shade trees. These two facts have given it the name of "The Bower City." Its court house, built in 1871, is the finest in the State, and is built of cut stone and cream-colored brick. It cost $100,000. It has six fine school houses, costing from $10,000 up; its high school cost $50,000. It has 12 churches, that cost, each, from $40.000 to $50,000. The Wisconsin Institute for the Blind is located here. It has several banks and several live newspapers. Of its manufactories, the Harris Manufacturing Company, with a capital of $152,000, and $33,000 surplus, employs 200 men in buildings that cover two (city) blocks of ground; one furniture factory employs 40 men, and another 20 men. The McLean Manufacturing Co. make a specialty of ladies' water-proof cloth and shawls. The Doty Manufacturing Co. employs $150,000 capital, and besides manufacturing agricultural implements, it makes punching and shearing machines, washing machines, step ladders, warehouse trucks, etc. A cotton mill, with 200 looms, and employing 130 hands, is in constant operation; one shoe factory, employs 50 men ; a boot factory, 30 men ; a cotton batting factory, 20 ; a pickle factory, 20 ; and a planing mill., 20 hands. The population of the city is over 12,000, it having increased over 1,000 in the year 1875. *Johnston, Johnston Centre* and *Emerald Grove*, are villages tributary to Janesville, and off the line of any railway. At this point we cross a branch of the Milwaukee & St. Paul R'y, of which we shall have more to speak when we reach HANOVER, on our St. Paul line.

Milton Junction, 99 miles from Chicago. We here cross the Prairie du Chien line, which gives you rail connections with *Whitewater, Palmyra, Eagle, Waukesha,* and *Brookfield* eastward, and *Edgerton* and *Stoughton,* etc., westward. Going to either of these points, you should buy your tickets to Milton Junction. The village is the seat of Milton College, one mile from the station, and is one of the most thriving educational institutions of the State. The village has 400 inhabitants, is 5 miles from Lake Koshkonong ("The lake we live in "), which is noted for its fine fishing. Along its shores are many Indian mounds. The Morgan House is at the depot. Who has not heard of this celebrated hotel and its more celebrated landlord?

Koshkonong, 104 miles from Chicago. The lake of the same name is one mile distant, and is 6 miles wide and 9 miles long. Its fish are black bass, pickerel, pike, yellow and silver perch, etc. Geese, ducks, brant and swans are unusually plentiful in its waters. Of ducks, we have canvas backs, red heads, mallards, wora, black heads and spike tails. Wild celery grows here in great abundance, and for canvas-back ducks this lake vies with the Delaware and Potomac rivers, and with Chesapeake bay. On the banks of the lake, Koshkonong House is built, and will accommodate 100 guests; The Bingham 30, and Koshkonong Club House 70. Another hotel, that will accommodate 200, is being erected. Tobacco is a staple crop in this part of Rock county.

Fort Atkinson, 111 miles from Chicago. The city was named after General Atkinson, who, during the Black Hawk war, built a fort and stockade here. It is in Jefferson county, which was organized in 1836 and has over 35,000 inhabitants. Fort Atkinson has 3,000 inhabitants, and is built on both sides of Rock river. *Rock Lake, Lake Mills, Ripley, Cambridge* and *Rose* lakes are near, and are all noted for their excellent shooting grounds, canvas back ducks being abundant in all of them. Considerable manufacturing is done in the city. The North-Western Furniture Company uses $150,000 capital, and employs 200 hands; a wagon factory employs 40 men; a foundry, 30 men; the flexible harrow factory, 40 men ; and a cheese factory, 20 men. The city has four schools and employs ten teachers. Five churches supply room for its worshipers. The Grand Mountain House, by J. H. Davis, gives homes for 50 guests, at $2.00 per day. There are several mineral springs near the city, two of which are especially celebrated for the cures performed by their waters. *Whitewater*, 9 miles, and *Cambridge*, 12 miles distant, are reached by daily stage, the first for 50 cents, and the last for 75 cents. *Hebron* is 9 miles off, and is reached three times weekly by stage for 50 cents.

Jefferson, 117 miles from Chicago, the county seat of Jefferson Co., is located in the centre of the county, and at the confluence of Rock and Crawfish rivers, with ample water power on the first named stream. The city has 3,000 inhabitants, two fine graded schools, fine county buildings, Bruenig's Hall, fitted up as a theatre, and capable of seating 600 persons; three banks, one newspaper, an excellent fire department, numbers of churches, one flour mill, one rope walk, a pork-packing establishment, six hotels, with another nearly completed, a fine city hall, and many first-class business blocks, built of cream-colored (Milwaukee) brick. It has several flourishing manufactories, amongst which we note The Wisconsin Manufacturing Company, furniture, using $80,000 capital, and employing 80 hands; the Jefferson Woolen Mill Co., employing 30 hands, and making 6,000 yards of cloth, besides selling 75,000 lbs. wool monthly; and Copeland, Ryder & Co.'s boot and shoe factory. Commencing in 1868 with $6,000 capital, they now use $20,000 capital, and employ 35 men; they sell annually $50,000 worth of boots and shoes, and proudly boast that they have never been obliged to stop work for want of a market or from "hard times" since the day they started. About $250,000 capital and over 300 men are employed in the various manufacturing establishments of this city. The Jefferson Liberal Institute, a high grade, non-sectarian educational establishment, is located here, as is a large Roman Catholic school, both of which are in a flourishing condition, and are largely patronized by the citizens of the vicinity and of the surrounding county.

Johnson's Creek, 122 miles from Chicago, has a population of 250, and is 1 mile from Rock river. It has a good school, two churches and one hotel. At *Aztalan*, 4 miles west, are many curious Indian mounds and ancient fortifications—one, 1700 by 900 feet, quite closely resembling a prone man.

Watertown, 130 miles from Chicago, is a thriving city of some 10,000 people, and is built on Rock river, whose waters are utilized by three dams across the stream. Over one hundred houses were built in the city in 1875, showing its rapid growth. It has many manufactories. It is the seat of two colleges—the German Lutheran Church controlling one, the other, "The College of the Lady of the Sacred Heart," being a branch of the University (Roman Catholic) of Notre Dame, Indiana. Two large public halls, "Turners" and "The Music," will seat 1,500 people. Twenty churches and three graded schools provide for the worship and tuition of citizens and children. Five large hotels accommodate the transient guests with first-class fare at reasonable rates. Five flour mills here make 1,000 barrels of flour daily, and furnish a market for much of the wheat that is so successfully grown in the surrounding county. *Lake Mills*, 10 miles south, and *Oconomowoc*, 12 miles east, are summer resorts, and are reached from this station over finely-graded roads.

A branch of the Milwaukee & St. Paul road is crossed here, and gives rail connections eastward for *Oconomowoc*, 13 miles, and *Pewaukee*, 25 miles, and westward for *Waterloo, Marshall, Sun Prairie, Lowell, Columbus,* etc.

Clyman, 138 miles from Chicago. Has a population of 1,400; is in Dodge county, and is a growing town, surrounded by a fertile and thickly settled county. *Hustiford*, 8 miles distant, is tributary.

Juneau, 145 miles from Chicago. The county seat of Juneau county, which was named after Solomon Juneau, an early settler of Dodge county, and has 48,000 population. The village has 500 inhabitants, is built on elevated ground three miles west of Rock river; has one grain elevator, a cheese factory, a fine public school, four churches, a county court house and two hotels. *Fox, Bear, Lost* and *Mud* lakes are contiguous to the village. The Wisconsin State Prison is in the northern part of the county, at *Waupun*. *Marysville*, 12 miles northeast, *Hustiford*, 8 miles, *Neosho*, 11 miles, *Danville*, 14 miles, and *Richwood*, are tributary towns off the lines of railroad. Large bodies of iron ore are mined and smelted at *Iron Mountain*, 10 miles northeast. The Wisconsin and The Northwestern Iron Companies work the vein, and the last named smelt 12 to 14 tons of iron daily. Winter's mineral paint is also made here.

Minnesota Junction, 148 miles from Chicago. This small village, 200 people, is an important railway junction, and gives us rail connections for *Beaver Dam, Fox Lake, Portage City, Waupun, Brandon, Berlin, Omro,* and *Winneconne;* passengers destined for these points should buy their tickets to Minnesota Junction, or to Burnett Junction (which see). At the depot at Minnesota Junction is found a good hotel, kept by Thomas Young, who accommodates guests at very reasonable rates, and furnishes excellent meals.

Burnett Junction, 152 miles from Chicago. This village of 200 people, is another important railway crossing point, and furnishes rail connections to a large country northward. It has two good hotels, an odd-fellows' hall and a good templars' hall. Fine shooting grounds are close to the village. Ducks, geese, swans and brant are found in countless numbers.

Chester, 160 miles from Chicago. A village with 100 inhabitants. It has one hotel, with a mineral spring in connection, good school, and much excellent shooting on the Horicon marshes, which are close by. *Kekaska, Maysville, Byron* and *Waupun* (the latter with a population of 3,000, and reached by daily stage,) are tributary, and seek the C. & N. W. R'y here.

Oak Centre, 165 miles from Chicago, is a village of 200 souls, in the midst of a fine farming country.

Oakfield, 168 miles from Chicago, has 400 inhabitants, one hotel, one school, two churches, three flour mills, and only one saloon—its people, being strictly temperate, discourage the use of spirituous liquors or their sale. *Darling's Gap*, a popular local summer resort, is 1½ miles from the station. *Mayville*, 14 miles southeast, is reached weekly (Wednesdays) by stage.

Fond du Lac, 176 miles from Chicago via this route, but only 148 miles from Chicago by our Chicago, Milwaukee & Fond du Lac Air Line route, of which we shall speak hereafter. This city, with a population of 18,000 souls, is located at the southern end of Lake Winnebago. The growth and prosperity of the city is largely dependent on its manufactures, of which it contains many of considerable importance. The city is built upon a prairie on the banks of the Upper Fox river, and within one mile of the lake. The river is deep, and navigable up to its forks, but to meet the necessities of manufacturers it has been bridged at various points, and navigation confined to the north channel. The scenery that surrounds the city is worthy of mention,—a ledge of limestone rock, elevated some 200 feet above the level of the prairie, and in many cases presenting perpendicular precipices 75 to 100 feet high, borders the eastern and southern margins of the prairie on which the city is built; from the base of this ledge hundreds of springs of cool, rippling water gush out, and meander over the gentle slopes of the prairie in narrow channels to the lake. Westward from the city the ground gradually rises, alternating with prairie and timber for some 25 miles. The surrounding country is fertile and thickly settled. The health of the city is and always has been good, probably in a great measure consequent upon the water supply, there being within the city limits over 300 artesian wells out of which the purest water constantly flows from the depth of 60 to 400 feet. Amongst its manufactures may be mentioned that of the celebrated La Belle Wagon, which employs 150 men; the sash, door and blind factory of C. J. L. Meyer, (which is the largest in the United States,) in which are used over 14,000,000 feet of lumber, and from which are shipped products exceeding $1,000,000 annually; a large steam bakery, a paper mill, an agricultural implement manufactory, employing 150 men, and several minor manufactories. Its public schools occupy 16 buildings, which cost $120,000, and are capable of seating 3,000 scholars. its high school building cost, in 1873, $45,000. It has 20 church edifices, many of which cost from $10,000 to $30,000 each. Its post office is one of the finest and most substantial buildings of the kind in the Union. In its masonic hall, four lodges, chapters and commanderies hold their meetings; and its odd fellows have a commodious hall, in which two lodges and an encampment conduct their work. The Patty House—its best hotel—cost upwards of $90,000, is four stories high, and can accommodate 250 guests. The American House cost $30,000, is first class in every respect, and can accommodate 100 guests.

Several yacht clubs navigate Lake Winnebago in elegant rakish craft, for prizes in sportive contests. Steamboats, with pleasure parties, often make excursions around the lake, which is 35 miles long by 12 broad—the largest lake *within* any State of the Union—whose borders furnish beautiful landscape views, and the most gorgeous scenery. Besides, Fond du Lac is surrounded with pleasant places of resort. Lake de Neveu, a beautiful sheet of water, is romantically situated about three miles southeast of the city. Eastward is Elkhart Lake, already famous for its natural beauties, and westward lies Green Lake, a noted summer resort. On all these lakes are pleasure boats propelled by steam, wind and man power. The waters of all these lakes furnish a plentiful and various supply of fresh-water fish, where piscatorially-inclined ladies and gentlemen can enjoy ample amusement in that line.

Fond du Lac county is situated in the eastern part of the State, 23 miles west of Lake Michigan. Its central line of latitude is 43° 45' north. It contains twenty-one organized towns, the two cities of Fond du Lac and Ripon, and sixteen flourishing

"The Point," at Duluth, Minn.—pp. 76, 91.

villages, and embraces a territorial area of about 720 square miles. Its population in 1875 was 50,241. This county is one of the most beautiful and fertile tracts of land to be found in the West. Its eastern part is rolling land, originally heavily timbered; the central and western portions undulating and rolling prairie and openings, the face of which is most beautifully picturesque. It is well watered, abounding in numerous streams and springs, and, in many localities, flowing fountains. Lake Horicon indents its southern border, and Lake Winnebago its northern. The county presents one continuous expanse of well-cultivated farms, with commodious and tasty farm houses, many of them very elegant buildings; spacious barns and good fences, which give every evidence of the wealth, thrift and prosperity of the inhabitants. It forms a beautiful scene, with its handsome buildings and their rural surroundings of grove and plain, and cultivated slopes and winding streams, blending into one picture, and stretching away as far as the eye can see.

At Fond du Lac we cross the SHEBOYGAN & FOND DU LAC RAILROAD, that runs from *Sheboygan*, on Lake Michigan, westwardly 78 miles to Princeton. This crossing being nearly at the middle of the line, will allow us to say a few words about the western end of the road, and to leave the eastern end until we reach it from Milwaukee. Then, going west from Fond du Lac, we change cars at a joint depot station, known as Fond du Lac Junction, and 4 miles out reach *Lamartine*, with 1,600 people; *Eldorado*, 9 miles, with 2,000 people; *Rosendale*

Green Lake is the next station, and is 6 miles west of Ripon, and one mile from the post office—*Dartford*—which is half a mile from the ever-beautiful and ever-attractive GREEN LAKE, so well known as a summer idling place. The natural scenery around Dartford is unrivaled in variety and beauty. Groves of primeval grandeur, far stretching prairies and extensive lake views greet the eye from every point. The grounds around the lake have been terraced, furnished with swings, promenades, and otherwise ornamented, to render them pleasant and attractive. The lake averages a length of 15 miles, and a width of 3 miles. Its banks vary from beautiful grassy slopes to high rocky cliffs,

The Northwestern Hotel, Marquette, Mich., on C. & N.-W.Ry.—page 72.

and *West Rosendale*, pretty little stations, and, 20 miles from Fond du Lac, reach RIPON, a beautiful little city of 3,500 inhabitants, with a history running back to 1844, when Warren Chase and his brother Fourierites, under the name of the Wisconsin Phalanx, settled close by, and called their village *Ceresco*. In 1850 they disbanded, and the Ripon of to-day began its existence. The city is in Fond du Lac county, which was organized in 1839, and now contains over 50,000 inhabitants. Most of the land is settled, and in a highly cultivated and productive condition. Besides two fine ward schools, with ten teachers, Ripon College, with fourteen professors, has its home here, and is in a flourishing condition. Eight churches, five temperance organizations, a masonic lodge, two odd fellows' lodges, and a lodge of Knights of Pythias, furnish religious, moral and benevolent food for the inhabitants. Ripon has an efficient fire department, a flourishing literary and library association, several newspapers, banks, manufacturing establishments and good hotels. It is a pleasant resort for the summer guest, and he who comes once wants to come again.

bordered with evergreens, presenting the greatest diversity of physical character, and affording unlimited natural advantages for pleasing and romantic rambles. Its waters are very pure, and so transparent that their pebbly bed may be seen at a depth of from 20 to 35 feet. A great variety and abundance of the finny tribe inhabit this beautiful sheet of water, and good fishing-boats and tackle for lovers of sport, and excellent sail-boats for seekers of pleasure, are furnished for the accommodation of visitors. The principal hotels are The Oakwood and The Sherwood Forest.

THE OAKWOOD is situated on the banks of Green Lake. The location of this much sought summer resort and delightful watering place is only one mile from Green Lake station and depot. Omnibus and carriages await the arrival of all trains.

The Oakwood House was opened June 15th, 1867, and is furnished in the style of a first-class house. The tables are unsurpassed by those of the best hotels in the United States.

Accommodations for all innocent and pleasant amusements have been amply provided. Great care has been given to furnishing pastimes both for the parlor and lawn, for persons of all ages, so that the most indifferent cannot complain of *ennui*.

In addition to former attractions, a new and beautiful steamboat has been placed on Green Lake. Parties can visit any of the attractive places on its shores on short notice, with pleasure and comfort.

Ponies, perfectly at home under the saddle, and in harness, expressly for ladies and children; horses, carriages and light buggies; beautiful shady groves; health, comfort and happiness—and all at reasonable rates.

To one of the most healthy locations upon the continent, shut away from the city where contagion spreads its blight and disease spends its fury, individuals and families may resort and spend a summer with invigorating and pleasurable results.

One journal says: "If our people had known of there being a place of this kind with such a beautiful lake, such fine fishing and duck shooting, rowing and sailing, shady groves, walks and drives, you would have been filled up from our city alone."

Another says: "The most beautiful sheet of cold spring water in the world, a perpetual cool breeze, fine fishing, good shooting, shady groves and free from MOSQUITOES; in fact, we pronounce it the most healthy spot in all America."

Another: "This is a most charming spot, and we who have spent the summer here are loth to leave it. If we could only take this beautiful lake with us, and have it where the eye could forever rest upon it, how charming it would be. The Green Lake fish are noted for being particularly delicious, and the fishers are busy filling orders for St. Louis and other cities; and it is so cool here, the thermometer has not once been above 90 degrees, and the air is bracing and pure."

Another calls it the Lake George of Wisconsin. "A modest world of land and water beauties—too little cultivated by hunters after charming scenery and healthful air. It is a fairy land of wonderful fascinations; and the weary of body and mind, or the despondent and languid invalid, and no less the strong and healthful, will find both body and mind invigorated, and the soul elevated, by a sojourn among the picturesque beauties of that lovely lake."

Green Lake, always locally regarded as "a thing of beauty" and "a joy forever," was unknown to tourists till eight years ago, when David Greenway, Esq., making a horoscope of its dark green waters, saw multitudes of pleasure seekers on its beautiful shores, and immediately made provision for the vanguard of his fancied host by erecting The Oakwood, since which time, year by year, Green Lake has grown famous, till now, there is no end of the pretty things said of it.

SHERWOOD FOREST, J. C. Sherwood, proprietor. This charming hotel, which was opened on the 15th of May, 1875, is embowered in and environed by a hundred acres of grand old oaks, lying with gentle grade along the north shore of Green Lake. It is within two miles of Green Lake station, on the Sheboygan & Fond du Lac Railroad. Omnibuses and carriages are always awaiting arrival of trains. The hotel is a large, inviting structure, with broad verandas, large, airy rooms and halls, and supplied with all the appointments of first-class summer resorts. It was commenced in the spring of 1874, partially completed, and partially opened for a few weeks last season. This, however, is its first *bow* to the public.

Gitche-Gumme, near Marquette, Mich.—page 72.

A billiard house and bowling alleys, together with the popular lawn games, are provided.

The whole forest is woodland lawn, gently sloping to the pebbly shore, and while the proprietor has opened some special avenues, nature has furnished uninterrupted drives and promenades everywhere. The scenery partakes of the beautiful, picturesque and almost romantic, rather than the grand and sublime. Nature here speaks in dulcet whisperings, where one might almost expect to greet nymphs and mermaids, satyrs and fauns. Here and there rustic seats and swings, pendant from the high, far-reaching branches, invite rest. The outlook from the grounds, as well as the piazza, is truly magnificent—a perfect kaleidoscope, taking in extensive prairies, woodlands and cultivated fields, as well as the entire lake, with its indentations and exquisite settings of bluffs and evergreens, grassy slopes and perpendicular ledges.

Of this place a writer says: "Sherwood's Point, on the west side of the lake, is widely known. It has probably been the scene of more picnics and celebrations than any similar area in the State. During the season of open air pleasures, there is a constant succession of carriages from Berlin, Ripon, Fond du Lac, and adjoining towns, and it is no unusual thing to find a dozen different coteries distributed about the grounds. Late last season, Mr. J. C. Sherwood opened a large and well-appointed hotel, as a nucleus of the delightful resort known as Sherwood Forest. The view from the verandas comprises a complete circuit of the lake and broken shores, while the immediate surroundings are especially pleasant. The drives are tastefully laid out, care being taken, in uprooting and trimming, not to detract from the rustic charm of the primitive woods. The generous patronage received by the Sherwood Forest, (in its then scarcely prepared state), as a debutante, is an assurance of its future. It requires no prophetic keenness of vision to see that Green Lake, with its attractive nooks, pure air and healthful climate, is developing into a resort no whit less recherche than that other popular inland watering place—Saratoga. In recognition of the beauties, some of its visitors have expressed themselves in a very substantial manner, by erecting pretty villas and nice summer cottages." The various other things combining to make the complement of such a resort will be found at the Forest, such as horses and carriages, boats and boatmen, baths, cold and hot; also, the kindly herd coming from the clover fields, to yield their sweet, rich milk to the Forest tables.

On the north side of the lake can also be found The Walker House. Whitmore Brothers will this summer finish and open another hotel, that will accommodate 100 guests. —— Collins has a fine farm house on the south side of the lake, and will accommodate summer boarders with the choicest "farm house" board. W. M. Lockwood has a steamer on the lake that will carry 100 persons.

"Green lake is three miles wide and fifteen miles long, and has less of civilization and more of weird natural grandeur than any of the Wisconsin lakes I have yet seen. It is never as mirror-like and tranquil as the transparent waters of Lake Geneva, but it is full of resonant airs, and deep, sobbing monotones, and harmonious sea-like music. Its borders are fringed with grand forest trees; not the transparent, slender, curled darlings of art, but the stately, indigenous growth of Indian soil. Huge boulders of rock lie in rows along its edge, as if, at some remote time, a race of giant children had played there, and set them out in even rows. The waters are full of fish—perch and pickerel and black bass. The season for summer visits lasts till November, and even then tourists go reluctantly away, lingering till they light out-door fires to keep warm while they pay their devotions to Nature. The woods, in October, are marvelously beautiful, after the frost has touched the trees, and each one hangs out its lovely, gay-colored banners of death. The air has at all times a health-giving inspiration, that goes down deep into the lungs, and diffuses new life into the tired, languid system, and you go home to the hotel with an appetite that fills the heart of the caterer with delight."

This is a favorite resort of the St. Louisians; so much so, that several wealthy citizens of that city have erected permanent homes on the shores of the lake, and now spend the summer months here.

The Only Route to Green Lake.

The only route by which you should attempt to reach Green Lake is via the Chicago & North-Western Railway. Take the train from the corner of West Kinzie and Canal streets, via the Wisconsin Division, and go to Fond du Lac; at that point you leave this road, and take the Sheboygan & Fond du Lac Railroad for Green Lake Station. Or, you can leave from the above-named depot, and go via the Milwaukee Division, to Milwaukee, then change cars, and take the train that runs over the Milwaukee & Fond du Lac Air Line, for Fond du Lac and Green Lake. The train leaving Milwaukee by this last-named route will have through cars for Green Lake, so that, by either route, you will have to make but one change of cars. All the trains of the Sheboygan & Fond du Lac Railroad connect both ways at Fond du Lac with all the trains of the Chicago & North-Western Railway. Green Lake is 26 miles west of Fond du Lac, and, via Milwaukee, is 174 miles northwest of Chicago, or 89 miles northwest of Milwaukee. If you cannot buy your tickets through to Green Lake, buy to Fond du Lac, and your fare will cost you no more than if you bought through. Green Lake is 6 miles west of Ripon, which is also a station on the Sheboygan & Fond du Lac Railroad. You should not be deceived into buying your tickets for Green Lake by longer, inferior, and more circuitous routes than the one named above. *This is the only direct route*, and the only one tourists should take.

"M. L. R.," in a letter to the *Chicago Tribune*, says:

"Here, in the heart of Wisconsin, secluded from the world of commerce and traffic, lies one of nature's most favored retreats. You hardly are aware of its existence, before you see the pale-green verdure of its hills, the deep, cool, delicious emerald of its forests primeval, and the rose-opal tint of its crystal waters. Of course you do not drop upon it from the skies, at least I did not, but arrived in the ordinary way, by the mechanical apparatus of the railroad. I started, fair and square, from the North-Western depot, in Chicago, and went by the way of Watertown and Janesville, to Fond du Lac. There I changed cars, taking the Sheboygan & Fond du Lac line to Green Lake. You can take your choice of leaving Chicago on the 9.30 A.M. train by Janesville and Fond du Lac, arriving here about 8.00 P.M., or go on the 10.00 train to Milwaukee, and have two hours to rest and refresh, making the same time here.

"Having reached the depot at Green Lake, we alighted, tired and hungry. A long-bodied, thin-legged, black coach waited to carry us to the hotel. Into it we filed, and rode up hill and down, stopping only long enough to shy a leathern mail-bag at an individual supposed to represent the postmaster, who stood in front of an unofficial-looking building, labeled Post Office. This was in the town of Dartford, the county seat, and quite a pretty village. We passed through it, and rode on through a line of dark woods, by a pleasant country road, till a mile of distance was between us and the depot, when the omnibus drew up with a flourish at the Oakwood House.

"It was not till I had breakfasted next morning, and stood, hat in hand, on the piazza of the Oakwood, that I realized what a lovely dimple in the bosom of Nature I had fallen into. On every hand rose grassy slopes or cliffs, of unmistakable grandeur. Wooded acres made a dark, rich background, against which were placed the beautiful villas of art and civilization; while far, far in the distance

City of Marquette, Mich.—page 73.
Reached only via C. & N.-W. Ry.

gleamed, with the opaline light, the waters of Green Lake, that nestled at our feet. At every glance some new feature of beauty was added; a white-winged ship; a tent, white and fair, amid the green foliage of the banks; the blue, curling smoke of an Indian encampment, just across the narrowest turn of the lake; and, directly near, the handsome grounds of Oakwood House, ornamented with swings and rustic seats, and summer houses, and croquet lawns, with a spice of evergreens in the air, and a buoyancy of atmosphere that made one glad of life, and health, and Heaven."

If thou art worn and hard beset
With sorrows that thou would'st forget;
If thou would'st read a lesson that will keep
Thy heart from fainting, and thy soul from sleep—
Go to the woods and hills! No tears
Dim the sweet look that Nature wears.

Leaving this charming locality, we push westward and pass *St. Marie*, a pretty village of 800 people, and 35 miles west of Fond du Lac, arrive at the end of the road, and at *Princeton*, a smart, busy, bustling city of 2,000 people. Having made this never-to-be-forgotten trip, with its more than pleasant sojourn at Green Lake, we can again seek Fond du Lac and hie us northward to

Vandyne, 185 miles from Chicago, a village of 100 souls, 2 miles from Lake Winnebago, having one school and one church.

Oshkosh, 194 miles from Chicago. Population, 17,000.

In 1673, Marquette started from Green Bay, and passing up the Lower Fox, came upon the lovely inland sea of Lake Winnebago, and was enraptured with the beautiful vision of nature that here spread before him, commingling woodland, opening and lake, glimmering like a gem in its emerald setting, and stretching away in the dim distance among the hazy points and headlands.

The present site of Oshkosh was the favorite stopping place of the early explorers, who were attracted by the great beauty and commercial advantages of the situation, and the delightful and fertile country adjoining, now known as Winnebago county.

The first settlers came as traders, and fixed a trading post there in 1818, near the head of Lake Buttes des Morts, where the Indian trail between Forts Winnebago and Howard crossed Wolf river. This was immediately before the Indians were forced to leave their ancient hunting grounds—a distinct period—a line between barbarism and civilization; an era of that wild, romantic mingling of the elements of barbaric and civilized life—the French and the Indian; of daring adventure and patient endurance. Here was the paradise of Indian life, his choicest hunting grounds, its waters teeming with fish, and its woods, pastures and rich prairies filled with game.

Here was fought one of the most bloody battles that ever took place, between the French, under the command of De Lovigny, and the warlike nations of the Sacs and Foxes. The Indians were fortified by ditches and palisades, which the French leader carried by assault. Hundreds of the Indians were slain in the contest, and were buried on the spot. The Tumuli or Mounds, indicating their burial place, gave to the spot the name of "Buttes des Morts" (Hills of the Dead), and which also originated the name of Lake Buttes des Morts, on the northwestern boundaries of this city.

Many were the wild scenes of frontier life that transpired here during the early occupancy of the French traders ; incidents that would make a volume in themselves, and which are interwoven inseparably with its history.

During the year 1836, a treaty was made at Cedar Rapids with the Menomonee Indians, by Governor Dodge, acting as commissioner, which resulted in the cession to the United States of over 4,000,000 acres of land, lying north of Fox river and west of Lake Winnebago.

The city was incorporated in 1853. At this time the population was about 2,500.

The *great event* for Oshkosh was the extension of the Chicago & North-Western Railway to this place, giving it connection by rail with the outside world. The first train arrived on the 13th of October, 1859.

Beaumont House, Green Bay—page 66.

The city of Oshkosh is situated on one of the finest commercial sites in the Northwest, at the mouth of the Upper Fox river, on the western shore of Lake Winnebago. It is a situation of great natural beauty, overlooking the picturesque lake and river scenery of the vicinity. Lake Winnebago and the Fox and Wisconsin rivers formed the great commercial highway of the Northwest before the age of railroads, and many a glowing description was then written of the beautiful lake and river country now called Winnebago county—of its lovely prairies, openings and woodlands, its fertile soil and salubrious climate. The site of Oshkosh is a tract with an elevation from 12 to 20 feet above the level of the lake. The city extends for a distance of nearly three miles from the shore of Lake Winnebago up the Fox river to Lake Buttes des Morts, occupying the tract between the two lakes, and covering a territorial area of nearly eight square miles.

Among the popular amusements are steamboat pleasure excursions to the various points on the lake, yachting and regattas, and drives through the beautiful surrounding country.

SURROUNDING COUNTRY.—The adjacent country, and that stretching away from here to the southwest for hundreds of miles, is the richest agricultural district to be found in the habitable world. Its surface is undulating prairie and openings, with its rivers and lakes skirted with timber. The scenery of this combined woodland, prairie, lakes and rivers is surpassingly beautiful; disclosing picturesque rivers which stretch away in the far distance like the varying pictures of a lovely panorama. The rivers and lakes abound in fish and water fowl, and the woodlands in game. The facilities for rural and aquatic sports have already made the locality famous for these enjoyments.

OSHKOSH AS A SUMMER RESORT AND WATERING PLACE.—This city possesses a rare combination of natural features for a delightful summer resort and watering place. The climate is not surpassed in healthfulness; the air is pure and dry; and the invigorating breezes from the lake temper the heats of summer; the scenery is lovely ; the lake a most magnificent sheet of water with beautiful shores, and good harbors that are accessible in every direction, thus affording the best of yachting facilities. The surrounding country is beautiful, with excellent roads, affording delightful drives and picturesque views of lake and river scenery. Wild game is abundant in the vicinity, and is composed of blue and green-winged teal, mallard and wood duck, snipe, woodcock, quail and prairie chickens. The waters abound in black and white bass and other fish, and brook trout are plentiful in streams within a day's travel.

The city has suffered fearfully from fires, but, like the fabled Phœnix, it has arisen from its ashes stronger and better after each calamity. As a lumber-making point it is surpassed by few in any land. The State Normal School and the Northern Wisconsin Insane Hospital are located here. It has a fine brick court house, a high school and several ward public school buildings, a fine masonic hall, a large number of churches, and many manufactories. Of its hotels, The Beckwith, The Revere, The Tremont, The International and The Seymour rank high. Wolf river is navigable for 150 miles from Oshkosh, and on it lines of steamers, connecting daily with the trains of the C. & N.-W. R'y, for *Buttes des Morts, Winneconne, Tuston, Morton's Landing, Fremont, Gill's Landing, Weyauwega, Royalton, Northport, New London*, and *Shawano*.

Another line of steamers also runs for *Omro, Eureka* and *Berlin* by the Upper Fox river.

State Hospital, 198 miles from Chicago, is the station for the State Hospital for the Insane, which is 50 rods from the shores of Lake Winnebago; cost $1,500,000, and can accommodate 600 patients. It is under the care of Dr. Walter Kempster, late of Utica, N. Y.

On an Island in Lake Winnebago, 1½ miles from the shore, is a summer hotel, by Joseph Heath, of Oshkosh, which can be reached hourly in summer by steamers from the hospital pier.

Snells, 202 miles from Chicago, is an unimportant station, with some 100 inhabitants.

Neenah and Menasha, 207 miles from Chicago. These two important cities are linked together here, as they are where located, as one station serves both, and although disunited municipally, are united in fortunes and in their hopes for the future. Together they contain about 7,500 people.

MENASHA, being situated at the foot of Lake Winnebago and Lake Buttes des Morts, and embracing part of Doty's Island, furnishes picturesque and entertaining scenery, unsurpassed by any Western town. The climate is unexcelled in salubrity, and no place on the continent is freer from epidemics. The air is mild and bracing and yields a vigor and endurance to the system, that is above all price.

outlet of Lake Winnebago. The present population is over 4,000. The city and town is without a cent of indebtedness, either bonded or otherwise, and consequently the rates of taxation are very low. The graded schools of the city are noted throughout this section for their thoroughness and efficiency. The streets are graded and graveled, and lined with good sidewalks. The business portion of the city is built up with fine brick blocks, and everything betokens thrift and prosperity. No city in the State can produce a better showing, in the way of growth and prosperity during the past season (1875) than Neenah, a *bona fide* list of new mills, stores, residences and improvements footing up $400,000 in round numbers. Four paper mills, employing 160 men; stove works, 40 men; seven

The Lakeside Hotel, Madison, Wis., on C. & N.-W. Ry.—page 80.

Lake Winnebago provides boating, sailing and bathing facilities. Steamboats ply on its limpid waters, and sailing vessels can always be had, furnishing ample means for pleasure excursions. Row boats are kept in connection with The National Hotel, and will always be at the service of guests, furnishing a most agreeable and healthy exercise on the ever placid waters of Fox river and adjacent bays of the lake. In connection with other sports, fish and game are plenty, and the sportsman need have no lack of pleasurable novelties.

Considerable manufacturing is carried on in the city, wood-working in various forms being particularly prominent. It has four flour mills, and attracts trade from the surrounding country for many miles.

Our depot is on Doty's Island.

NEENAH.—The city of Neenah is located in the county of Winnebago, and most romantically and beautifully situated on the Fox river, and at the

flour mills, stave and barrel factories, plow works, twelve churches, a public ("Germania") hall, that cost $15,000, and will seat 1,000 persons; several good school houses, a hotel—The Russell House—just finished, that will accommodate 100 guests, together with its miles of busy streets—strongly attest the character of the city we have in Neenah. Wildfang's mineral spring is near the city, and has more than a local reputation for its remedial powers. Riverside Park, a finely cultivated and adorned public park, will well repay a visit; it is on the banks of Fox river. No locality can offer better facilities for fishing, boating and shooting than can be found in this vicinity.

West Menasha, 209 miles from Chicago, is a joint depot at the crossing of the WISCONSIN CENTRAL RAILROAD, that here gives us rail connections for *Gill's Landing, Weyauwega, Waupaca, Amherst, Stevens' Point, Marshfield* and *Worcester.*

Appleton, 214 miles north of Chicago. The Lower Fox River Valley embraces a section of country situated between Lake Winnebago and Green Bay. From northeast to southwest it extends a distance of 50 miles, and from northwest to southeast about 40 miles. The valley is intersected by the 44th parallel of latitude, and its climate, therefore, is similar to that which obtains in Southern Minnesota, Central Michigan, Central New York, and in the southern part of Vermont and New Hampshire. From the time of its earliest settlement it has been noted for its health-giving elements. Even in early times it was free from sectional epidemics.

As a place of residence, the Fox River Valley presents every attraction which is at all desirable.

Pyramid Rock, Devil's Lake, Wis., on C. & N.-W. Ry.—page 81.

The scenery which borders the majestically-flowing stream, the variegated beauty of woodland and meadow, and finely-cultivated farms, the pleasant undulations of valley and hillside, the roar of the cataract, the grace and curve and dash of the swift-rushing current, all combine to minister to the esthetic as well as to the practical wants of the people of this valley.

In the centre of the valley of the Fox, through which lay the celebrated pathway of "La Pere Marquette," down to the Mississippi—a valley which is thickly sifted with the ashes of the past, and is the heart of the historic interest of the State; the scene of her most bloody Indian wars, and the home of half her legends and traditions—in the centre of this valley has sprung up a swift civilization which has its outcome and expression in Outagamie county. The capital city of this county is the old "Grand Chute" of early times, or the APPLETON of to-day, a town long known to many tourists for the beauty of her surroundings, and in business circles for her energy and enterprise. Wisconsin can boast no more charming summer resort than is this little city, bathed by a broad and rapid running river, and on the east approached by wild ravines and brilliant forests; on the west by fields of yellow wheat, gay apple orchards, and the finest farm lands of the State.

The well-known Telulah Springs are at the eastern extremity of the city, in a charming point on the brink of the river, and at the foot of a magnificent natural beech and maple grove of full 50 acres. The water of these springs, which is crystal-clear, pours from the hillside near the stream, and has been carried into reservoirs, about 14 feet above the level of the river, the amount of the supply being quite 6,000 gallons every day. As stated by an analytical chemist, "Telulah Spring water contains the same salts in about the same proportion as the Bethesda," and like that celebrated spring, in curative qualities is unsurpassed, having *peculiar* efficacy in Bright's disease, diabetes, all kidney affections, dropsy, etc. This spring, together with Bethesda, holds high rank even in a State which flows with fountains, and is filled with mineral and medicinal waters. The spring lies near the foot of the Grand Chute rapids, formed by the swift decline in the river bed of 50 feet within a mile, and its surroundings are lovely and remarkable. The formation of the valley in which it is found is curious, and its story of the greatest interest. Some of the remarkable "burial mounds" of the State are within the distance of a pleasant ride, and near these are several of the rock-traced pictures and inscriptions of a pre-historic race. The river abounds in fish, the wild rice tracts are filled with ducks, and the woods with much small game. APPLETON is easily accessible to the great centres. It has now a population of about 8,000, and as a manufactnring point, has great importance in the State. It is well shaded, and is threaded by delightful drives, and filled with pleasant homes. In educational advantages the city stands without a peer within the State. Lawrence University is here located, and the general school system is of the highest grade. The tone of society is moral to a high degree; the citizens are law abiding and industrious, enterprising, ambitious and hospitable. Finally, the climate is delightful. The heats of summer and the frosts of winter are tempered, both, by nearness to the great lakes of the North, and altogether no more delightful watering place, or charming summer home can be discovered anywhere within the limits of a noble State. Hotel and boarding house accommodations are ample and first class.

Little Chute, 219 miles from Chicago, is a German village of 200 persons.

Kaukauna, 221 miles from Chicago. Population, 800.

Wrightstown, 226 miles from Chicago. Population, 1,400. These are thrifty villages, surrounded by a fertile farming country, and good shooting and fishing grounds. Deer and bear are not scarce, while woodcock, snipe, ducks, geese, partridge, pheasants and smaller game abound. Otto Guttrer, a noted hunter, lives at Wrightstown, and is always glad to show the stranger where game is to be found. This village has some large saw mills, in one of which 60 men find work *day and night*. The American is its best hotel. *Snidersville, Hollandtown* and *Askeaton* are tributary villages.

Little Kaukauna, 231 miles from Chicago, is merely a way station.

De Pere, 236 miles from Chicago, is a thriving manufacturing city of 4,000 people, built on both sides of the Upper Fox river, and is reached by the largest lake steamers. Two extensive iron smelting furnaces here employ many men, and weekly produce large quantities of fine pig metal. The De Pere iron works manufacture railway cars. The city has fine schools, public as well as sectarian; eight churches, and one fair hotel. The Oneida Indian reservation is 3¼ miles west, and has on it 1,600 semi-civilized Indians.

Fort Howard and **Green Bay,** 242 miles from Chicago. FORT HOWARD is on the west side of Fox river, one mile from its mouth, opposite to Green Bay, and connected with it by four bridges. It was an early military post, hence its name, and yet has some citizens who were drawn here by its soldier attractions. It has one hotel, a newspaper, and a fine growing business. The population consists of about 4,000 souls.

GREEN BAY is noted as having been one of the first settlements made by white men—here the banner of the Cross was first erected, and here the first mass said, in the territory now included within the limits of the State of Wisconsin—and is almost without a rival in the State in the inducements it offers to summer tourists, or to those who desire a cool and pleasant retreat from the heat and malaria of the South. The ancient settlement has nearly passed away, but there remains sufficient to recall the memories of the past; while the modern city, with its spacious and elegant hotels, its fine school houses and other public buildings, its large and well-filled stores, and its beautiful private residences, make a pleasing contrast with the remains of the past.

The city is surrounded on all sides but one by water; lying in the point of land at the confluence of the Fox and East rivers, and about a mile from the mouth of the former. Both of these rivers are navigable for steamers, the Fox river being navigable for the largest class of lake vessels. It has also connection, through the GREEN BAY & MIN-

The Cliff House, Devil's Lake, Wis.—page 82.

NESOTA RAILWAY, with *Winona, St. Paul* and *Minneapolis*, and all the magnificent scenery of Northern Minnesota. It is connected with both shores of Green Bay by comfortable and convenient steamers. A line of steamers connects with the trains of the Chicago & North-Western Railway, and makes tri-weekly trips up the east coast of Green Bay, making landings at Fish River, Sturgeon Bay, and other ports on that shore.

Green Bay, with its suburbs, contains a population of 12,000 to 15,000 persons. It is noted for the healthfulness of its climate—enjoying almost entire immunity from all epidemic diseases. The city is laid out with great precision and regularity—its streets being all broad and straight, and the most of them are shaded by rows of magnificent old maples, elms and poplars on either side, that, in some cases, interlace their boughs in the centre; this gives to the place a charming rural aspect, while at the same time it has all the advantages, comforts and refinements of a large city. The water supply is excellent, being mostly clear, cold, living springs, gushing out from the surface of the ground, or deep artesian wells. The days are comfortably warm, and the nights always deliciously cool for sleeping.

For amusements, there are magnificent drives extending in every direction from the city, with sylvan, picturesque scenery, beautiful cascades, and everything to please the eye. The Fox river is here about 1,500 feet wide, and 25 to 30 feet in depth, spanned by three handsome carriage and foot bridges, free to all. The river gradually expands out into Green Bay, a beautiful sheet of water, 120 miles long, with an average width of 15 miles; this gives unexcelled advantages for yachting, an amusement much indulged in by the citizens and visitors. Steam yachts also ply between the city and points of interest in the vicinity. The bay has a gently shelving, gravelly or sandy beach, and bathing in the pure, crystal waters is a favorite pastime. There are also excellent fishing grounds and plenty of fish, with good hunting in its season.

There are three large, first-class hotels in the city, viz: The Beaumont House, terms, $3 per day and $17.50 per week; Cook's Hotel, $2 per day and $8.50 to $12 per week; and The First National Hotel, $2 per day and $9 to $12 per week. It has seven newspapers, fourteen churches, many fine schools, three public halls, a court house that cost $40,000, and some manufactures.

THE GREEN BAY & MINNESOTA RAILROAD,

Running, as it does, from Green Bay westwardly across the State of Wisconsin to the city of Winona, on the Mississippi, in Minnesota, has opened up a country long destitute of much needed railroad facilities. Starting from Green Bay, it passes through the counties of Brown, Outagamie, Waupaca, Portage, Wood, Clark and Trempealeau.

Skillet Creek, Devil's Lake, Wis.—page 83.
(From Photograph by Hoard & Tenny, Winona, Minn.)

Passing westward from Green Bay, 10 miles out we reach *Oneida*, the village of the Oneida Indian Reservation, with a population of about 1,600. *Seymour*, 17 miles from Green Bay, is in Outagamie county, and 20 miles from its county seat, *Appleton*, which is reached by stage, fare $1. *Shawano*, 25 miles north, and *Angelica*, 12 miles north, are reached by stage, daily. Seymour has a population of 1,500, two good schools, five churches, a stave and barrel factory, employing 75 men; a wagon stock foundry, employing 20 men; a hub and spoke factory, employing 25 men; a spoke factory, employing 15 men, and a lumber and shingle mill, employing 30 men; two hotels— The Wisconsin House, by Louis Fisher, and The Seymour, by Otto Bechener, each with 15 rooms, and charging $1.50 per day—furnish accommodations for transient guests. The railroad was built through the village in 1871. The surrounding country is heavily timbered, and the forests are full of deer, bear and small game. *Black Creek*, 24 miles out, and *Shiocton*, 31 miles, are small villages. *New London*, 39 miles from Green Bay, having a population of 2,500, is in Waupaca county, 20 miles from the city of Waupaca, the county seat, which is reached, during the season of navigation, by steamers on the Wolf and Waupaca rivers, and by stage during the winter. New London is built at the confluence of the Wolf and Embarras rivers. The surrounding country is heavily covered with hard wood timber, and has a deep, black soil, which is very productive under cultivation. The city has two large ward school houses and one German academy, six churches, several manufactories, and six hotels. *Northport, Royalton, Ogdensburg, Scandinavia, Amherst,* and *Plover*, are thrifty villages, with a population of from 100 to 1,200 each. *Grand Rapids*, 96 miles from Green Bay, with a population of 2,000, is the county seat of Wood county which was organized in 1856, and has a population of 8,000. The county is heavily timbered with hard woods. In the village are three churches, two schools, one occupying a building which cost $20,000, and will accommodate 600 scholars; three public halls, two hotels, and six saw mills. In the vicinity there is over 35,000 acres of cultivated cranberries. *Dexterville*, 110 miles from Green Bay, is a flourishing village of 2,000 people. *Merrillan*, in Jackson county, is at the crossing of the West Wisconsin Railway, which furnishes direct rail connection for St. Paul, 130 miles north. The village has a population of about 500 persons, two schools, a flouring mill, and a saw mill. *Arcadia*, 192 miles from Green Bay, is built on the Trempealeau river, has a population of 1,000, two schools, four churches and three hotels. There are many trout streams in the vicinity, and large numbers of brook trout are taken here every season. At 214 miles from Green Bay we reach the city of Winona, which will be described hereafter. Having hurriedly made the trip across the State, we now return to Fort Howard, and pursue our journey northward.

On the Baraboo, near Elroy, Wis.—page 85.

Duck Creek, 247 miles from Chicago; an unimportant station.

Big Suamico, 251 miles from Chicago. Has two hotels, one school and two saw mills.

Little Suamico, 257 miles from Chicago. Unimportant.

Brookside, 262 miles from Chicago. A new and small place.

Pensaukee, 266 miles from Chicago, is in Oconto county, and in the midst of the pine lumber country. It has 300 population, one first-class brick hotel, that has 100 rooms; one school, and one church. *West Pensaukee* is five miles distant. Game of all kinds abound in this vicinity.

Oconto, 271 miles from Chicago. This city, of 5,000 people, is on Oconto river, two miles from its mouth. *Oconto Falls* are 16 miles distant; *Stiles*, 12 miles west, and *Gillettown*, 30 miles west, are reached by stage. This city, with Peshtigo and many other villages and a large expanse of country, were burned over in October, 1871. Hundreds of persons perished, and millions of dollars worth of property were consumed. Many marks of this terrible calamity are still plainly visible. In the city is the county court house, jail, and other county buildings; six schools, three public halls, seven churches, many lumber mills, and four hotels.

Caviots, 280 miles from Chicago, is an unimportant station.

Peshtigo, 284 miles from Chicago, is on Peshtigo river, seven miles from its mouth. Lumbering, and commerce incident thereto, occupy the time, talents and capital of its citizens. Thirty-five miles above the city are Big, or Chameleon, Falls, 90 feet perpendicular, and on same stream are Roaring, Caldron, and Eagle's Nest Falls, nearly as great. Thunder Lake, River Medicine, Gravel and Trout Lakes, are near, and are full of fish. Brook trout are caught in great abundance in many of the streams of the vicinity. Deer, bear and other game are plentiful. The city has several good hotels, where sportsmen are lodged and fed at very reasonable rates.

CHEAP LAND FOR THE FARMER.

The **Chicago & North-Western Railway Company** have for sale, in the States of Wisconsin and Michigan, 1,003,978 acres of Farming, Timber and Pine Lands, in tracts of 40 acres and upwards, at from $2 to $12 per acre. The timber on these lands consists—according to locality and soil—of pine, maple, beech, white oak, red oak, birch, ash, basswood, hemlock, and cedar, which is valuable for charcoal and manufacturing purposes.

Willow River Falls, near Hudson, Wis.—page 88.

Large tracts of these lands are in the immediate vicinity of the iron mines of Michigan and Wisconsin, and from the charcoal alone that can be manufactured from the heavy growth of timber thereon, parties purchasing can pay for them at the prices charged by the Company for said lands, and have money left to enable them to convert the lands from which the timber has been taken for charcoal purposes, into productive farms, for the products of which they can at all times obtain the highest market prices in the mining and lumbering districts in the immediate neighborhood of these lands.

Of the above lands, 639,750 acres are in the State of Michigan, adjacent to and on each side of said Company's railroad, which has been fully completed and is now in successful operation between Lake Superior and the Wisconsin State Line ; and the balance of said lands, 364,228 acres, are in the State of Wisconsin, between the Michigan State line and Township line No. 30, and between Ranges 10 and 18 East, and are bounded on the north by the Brule and Menomonee rivers, and are traversed by the Wolf, Oconto, Peshtigo, Pine and other rivers, on which the pine timber taken from these lands is annually floated to the various places of manufacture thereon.

Marinette, 291 miles from Chicago. This city, of 4,000 people, is on the south side of the Menomonee river, which here forms the boundary between the States of Wisconsin and Michigan. The business of the city pertains to lumbering in some form. It has ten saw mills employing over 3,000 men, and manufacturing 150,000,000 feet of lumber yearly; one blast furnace employs 80 men. In the city are three schools, four churches, two public halls and two hotels. Several trout streams are near. Crossing the Menomonee river on a fine bridge, we reach the depot for the city of

Menomonee, 293 miles from Chicago, and are in the State of Michigan. Here, also, "lumbering" is the leading business. It has five large saw mills, that employ 600 men; an iron furnace, employing 75 men; a court house, that cost $30,000; a brick and stone town hall, that cost $6,000; four schools, four churches, and two good hotels. Population, about 4,000. Without delaying long at BIRCH CREEK, WALLACE, STEPHENSON, GRAVEL PIT, BAGLEY, KLOMAN, SPALDING, FERRY, BARK RIVER, or FORD RIVER, which are mere side tracks, we hurry on to

Escanaba, 357 miles from Chicago. This is one of the pleasantest summer resorts there is in the West. It is situated at the head of Little Bay Des Noques, at the north end of Green Bay. The water of the bay, clear as crystal, washes the streets of the city on two sides, while the Escanaba river forms the third, and the aromatic "piney woods" close well down on the other side. Good hotels offer quiet and comfortable quarters for tourists who may wish to spend days or weeks here fishing, boating or bathing. White Fish Bay in this vicinity offers rare sport for fishermen, and every little stream (and they are numerous) is almost alive with the ever beautiful brook (spotted) trout. From Escanaba excursions are fitted out in various directions. Those not caring for fishing can take to the "woods," and find bear and deer in abundance, to say nothing of ducks, geese, brants, partridges and smaller feathered game. This is now a favorite summer resort to the people of Chicago. It has a population of 3,000, and is adjacent to the vast mineral regions, for which this section of country is renowned. The hotel accommodations are unsurpassed. The Tilden House is the largest, and first-class in all its appointments, and located immediately on the bay shore; surrounded by beautiful groves and parks, laid off in flower beds, and beautiful serpentine walks and carriage drives; being well supplied with boats—both rowing and sailing—fishing tackle, and professional guides in readiness to convey guests to the trout streams. The Luddington House has accommodations for 100 guests. The climate of Escanaba is unsurpassed. During the hottest of the summer months the ther-

Pulpit Rock, on the St. Croix, near Hudson, Wis.—page 88.

mometer ranges at about 80 degrees, averaging but 65 degrees during the entire summer season. The place is rapidly becoming one of the most popular summer resorts of the Lake Superior district, and, from present indications, the coming season promises to eclipse all previous ones in point of visitors from all sections of the country, To sportsmen, fond of hunting or angling—the naturalist in quest of the curious and wonderful in nature, in connection with the iron, silver, lead, copper and gold deposits of Lake Superior—the business man, seeking rest and health in a pure, invigorating air—Escanaba offers unsurpassed advantages. At Escanaba are extensive mineral docks owned by the railroad, and *into* which (through the spring, summer and fall months), from 700 to 800 cars, *daily*, of iron ore and pig iron, hauled from the iron regions around Negaunee and Ishpeming, are deposited, the daily average being about 7,000 tons. From these docks vessels load for all the ports of the lower lakes.

The country beyond Escanaba is not very inviting, but contains many fine brook trout streams, and deer, bear and other game and fur-bearing animals. The sportsman, fisherman or trapper will find ample employment and sport here. Passing along the classic shores of Goose Lake, we soon reach

Negaunee, 419 miles from Chicago. Here we are in the midst of the celebrated iron regions of Lake Superior. Surrounded on all sides by the mines and furnaces of some thirty or more mining companies—this busy city does not present an attractive appearance to the fashionable visitor or to the "kid glove" tourist, but to him who would view nature in her wildness, or who would go with the hardy, industrious miner into the mines, and seek out the precious gems that are found there, this place has an abiding attraction. The city contains over 4,000 people, is built in a narrow valley, surrounded by high and broken hills, and is 1,400 feet above Marquette, which is only 13 miles distant. It is well supplied with schools, churches, hotels, newspapers and business houses. In the vicinity are many romantic and picturesque spots, well worth visiting. Game is abundant and brook trout more than plentiful. *Escanaba River, Little Lake, Cascade, Lake Michigammi* and *Menomonee River* are within visiting distances, and a visit to them will amply repay the tourist. Of all the gems of this wild country, you must not fail to see *Teal Lake*, as beautiful a body of water as eye ever looked upon. We reproduce a scene on the lake, that has been painted by Edward Schrottky, a rising young artist of this place. Our wood-cut does poor justice to the beauty of the picture or of the lake. On the farther side of the lake, and to the left of the picture, may be seen a house. Its history is not unromantic. Many years ago, an Eastern gentleman, with an only daughter, about 20 years of age, settled at Chicago. The moist air from Lake Michigan did not agree with the lady, and she daily faded. An Indian chief, at Fort Dearborn, told the father, of the pure, dry air of the hills of the great northern lake, and drew no mean picture of the country about Negaunee and Teal Lake, and urged that the daughter should be taken there. Anxious to adopt any means that seemed to promise hope to the almost dying girl, the lumber for a house was prepared, and with an ample supply of handsome, costly furniture, was placed on a vessel, chartered to run as near Teal Lake as possible. In due time this vessel reached the port where Marquette has since been built. Friendly Indians "packed" the cargo of the vessel over almost pathless wilds, 13 miles to the site shown in our picture, and in course of time the house was built, furnished and occupied by the invalid and her father. A happy year was passed; bloom again came to the wan cheek and fire came to the dimmed eye; but, alas, only to mock the hopes of the doting parent. With the coloring of the leaves the next fall, the father bore the body of his dead child to his far-off Eastern home, and abandoned house, furniture and all. The Indians, with superstitious dread, kept away from the place, and everything remained as the owner had left it until a few years ago, when the white man prospected the country, and settled here to rob the hills of their mineral treasure. Having none of the scruples of the untaught savage, he did not respect the home of the dead girl, and soon stripped it of its contents, so that to-day the house alone is left. It stands there, a monument to the now dead and almost forgotten father, who, in its building and furnishing, expended over $80,000. The place is known as "The White House."

On the St. Croix, near Taylor's Falls, Minn.—page 88.

Ishpeming, 422 miles from Chicago. This city, of over 6,000 people, is in the same iron region as the last named. Many mines are close to its limits and within the city proper—the Cleveland, producing 150,000 tons yearly; the Lake Superior, 150,000 tons; Barnum, 50,000 tons; Pittsburgh and Lake Angeline, 40,000 tons each. Deer Lake furnace, two miles off, produces 10,000 tons yearly of charcoal pig metal. In the city are five churches, one school, with 11 teachers, occupying a building that cost $52,000. The Barnum House is a first class hotel, kept by Robert Nelson. It has 90 rooms, is lighted with gas, supplied with hot and cold water and bath rooms, heated with steam throughout, finely furnished, and cost, with its furniture, some $80,000. It was opened in June, 1875, and is admirably kept. Ishpeming is the northern terminus of our line.

Marquette, 435 miles from Chicago, though not directly on the Chicago & North-Western Railway, is reached by rail by that route only, and is so closely identified with this line, that we almost call it our terminal station, and largely treat it as if it were so. Marquette is situated on the south shore of Lake Superior, at the eastern terminus of the MARQUETTE, HOUGHTON & ONTONAGON RAILROAD, and is the centre of the great iron region of Lake Superior. The principal business interests are those connected with mining. It is well supplied with excellent hotels and large summer boarding houses, where comfortable, well furnished rooms and unexcelled board can be procured at very reasonable prices. The city is beautifully located on the Bay of Marquette, which is a deep indentation of the shores of the lake. The town is well built, its streets wide, clean, and well paved. Its people are refined, educated, and extremely sociable and kindly. On the bay you have unequaled facilities for boating, and its waters are filled with *gamey* fish, which seem eager to reward the angler, as they are caught in great abundance with but little labor. A few miles out in the bay are several large islands covered with virgin forests. These islands are favorite resorts for picnic parties, that reach them by sail boats, by steamer, or by small row boats, of which any number almost may be hired in Marquette at any time.

For the invalid or for the resident of our Southern or Eastern States, Marquette offers many inducements as a summer resort. Its air is pure and clear, its days not hot, its nights pleasantly cool, and yet not cold, and its healthfulness unquestioned.

From Marquette you can take steamer for Sault St. Mary, for Isle Royal, St. Ignace Island, Fort William, or any point on the north shore of Lake Superior. On that shore you will find nature in all her wildness. The white man's arts and ways have not yet penetrated its wilds, and the Indian with his peculiar ways can be found without seeking far. This Indian is not the savage of the plains or mountains, but he who has been tamed by the kindly teachings of the patient Catholic missionary, who has been a dweller in the tents of the uncultured child of the forest for generations, and who has lived there really and truly for the Indian's good, and not for the white man's aggrandizement, as is too often the case with the so-called friend of the Indian. No finer trout fishing is to be found anywhere on the broad earth than can be found on the north shore of this great inland ocean. Speckled trout, weighing from five to twelve pounds, are often caught by the few adventurous spirits who

"The Dalles," on the St. Croix, Wis.—page 91.

have for several years sought these favored shores. The rivers *Nipigon* and *Michapacoton* are the best known of the trout streams of the north shore. Guides to these streams can be easily hired at Marquette, and fishing parties be fitted out with little expense or labor. And here we might drop a hint that may be useful to the stranger: Take an Indian for your guide if you go to the north shore to fish; see that you get one that does not love "fire water," and one that is not afraid of work. Plenty of lazy white men will tender their services, and boast of their knowledge and skill, but trust them not. They are utterly worthless, either in your boat or out of it.

The best hotels at Marquette are The Cozzens, Alfred Cozzens, proprietor—it can accommodate 150 guests for the summer—this house has a number of summer cottages fitted up for the use of guests, who may prefer them to the rooms of the hotel—and The Northwestern Hotel, Farnham & Lyons, proprietors. This house is situated close to the waters of the bay, and is a charming location for a summer home. Mesdames Williams and Sherman keep excellent boarding houses. The rates for private board range from $6 to $12 per week. A daily line of Pullman Palace Cars is run between Chicago and Marquette, by the Chicago & North-Western Railway Company.

Marquette, as a watering place, cannot well be excelled. Romantic scenery surrounding one on every side, a cool, bracing atmosphere, which, to those who may be suffering from the heat of a summer sun, is, as it were, the "balm of Gilead." In the foreground a beautiful bay spreads away to the distant shore (which is often compared to the bay of Venice), whose silvery waters often lie like an immense mirror beneath the rays of the setting sun, and when dotted with vessels and steamers, presents a scene worthy the pencil of an artist. Salmon trout abound in its waters, and are often taken by trolling, weighing from five to twenty-five pounds each. One person not unfrequently captures from one to twenty fish per day, in the season. There are a number of streams in the vicinity, where the speckled beauties are awaiting the fly of the angler.

The Falls of Minnehaha, Minn.—page 90.

Marquette has a population of about 8,000. It is lighted with gas, and is supplied with water from the cool, crystal lake by the Holly water system.

To the invalid or tourist, needing a few weeks' recreation, we recommend them by all means to seek the pure air and splendid climate in and around the fair city of Marquette. Sailing over the broad, clear waters of Lake Superior, trolling for the large thirty-pound lake fish, beating the mountain streams for speckled trout, visiting the rolling mills, furnaces, mines, and other objects of interest, will serve to pass away several weeks in an amusing and profitable manner. The hotels here are well kept, very comfortable and charges reasonable.

We quote from the *Mining Journal:* "The people of Marquette are remarkably well favored with the grand in nature—in the hills and valleys, the swift-flowing river, and the rivulet, the expanse of lake and stretch of shore line, the rising plain and unnumbered tints of foliage, by which the city is surrounded. It would be difficult to select a point that offers a greater diversity of striking and beautiful scenery, in the midst of a moving commerce, which is asserting itself as the most powerful in the world. A finer picture never covered the canvas of an artist than is presented by Marquette from the centre of the bay, with the docks, and ships, and steamers in the foreground, bustling with life, and the city dropping from the high land to the right and left, on both sides of the bay, with a horizon of hills to the extreme right and left in the background."

Marquette is the county seat of Marquette county, which was organized in 1845, and has a resident population of 20,000. The city contains a county court house and jail, two public halls—Mathews and The Opera House, which will seat 1,000 persons; five churches; a union high school, three ward schools, a convent and Roman Catholic seminary, three banks, two foundries, four blast furnaces, one rolling mill, one steam forge, and several other manufactories. The machine and car works of the Marquette, Houghton & Ontonagon Railroad Company are located here, and give employment to a large number of skilled mechanics. Five extensive docks for the shipment of ore have been built and are maintained here at large expense. Dead, Chocolay, Little and Garlic rivers are near by, and are noted trout (brook) streams. Returning to Ishpeming from Marquette, we find the Marquette, Houghton & Ontonagon Railroad running westward, and towards Ontonagon. It runs through a wild and mostly uncultivated district, but one that is well worthy of a visit. Iron mines and furnaces are on every hand; mountains of iron are on every side, and the roaring of the rapid running river is heard many times while passing from Ishpeming to L'Anse.

Lake Michigammi, 38 miles from Marquette, situated on the line of the Marquette, Houghton & Ontonagon Railroad, in Marquette county, is one of the most beautiful sheets of water to be found in the country. The shore is very irregular, presenting many points of beauty; the lake contains many wooded islands, which add much to the picturesqueness of the scenery. A steamer runs on the lake from Michigammi to the islands. At Michigammi are the celebrated Michigammi and Spurr iron mines. The Hamey, Hoskins and other mines, but partially developed at the present writing, are located near Michigammi.

L'Anse, 63 miles from Marquette, in Baragey county, is a new town, situated on Keweenaw bay, and at present is the western terminus of the Marquette, Hougton & Ontonagon Railroad, but surveys for the extension of the line to Ontonagon and Houghton have been made. The harbor is one of the finest on the whole chain of lakes. There are two churches, one school house, one bank and several stores. Arrangements are now being made for building a dry dock and a blast furnace. The railroad ore pier and merchandise dock and machine shops give employment to a large force of workmen. On Fall river and L'Anse bay is to be found as fine brook and salmon trout and white fish fishing as there is in the country. Methodist and Catholic Indian mission houses are situated about four miles from L'Anse, on opposite sides of the bay.

The following named towns are situated on the line of the Marquette, Houghton, & Ontonagon Railroad: Marquette, Morgan, Negaunee, Ishpeming, Greenwood, Clarksburg, Humboldt, Republic, Champion, Michigammi, Spurr, Sturgeon, Summit and L'Anse.

Although the season of 1875 was one of very great depression, and was particularly unfavorable to the iron interests, the following statistics of the iron ore traffic may be interesting: Produced, by Republic mine, 127,000 tons; by Lake Superior mine, 114,000 tons; by Cleveland mine, 109,000 tons; by Jackson mine, 106,000 tons; by Champion mine, 47,000 tons; by Michigammi mine, 45,000 tons; by Spurr mine, 42,000 tons; by Saginaw mine, 45,000 tons; by Kloman mine, 35,000 tons; by Barnum mine, 41,000 tons; by other mines, 225,000 tons. Total, 936,000 tons. In addition to this, there was manufactured and shipped by the charcoal furnaces of this district, 90,500 tons of pig iron. The aggregate production of iron ores of the mines in this region from 1856 to 1875, inclusive, was 9,648,281 tons. The aggregate product of pig iron from 1858 to 1875, inclusive, was 719,351 tons.

Names of iron mines and furnaces, with location, on the Marquette, Houghton & Ontonagon Railroad: Marquette and Pacific furnace, Marquette; Carp furnace, Marquette; Grace furnace, Marquette; Bancroft furnace, Bancroft; Morgan furnace, Morgan; Rolling Mill mine, Negaunee; McComber mine, Negaunee; Jackson mine, Negaunee; New York mine, Ishpeming; Cleveland mine, Ishpeming; Lake Superior mine, Ishpeming; Lake Angeline mine, Ishpeming; Saginaw mine, Saginaw; Winthrop mine, Saginaw; Shenango mine, Saginaw; Greenwood furnace, Greenwood; Michigan furnace, Clarksburg; Washington mine, Humboldt; Edwards mine, Humboldt; Franklin mine, Humboldt; Hungerford mine, Humboldt; Republic mine, Republic; Kloman mine, Republic; Peninsula mine, Republic; Metropolis mine, Republic; Erie mine, Republic; Cannon mine, Republic; Keystone mine, Champion; Champion mine, Champion; Michigammi mine, Michigammi; Harney mine, Michigammi; Spurr mine, Spurr; Steward mine, Spurr.

Again referring to L'Anse, we would say, that here close connection is made with the staunch iron steamer "Ivanhoe," belonging to the L'Anse, Houghton & Hancock Transit Company, which runs to the port of Houghton, the distributing point for the copper district, embracing Houghton county and a part of Keweenaw Point. The steamboat trip from L'Anse to Portage lake occupies about three hours, the steamer passing through the beautiful sheet of water known as Keweenaw bay, and the picturesque Portage river and lake, all of which are renowned for their scenic effects, etc. Portage lake is noted as the site of a number of thriving industries, which include stamp mills, copper smelting works, foundries, machine shops, candle factories, copper rolling mill, saw and planing mills, etc., etc. Portage lake has two thriving towns, Houghton and Hancock. The former is the

The Falls of St. Anthony, Minn.—page 94.

county seat of Houghton county. Its situation, on the side of a hill, is an attractive one, and its excellent hotel, one of the best—The Northwest—makes the place a desirable summer resort. All the great copper mines of Lake Superior can be reached from this town within an hour and a half. On the opposite or north side of Portage lake is the flourishing town of Hancock, which is the western terminus of the Mineral Range Railroad, a line of narrow gauge railway, in operation between the famous Calumet and Hecla mine and Portage lake. During the season of navigation, all points of interest on Lake Superior, including the silver mines of Ontonagon, the copper mines of Isle Royal, the North Shore silver mines, Duluth, Bayfield, Superior City, etc., can be reached from Portage lake, it being the eastern and southern terminal point for a line of steamers, calling at all the localities named. The climate of Portage lake in the summer is one of the most delicious on the American continent, and, aside from its great attraction as the site of the largest copper industry in the world, the tourist or pleasure seeker will find much to interest in studying the scenery on either side of the lake. The section also affords some excellent trout streams.

Names of silver and copper mines in the Lake Superior country, which may be reached via Marquette, Houghton & Ontonagon Railroad, and steamers from L'Anse: Copper—Calumet and Hecla, Copper Harbor, Atlantic, Hancock, Eagle River, Pewabic, Allouez, Franklin, Osceola, Phœnix, Quincy, Albany and Bos. Silver—Superior, Cleveland, Collins, Ontonagon, Pittsburg, Excelsior, Scranton, Luzerne, and several others.

PORTAGE LAKE is an irregular body of water, about twenty miles in length, extending nearly across Keweenaw Point to within two miles of Lake Superior. Steamers and sail-vessels drawing 12 feet can pass through Portage Entry, and navigate the lake with safety. This body of water was an old and favorite thoroughfare for the Indians, and the Jesuit Fathers who first discovered and explored this section of the country. During the winter months the atmosphere is very clear and transparent in the vicinity of Houghton, and all through Keweenaw Point; objects can be seen at a great distance on a clear day, while sounds are conveyed distinctly through the atmosphere, presenting a phenomenon peculiar to all northern latitudes. This is the season of health and pleasure to the permanent residents.

PORTAGE AND LAKE SUPERIOR SHIP CANAL. This important work was commenced in 1868, and finished in 1873, at a cost of about $2,500,000. Its length is 2¼ miles, with piers 600 feet in length, extending out into Lake Superior on the north, affording a safe entrance for downward bound vessels. The canal is 100 feet wide, 15 feet deep, with banks rising from 20 to 35 feet above the water. At its southern entrance into Portage lake, 8 miles above Houghton, it runs through a low marshy piece of ground, then enters the lake about half a mile wide. Below Houghton it connects with the Portage Lake and River Improvement, 14 miles in length, making the distance across from lake to lake, 24 miles.

HANCOCK, Houghton county, Michigan, is situated on the north side of Portage lake, opposite to the village of Houghton, with which it is connected by a steam ferry and a bridge. The town was first laid out in 1858, and now contains about 2,000 inhabitants, including the mining population on the north side of the lake, its sudden rise and prosperity being identified with the rich deposit of native copper in which this section of country abounds. The site of the village is on a side-hill rising from the lake level to a height of about 500 feet, where the openings to the mines are situated. Here are one congregational, one methodist, and one Roman catholic church; two banks, two public houses, the *Sumner Mine* and stamping-mill, a number of stores and warehouses, one steam saw mill, one barrel factory, one foundry and machine shop, and other manufacturing establishments. In the vicinity are four extensive steam stamping mills, worked by the different mining companies—the Quincy, Pewabic and Franklin.

The Mills at Minneapolis, Minn.—page 90.

FROM MARQUETTE TO DULUTH, VIA STEAMER.

From Marquette, or from Houghton, you can take steamer to Isle Royale, Silver Islet, and Duluth.

The steamers leave Marquette in the morning, and pass by the Huron islands, Manitou Island, Keweenaw Point, past Fort William, Eagle Harbor, Eagle River, Ontonagon, the Pewabic Copper Mines, Copper Harbor, Ashland, Bayfield, and so up to Fond du Lac and Duluth. We have an attractive trip, on magnificent boats, over the largest lake in the world. Lake Superior is noted for its clear, cold water (it being so clear that from the deck of the steamer you can plainly see the great lake trout playing in the water forty feet below the surface); you pass within sight of the shores of the lake, which are in many places mountainous, and clothed in the verdure of the pine, hemlock, spruce, fir, and other evergreen trees. A more delightful trip for the hot days of summer cannot be had within the bounds of the American continent. The steamers are large, staunch, finely equipped, and commanded by officers whose superiors in courtesy and kindness cannot be found anywhere.

You can visit Duluth and Marquette during same trip, going to Duluth via St. Paul, and returning via Marquette, or *vice versa*, if you procure the round trip tickets issued by the Chicago & North-Western Railway, at Chicago. The following letter gives some idea of a trip by steamer on Lake Superior:

"'To Duluth via the North Shore and Silver Island,' is an announcement I read in a Marquette newspaper on Monday last. I lost no time in securing passage on the splendid steamer St. Paul, of Ward's Lake Superior Line. Leaving Marquette on the following morning, favored by a cloudless sky and an unruffled sea, the run to Houghton and Hancock was enjoyably made in about eight hours. Several substantial stone buildings are being constructed in Houghton, while the narrow-gauge railroad from Hancock to the Calumet Mine—a distance of twelve miles—and the lively business it does, give to Hancock a metropolitan aspect.

"As the day was fading into night, our boat steamed down the copper-colored lake (Portage lake), amid rugged scenery—forest-covered hills towering on each side, and, eight miles distant, entered Portage Lake canal. This cut is without locks, is one hundred feet wide, two and one-quarter miles long, has a good depth 'of water, and cost $2,500,000. At its Lake Superior end a locomotive head-light, perched upon what resembled a primitive pigeon-coop, lighted us out into the lake. With the prow of our vessel turned northward, and the Captain's assurance that daylight would bring us to Silver Islet, the hundred or more excursionists turned into their berths.

"Isle Royale first came in sight. The vast mineral deposits there discovered, attract to it much attention. It is situated within thirty miles of the north shore, and a natural wonderment is how it came to be included within the United States. The simple fact is, that when the treaty defining the boundary line was made, the British Commissioner did not know its value, while Benjamin Franklin, the American Commissioner, did. During his residence in Paris, as Ambassador of the United States, he had discovered among the French archives the reports of Jesuit explorers, dating back to 1630, which announced the existence of rich copper-deposits on this island. Keeping this information to himself, when the treaty was being drawn up, he, without assigning a reason, insisted upon this island being secured to the United States. The British did not deem it worth while to object. Franklin then wrote home that he had secured for the Republic all the copper the country would ever need. He had then no idea that rich deposits of the same ore would be found throughout Keweenaw Point.

"The island is about fifty miles long by ten in width. Its surface is rugged, and inviting only in midsummer. Its shores are indented with numerous bays and inlets, capable of floating the largest craft. Near the middle of the island are two lakes —Desor and Siskawit.

"A vein of silver was opened in the western end

White Bear Lake, Minn.—page 91.

of the island, and, as it lies on the same range as Silver Islet, it is believed that silver ore predominates. But the fabulous reports about Silver Island —of pure silver nuggets, large as a man's head, found in its matchless vein—engrossed our curiosity and challenged our belief. To the Indians it was not unknown. For many years they had exhibited silver specimens to the citizens of Ontonagon, on the south shore, but could not be induced to reveal the location of the mine.

"Among the thousands of islands of varying size which cluster along the north shore, Silver Islet seems like a mere speck on the surface. At no point was it more than five feet above the level of the lake, while its dimensions were less than eighty feet square. When its marvelous value was discovered, the obstacles in the way of opening the vein seemed insurmountable. The islet is about a mile distant from the main land, upon which the settlement is located. More than five hundred feet of crib-work has been thrown out in the form of a square, starting from the middle of the islet, and running southeast. Inside this protection, and around the richest part of the vein, a coffer-dam has been constructed. A shaft has been let down to the sixth level—about four hundred feet—at which depth good ore is now being mined. The operations of silver and copper mining are similar. The opening of the shaft rarely exceeds six feet square. The veins are reached by what are termed "levels." On Silver Islet they are about seventy feet apart. After a vein has been followed as far as thought profitable, the shaft is sunk ten feet deeper, when the vein below is reached. The waste material thrown out has been used to fill in around the island, thus largely increasing its dimensions. Upon this made ground, and upon piles driven in, numerous buildings have been erected. Loosely lying around the islet are piles of rocks taken from underground which are said to contain more silver than is found in the most profitable mines in Nevada and Colorado.

"Six miles west of Silver Islet, Thunder Cape juts far out into the water, and looms up fully 1,350 feet above the level of the lake. This bold promontory presents a grand aspect—the most striking on the north shore. It marks the entrance to Thunder Bay, in which Prince Arthur's Landing and Fort William—both considerable settlements—are situated. In some places Thunder Bay rises from the water almost perpendicularly, presenting a basaltic appearance, while it is rendered more awful from its having upon its summit an extinct volcano. The Canadian Government has located a lighthouse at its highest point. From its summit magnificent views are obtained of the majestic scenery in the vicinity. Islands, varying in length from one hundred feet to half that number of miles, are seen as thickly strewed as are the Thousand Islands of the St. Lawrence. Within a dozen miles north they are counted by hundreds.

"Indian tribes still roam over the vast territory from Lake Superior to Hudson's Bay on the north. The mountainous peaks they regard with especial veneration and awe, associating with them fabulous legends. They believed the thunder-clouds were gigantic birds, whose nests were on the highest hills, and whose cries were heard afar off. The head they assumed resembled an eagle's, having on one side a wing and a paw, and on the other an arm and one foot. The lightning was supposed to issue from the beak through the paw, by which it was launched forth in fiery darts over the country. From this superstition the locality became invested with the name Thunder.

"Bounding Thunder Bay on the south is Pie Island. The Indians name it after the Tortoise. It is eight miles long by five miles wide, and in one place rises to an altitude of eight hundred and fifty feet. The highest point is basaltic, resembling the Hudson river palisades.

"Westward, along the shore, the prospect is ever pleasing. There is the same rugged, mountainous shore, covered with spruce, pine, birch, balsam, and cedar trees. About one hundred and twenty miles northeast from Duluth, the boundary line is

Oak Grove House, Cedar Lake, Minn.—page 91.

defined by a small trout stream, called Pigeon river, which empties into a beautiful bay of the same name. Our very obliging captain, Albert Stewart, ran into the bay to the mouth of the river—five miles from the lake—simply to enable us to view the grand scenery and the insignificantly small boundary line. Majestic hills, covered with thick foliage, encircle the bay. About a mile up the river, water falls ninety feet into a chasm, then rushes through a gorge into the bay. At this remarkable spot one white man—Capt. Parker—dwells, fishing and hunting in British or American territory, at his pleasure.

"Ten hours subsequent sail brought us to Duluth."

Please retrace your reading a few pages, and you will find that at Harvard Junction, 62 miles from Chicago, a line of this road diverged westwardly. This we will now follow up and see of what it consists.

THE CHICAGO, MADISON & ST. PAUL LINE.

When first opened, this was known as "THE ELROY ROUTE," and was named from the City of Elroy, through which it passes. This through line consists of the

Chicago & North-Western Railway from Chicago to Elroy, (Wisconsin Division Chicago to Harvard Junction, and Madison Division Harvard Junction to Elroy), and the West Wisconsin Railway from Elroy to St. Paul, with the St. Paul & Pacific Railroad to make up its Minneapolis extension. The line is here, as it should be, treated and looked upon as one line, as it is so operated, advertised and fostered. It is essentially a great through route, and as far as the public see, know, or can feel, is but one railroad. Its trains of Pullman Palace Drawing Room Sleeping cars run through without change twice daily between Chicago and St. Paul, and no break is made in the journey. *We would here say this is the only road that runs Pullman Palace cars between Chicago and St. Paul by any route.*

Leaving Chicago from the Wisconsin Division depot of the Chicago & North-Western Railway, on the corner of West Kinzie and Canal streets, the route of its trains follows the line of the route we have described for the Green Bay & Lake Superior Line, as far as Harvard Junction, 62 miles from Chicago; thence it passes through Rock, Dane, Sauk, Juneau, Monroe, Jackson, Eau Claire, Dunn and St. Croix counties, in Wisconsin, crosses the St. Croix river at Hudson, and passes through Washington and into Ramsey county, in Minnesota, to St. Paul and to Hennepin county, at Minneapolis. Along this line is some striking scenery—first, the beautifully cultivated and fertile valleys of Rock county; then the charming lake region in Dane county, and around the capital of the State,

Lake Minnetonka, Minn.—page 90.

Madison; then the broken and picturesque valley of the Wisconsin river, followed by the wild, weird, grand and awe-inspiring scenery along the Baraboo river and around that mystery, Devil's Lake; succeeded by the striking views along the valley of the Baraboo, and the almost mountain county of Monroe, soon left for the resinous "piney woods," with their logging camps, and streams filled with rafts or lined with mills; to be again followed by the fertile wheat fields of St. Croix county, and the ever beautiful and romantic valley of the St. Croix river, with its "Dalles," Castle Rock, Willow Falls, etc.; and at last Minnesota, that land of lake and pure running streams. No other route can show a tithe of the attractions that are here offered, not only to the summer tourist, or the transient guest, but also to the staid business man, or to him "who comes to stay." Prairie and lake, valley and mountain, breezy odorous woods, and quiet vineyard and farm scenes, follow in charming succession, so that none can complain of sameness or monotony. To the lover of the quiet, as well as to him who delights in the grand and sublime, this route offers peculiar charms, and none pass over it once without desiring to do so not only again, but again and yet again, so great are its attractions.

THE ROUTE TO ST. PAUL AND MINNEAPOLIS.

We will leave the Wisconsin Division at Harvard Junction, and pass northwestwardly on to the Madison Division with the through Chicago and St. Paul train. At **Roscoe**, 85 miles from Chicago, we reach a pretty village of 600 people, in Winnebago county, Illinois, on Rock river. Two large creeks, the North and South Kinikinick, here enter Rock river, and furnish a very fine water power, that, as yet, has been utilized but little—two flour mills and two plow factories only being in operation on it. The village contains one school, with three teachers; two churches and two hotels. Saloons, or "whisky shops," are not tolerated; liquor is not permitted to be sold within a mile of the village. Four miles east of Roscoe are seven springs, from which it is claimed seven varieties of medicinal mineral waters flow.

Beloit, 91 miles from Chicago. Here we have a fine manufacturing city of 5,000 people. It is on Rock river, a portion of the city being in Wisconsin and the other portion being in Illinois, the State line actually passing through the freight houses of this road. The society of Beloit is above the average, and is claimed to be so from the fact that it is a "college town," and the seat of fine educational institutions. Beloit College, founded in 1847, has nine professors and an average yearly attendance of 200 students, is the pride of the city, and has been designated "The Yale of the West." The public schools of the city rank high; its high school building, said to be the best in the State, cost $30,000. The city contains several large paper mills, agricultural implement factories, a scale factory, wind mill factory, and a variety of other manufactories, which, together, employ over 700 men. The iodo-magnesian springs are coming into note, by reason of their unquestioned remedial virtues. The springs are owned by a company, having ample capital to thoroughly develop any merits found in them. The country surrounding the city is charmingly diversified and highly cultivated. Rock river here, besides supplying ample water power, also furnishes fine boating and most excellent fishing.

Afton, 98 miles from Chicago, is a village of 150 people, one-quarter of a mile from Rock river. It has one flour mill, one school and one church.

Hanover, 104 miles from Chicago. This city was originally called Plymouth, after the town of that name in Massachusetts. The earliest settler, a Mr. Janes, who gave his name to the city of Janesville, found a large sandstone rock that was easily worked, and out of it he burrowed a house, with three rooms, and lived in it for 15 years. This singular and unique house still stands, and can be seen from the train as it passes near the village. The village is built on both sides of Bass creek, contains about 200 people, and has two hotels—The Fincham and The Gilbert Houses. At this point we cross the SOUTHERN WISCONSIN DIVISION of the MILWAUKEE & ST. PAUL RAILWAY, and form the short and direct route between Chicago and *Orford, Brodhead, Juda, Monroe*, and the many villages tributary thereto. Close connections are always made here, and passengers destined for the above-named points should buy their tickets to Janesville or Hanover, over the Chicago & North-Western Railway.

Footville, 107 miles from Chicago, population, 400. For three years this was the railway terminus, and at that time had a large and lucrative trade. It now contains two large cheese factories, good schools, three churches, and two hotels. An immense honey-combed rock, known as "The Queen of the Prairie," is a local curiosity.

Magnolia, 111 miles from Chicago, is a village

Lake Minnetonka, Minn.—page 90.

of 300 people, and is surrounded by a rich prairie farming country.

Evansville, 116 miles from Chicago, has a population of 3,000, and is an important stage centre. A tri-weekly line runs to JANESVILLE and *Union* (which is one of the oldest towns in the State, and before the days of railroads was the most important town on the stage line between Milwaukee and Mineral Point), and a daily line to *Albany*, 18 miles east. The village is built on elevated ground on the banks of Albues creek, and is a place of considerable manufacturing importance; a wind mill factory, employing 30 men; a furniture factory, 25 men; a boot and shoe factory, 75 men, and using $100,000 capital; and ten or twelve cheese factories. The public school building cost $16,000, and "The Seminary," $10,000. One public hall will seat 500 people. The Spencer House is the best hotel, has 25 rooms for guests, and charges $2 per day. A line of railroad, some years since, occupied the attention of the citizens of this city, Janesvile, and the country between them, but at present no trains pass over the intervening space.

Brooklyn, 122 miles from Chicago, has a population of 300, and is in Green county, 30 miles from Monroe, its capital. One cheese factory here makes 1,200 lbs. of cheese daily, all of which is shipped to Hull, in England. *Belleville*, *Dayton*, and *New Glarus* are tributary, and reached from this point.

Oregon, 128 miles from Chicago, formerly called *Rome Corners*, is a village of 500 people, having one graded school, two churches, and one hotel.

Syene, 133 miles from Chicago, is not an important station. *Verona Corners* and *Paola* are tributary. *Lake Waulusa* is 2½ miles distant, and affords fine fishing.

Madison, 138 miles from Chicago. The city is pleasantly situated on an isthmus about three-fourths of a mile wide, between lakes Mendota and Monona, in the centre of a broad valley, surrounded by heights from which it can be seen at a distance of several miles. Lake Mendota lies northwest of the town, is six miles long and four miles wide, with clean gravelly shores, and a depth sufficient for navigation by steamboats. Lake Monona is somewhat smaller. A great many efforts have been made to depict the beauties of the location; but no words can convey an adequate idea of what is, indeed, indescribable. The reason of this is that every new point of observation creates a shifting panorama—that no two exhibit the same scenery. From any considerable elevation, a circuit of nearly 30 miles in every direction is visible. Four lakes lie embosomed like gems, shining in the midst of groves of forest trees, while the gentle swells of the prairies, dotted over by fields and farms, lend a charm to the view which words cannot depict. From the dome of the Capitol to the dome of the State University, the whole bearing and aspect of the country is so changed as scarcely to be recognized as identical. On the west, the lofty peak of the West Blue Mound, 25 miles away, towers up against the sky, like a grim sentinel guarding the gateway toward the setting sun, while the intermediate setting is filled in with swelling hills, majestic slopes, levels, and valleys of rivers and rivulets. Madison is the centre of a circle, whose natural beauties compass all that is charming to the eye, grateful to the senses, pleasing to the imagination, and, which, from their variety and perfection, never grow tedious or tiresome to the spectator. The

The Dalles of The St. Louis, near North Pacific Junction, Minn.—page 91.

good taste of the citizens has preserved the native forest trees, so that its dwellings are embowered in green, and buried in foliage in the proper season, to that extent that the whole city cannot be seen from any point of view. It is, in itself, unique, like its surroundings, and the transient traveler gains no conception of the place by barely passing through it. Madison has many good hotels—among these we may confidently name The Park House, M. H. Irish, proprietor, and The Vilas House, P. B. Parsons & Co., proprietors. The Lake Side House, W. Roos, proprietor, on south side of Lake Monona, has one hundred rooms and four cottages for rent, all fitted up in good style. The proprietor of this house owns a steamboat, that plies between Madison proper and his hotel, at such hours of day or night, as may best accommodate his guests.

The *Tribune*, of Chicago, says:

"There is no more charming or agreeable route for summer travel than the one that leads hither by the Chicago & North-Western Railway, for it runs through a country rich in farming privileges, and in wild natural beauty, and through towns and villages which are all connected, by their commercial interests, with the Garden City, through that great life-giving artery, the railroad—the second home of all American people. The trip is short and pleasant. The five-hour ride is pleasantly diversified by the occasional stoppages at stations, the getting off or on of passengers, and at noon by sitting down to a good dinner at Harvard Junction. Even Charles Dickens himself would have been satisfied with the cooking and appointments. You do not have to bolt your food, or amble up to a high counter and make a shy, hit or miss, at a tall stool, whereon you sit to eat soggy doughnuts and drink inky coffee; but you are seated comfortably, your order is quickly filled, and your food is excellent. * * * * But we have arrived at Madison. We are running smoothly between two lakes apparently, for water, water, is everywhere. There is a shore, dimly outlined with houses and trees, a great stretch of blue, rippling water, and a compact little town, built around a beautiful park, with a State House of surpassing beauty; for this is the capital of Wisconsin, the political centre.

"One of the loveliest drives here is that which leads through the grounds of the State University—a prominent and elegant building. This drive is the pet resort of residents and tourists, giving exquisite views of three different lakes, a full and complete panorama of the town, and looking down on the stately white dome of the Capitol, from which it ascends in a straight and direct line for one mile.

"A very popular place of resort for pleasure is the Lake Side Hotel, just across Lake Monona—the second and most beautiful of the lakes. A pretty little propeller runs every fifteen minutes from the city, and lands passengers a few yards from the hotel. The grounds are spacious, highly cultivated, and devoted entirely to the amusement of guests. There is a large concert-hall, where the Madison Band discourses sweet music, and visitors sit around at small tables and drink lemonade or beer. The house is large and commodious.

"The lakes here abound in choice fish,—pickerel, bass, pike, perch, and whitefish. Men and women make it a business to go out trolling for fish. They sit in the boat and row about gently, letting the line drag after, with its metallic spoon whirling in the clear water, and enticing silly fish to their cruel end. * * * *

"The broad full moon has risen, and is looking down on the silent, sleeping town. It is midnight. The white houses gleam through the green foliage in serene beauty. The fair, white dome, with its many panes, rises far above its less aspiring neighbors, and peers, white and solemn, out of its fair, green setting. Far away, the blue waters roll their endless volume of sound. From across Lake Monona comes the "tune-turn" of the band, at its last tune. It is not more musical than the harmonious blending, softened by distance, of the cricket's chirp and the frog's croak. Good-bye, pretty lakes! Good-bye, Madison, sitting like a queen on your green hills in the moonlight."

Mendota, 143 miles from Chicago, is the station for the Wisconsin hospital for the insane, which is located half a mile from the station, on the shore of Lake Mendota.

Waunakee, 148 miles from Chicago, is a village of 300 people, in Dane county.

Dane, 153 miles from Chicago, also in Dane county, is a small German village.

Mineral Springs, Sparta, Wis., on C. & N.-W. Ry.—page 96.

THE CHICAGO & NORTH-WESTERN RAILWAY.

Lodi, 158 miles from Chicago. This village, of 1,600 population, is in Columbia county, which was organized in 1846, and has a population of 29,000. The county seat is at Portage, a city of 5,000 people, 18 miles from Lodi, and reached by daily stage. *Crystal lake,* a beautiful body of water, one mile square, is five miles distant, and is reached by a pleasant road. Spring creek runs through the village of Lodi, and furnishes excellent water power, which is utilized by two large flouring mills. *Poynette,* 10 miles, and *Prairie du Sac,* 10 miles distant, are reached by stage daily; fare to either place, 50 cents. Lodi has a brick school house, that cost $15,000; four churches, a large broom factory, a cheese factory, and two good hotels.

Okee, 161 miles from Chicago. An unimportant station.

Merrimac, 164 miles from Chicago. This village, the county seat of Sauk county, is built on an elevated bluff on Wisconsin river, (which is here crossed by the railroad on a bridge that cost $100,000). It has 200 people, two hotels, good schools and churches, and a fine trade with surrounding country. *Prairie du Sac* and *Sauk City* are tributary. *Palfrey's* and *Dorwood's Gorges,* four miles distant, are worth visiting.

Devil's Lake, 172 miles from Chicago. Prominent among the summer resorts of the Northwest stands the Devil's Lake, in Sauk county, Wis., 36 miles north of Madison. It is reached directly by two daily lines of palace cars, that leave Chicago morning and night, and stop in front of the hotel that has been opened for the use of the summer tourists who flock to the place.

The bluffs of the Wisconsin, at the point where the Baraboo river embouches into the valley, are 600 feet in height. In the midst of this enormous rocky stratum is a deep fissure or gorge, depressed over four hundred feet from the surface, hemmed in by mighty precipices, which constitute the basin of a body of water about a mile and a half in length by a half mile in breadth, known as Devil's Lake. It reposes like a dewdrop in its mighty casket, and from its profound depths reflects the dark shadows of the beetling crags that environ it. The level of the waters is one hundred and ninety feet above the Wisconsin river, and it is supposed that the bottom reaches below that of the river. There is not in the West a sample of as bold, rugged and striking scenery, or any more pleasing to the tourist. A two hours' ride on the cars from Madison will land the visitor upon the shore, and a small steamer will give him every opportunity for exploration. The whole section is wild and full of interest.

The lake is one of the most wonderful and romantic spots in existence, and nothing to compare with it can be seen east of the Rocky Mountains. It has an abiding attract'on for tourists, who return to it again and again, to admire and enjoy it, to wonder at it, and to puzzle over it. Here, ages ago, probably some terrible internal convulsion rent the earth's surface, and piled various strata of rock, of immense s'ze, from 300 to 600 feet high, and disposed it in every conceivable fantastic form. Within the basin thus made lies nestled a beautiful, placid lake of clear, pure water, which reflects on its mirror-like surface the rugged and awe-inspiring

Trout Falls, Sparta, Wis., on C. & N.-W. Ry.—page 97.

barriers which environ it. It has no visible inlet or outlet. It abounds in fish. Increasing numbers of tourists include it in their round, now that it has become so easily accessible by rail.

This beautiful body of water is surrounded with precipitous mountains on every side, except at two points, one being at the southern end, where the railroad enters the lake basin, and the other at the northern end, where the railroad finds exit from the basin of the lake. On every side of the lake you see "rock piled on rock" in every conceivable form, and in immense columns, pillars, piles and masses of very great magnitude and height. The railroad runs along the shore of the lake on a bed that was literally blasted out of the sides of the mountain. From the car windows all the beauties of this wonderful and weirdly mysterious region can readily be seen.

We copy the following letter, as it gives the views of one who was last year at this delightful summer resort, and who was so much pleased, that he wrote, hoping it would induce others to go there, and enjoy what the writer had already experienced:

"Call this satisfaction. The north corner of a light, cool gallery, from which, in the third story of the Swiss hotel, it is literally one step into a young wood, whose dancing shadows almost play upon this page, and at whose feet lie scattered bowlders from the shattered rocky wall of the height that shuts the view, two rods from my chamber window. This in the rear. The other hand shows a blue lake, crisping and brilliant in the wind that sweeps from the west, cleft straight for the Cliff House, setting every fibre of the slim young poplars and

Perch Lake, Sparta, Wis., on C. & N.-W. R'y.—page 97.

black oaks astir, while the nervous willows tingle in a shivering delight down on the sand. If one could make you feel the brightness, the delight, of this late summer morning, that here wears the freshness of spring, there would be a hegira of linen coats and straw hats for Devil's Lake that would make the Chicago & North-Western Railway glad. It is good fortune to catch the up-train one minute before starting, and go rolling off on the smooth track of the North-Western Railway, through the rich valley of Rock river, green and golden after the rains, in the splendor of harvest, where the glassy lights on the varnished oak boughs glitter for miles of sloping woodland; past the embowered dome at Madison, where everything wears holiday air, and the wide, cool lakes tempt one for a day and a week to find the certainty that this capital is one of the loveliest towns for summer-faring, West or East, with its gardens and sails, and beautiful girls, and fun-loving people. But I had it in heart to see this lake among the Wisconsin hills, which had been neighbor for ten years, and yet I had to come from the seaboard to visit after all. One good American wasn't going away from home forever, without knowing something about Wisconsin's blue-green woods, and strange, isolated cliffs, and mysterious lakes, and seeing them at their loveliest, in this burning summer, never perhaps to look upon them again. I did not know Wisconsin was so beautiful.

"It gave one a happy heartbreak to ride through that region of bluff, and oak slope, and pointed knolls, that the railroad opens up on either side, after leaving the little station of Dane, beyond Madison. There is a fullness of sunshine here, a strength in the light, with which hazy Eastern summers do not compare; and there seemed such boldness in each wind-turned hill, and the gallant woods glittered and flung their crests like the staunch regiments that did honor to the State, till the pleasant country seemed glad in its own luxuriance. Was there a glamour in the eyes that looked, or will somebody say that airy bridge across the Wisconsin, beyond Lodi — over which the train runs at foot pace, giving passengers time to mark the meeting of two streams, whose banks were wild with young, bright forest—is not a pretty picture? The wind-work of the plains begins here in miniature. It has rounded, pointed and smoothed off the sand-hills in odd, isolated pinnacles and domes, that rise beyond the line of woods crowding to the water's edge, accenting a scene that would be fair to linger over, if it had only the slight, high bridge spanning a gulf of green, cleft by broad, clear waterbeds, whose very sand-bars the water-beech and willow have turned into beauty. The town of Lodi, which dates from ante-railroad times, looks like a New England village set among bluffy hills and smothered in orchards and gardens. The railroads have changed the air of interior towns much for the better. Farming in a small way was running itself out, and all the industries that depended on it; but the road gave things a smart fillip, and knocked them into shape again. The low element that follows railways has hardly had time to put in an appearance, or else has been sent straight back again. The groups about the stations were of pretty, bright-eyed girls, cheery gossips, in trim seersucker and white cuffs, waiting to see a friend, and easy-goers reading the Chicago papers thrown off the train.

"Another hour of threading the green wilderness of the Wisconsin, and, as the sun was hanging low, the train passed a charming bit of a scene, a nook of vineyard between cliffs whose tops could not be seen, a corner of luxuriant garden, with long grape-trellis down the middle, and a screen of tall trees between it and the western height. It was an acadian picture, and the figures in summer dresses and light hats, strolling in happy leisure, did not injure the effects. We turned the corner of the cliff which shut out the lovely place, and the cars were running on the very edge of a magically-clear lake, whose heights of tumbled bowlders were almost in reach from the windows on the other side. It was lonely and lovely beyond words. That those rich midland counties should hold in their heart such a desolate, witching mystery, was like a strain of Chopin in Mendelssohn's music. The loneliness enhanced the beauty.

"The next minute the train was stopping by a platform at the upper corner of the lake. 'Cliff House' was shouted, and a Swiss cottage, with bright dresses on its ample galleries, came to view through the trees.

"Don't make the mistake of supposing the lake, the Cliff House and Baraboo are mixed up together; but get your trunks checked for Devil's Lake direct. Baraboo's tree-lined streets sleep three miles farther up the hills. Leaving trunks and checks to the providence of the Railway Company, I saw the lake on one side, the hotel on the other, dropped off the train, and never have been sorry for making up my mind in half a minute on that matter.

"The house is so pretty; and it's something to see a summer-hotel that isn't an eye-sore. This ample Swiss cottage, with wings and galleries to catch the breeze, built into the slope of the cliff behind, with croquet-ground in front, and just room for the railroad to pass between it and the lake, charmingly suits the spot. The inmates live on the deep galleries, between the breeze off the lake and the rustle of the forest beside it, but the rooms are carefully provided, enough to make an after-dinner sojourn actually pleasant. It is such a contrast to a dozen or two summer-hotels East, that I could name. Don't I know their miseries—the hard beds, worn carpets, and dilapidations generally; the odious kerosene; the fried potatoes—greased potatoes rather—and frightful pastry and pies; the pert, curious waiter-girls in Sunday finery the week long; the landlord, whose business seems to be, putting off till next day whatever should be done to-day; in fact, all the drawbacks that make people very glad to be at home again? Something of the sort I was prepared to endure, but the Swiss cottage, set down here in the wilderness, put all such ideas to rout. Its cool, clean halls and stairways; the casings finished through the house in varnished pine, that looks almost as handsome as California laurel or satin-wood; the dainty neatness of every fastidious nook and corner, do not prevent one's room-door from opening on fresh Brussels, and easy chairs, and French bedsteads. Actually, we have snowy toilet covers, and walnut in the bed-rooms, instead of much worn paint. The beds, lily-like and soft, don't require that one must be tired to death to rest on them, and the quilts are not of the honeycomb description. To look round one's room, faultless in dainty order, and think of the scoffing care bestowed on certain grand hotels in Saratoga and by the seaside, results in unmitigated happiness for the time. The same bright and

Castle Rock, Sparta, Wis., on C. & N.-W. Ry.—page 97.

shining freshness is on everything, even to the hall-lamp, which delighted my eyes with its brilliant neatness. But there! you don't perhaps deify immaculate housekeeping in detail to this extent.

"You can judge how finding such a deliciously-comfortable home left one's mind free to enjoy the scenery. People say it is like Windermere; and, if desolate fell, and scaur, and crag, belong to that region, there are enough of them here. That's the charm of it to me—its intense loneliness. Banks, 500 feet high, guard it on east and west, with a lower cliff walling in the south, with a pass at each end for the moon to rise through and the wind to creep in. These banks, topped with cliff, broken into many a needle and archway, are slopes of disheveled bowlders, greenish-gray with lichen, and sparsely relieved with growth of pine and black oak, where it gets a shelving foothold. The crags look out of the soft woods, and faces of broken rock, which no kind forest can ever cover, keeping barren reminder of the awful upheaval that shattered the fiery cliffs of porphyry, and hurled them in heaps like those of Samaria. In the crater of the mountain this lake was left, fed through the crevice deep down in its heart, and filled from unknown levels. That day of the Titans is over, and to-day we have this inclosed lake, whose sheltered air and limpid waters have incomparable softness. Such another place for invalids is not to be found in this Northern climate. The air at this height—the rim of the lake is 300 feet above the level of the Wisconsin, I am told—is always lively, always cool, yet tempered to that

anything of that sort, that might disparage other watering-places; but the fact is that, as far as air and water are concerned, we have simply the best that is to be procured.

"Talk of the boating on Lake Michigan, or Erie, or Tahoe. Here is water that one can see through like quartz-crystal of the clearest sort, at fifty feet depth. It looks the color of hock nearest the shores, as boats put out in it; and the tint deepens till, past the half-way tree, floating down, in 175 feet soundings, it is the deep, clear green that tells of absolute purity in any volume of water. I hope never to be called one of the impressible ones, but I am in love with this sacred lake of the Devil, and shall be till I die.

"How we amuse ourselves is an open question—there is so much to be done and seen, if one goes at it in an intelligent way. A steamer, that will hold about fifty chairs on its deck without guards, goes round the lake several times a day; and new-comers twist their necks under West Cliff, trying to get a look at the Turk's Head, which looks like a bust of Lincoln in gray rock, ready to topple over. Rounding home, the boat stops at the vineyard in the southeast corner, where, at bonnie Kirkland, whose grapes you have often tasted from paper boxes, a wine cellar, shaded by trees and crowned with vines, fronts the building on the lawn. A most lovely rustic spot is this farm of the Kirk Brothers, who make it a pleasure ground for the region. The interval between East and South Cliffs, half a mile wide, runs back for two miles, inclosed by high hills; and in this sunny corner, with the warmth reflected from the glowing rocks of East Cliff, where only south and west winds can draw through, ripen acres of such grapes as you never dreamed of in Wisconsin. The grounds about the house are lovely and home-like; a field of honeyed clover, that no

The Warner House, Sparta, Wis., on C. & N.-W. Ry.
Page 97.

delicious softness found on the magical shore of Old Plymouth, that always keeps ten degrees warmer than Boston, thirty miles above; or in the vineyard-belt of Ohio. The water is purity itself—so clear, that not a trace of sediment is left along the margin anywhere; and soft to that degree it seems as if distilled. I can imagine no greater luxury in the way of bathing than to run out on the mile of sand-beach at either end of the lake, that slopes inward for rods without getting beyond depth, and let the waves lave one like any chrisom-child. The water is delicious beyond compare. One notices it in the wash-basins the first thing; and I never can sit in a boat here without letting a hand trail in the tide, that is like cleaving velvet. I don't wish to make any impertinent claims, or

one is afraid to walk in, shaded by high nut-trees and oaks; the whitewashed cottage in the centre, wearing a cornice of Wisconsin ivy, with its dark and light green trails, richer than Corinthian temple ever boasted, with grape-roofed arbors, standard roses in basket trellises of rustic work, the wine-press and bee-hives, the straw-racks and dove-cote appearing through the trees, with their feet in the perfect sea of blossoming clover; a picture of farm-house plenty and adornment that a poet would revel in. Back of the orchard slopes the vineyard, trimly kept, and richly green at present; but nearer is a tunnel of foliage, the great grape arbor, three hundred feet long, and the largest in the State, before the railroad cut away half its length. Enough is left to give the place an Old-

World look, as if it were a homestead in France; and one half expects to see a girl in a scarlet kirtle and high cap come out to complete the picture.

"One would think artists would make this a favorite haunt. If softest sky, bold forms, and porphyritic colors of rock, set off by changing forest and fair reach of bending lake, are worth anything to artists, they can find them here.

"It is a night of cool, delicious cloud as I finish this. There has been breezing on the balconies, music and Chicago fire in the parlor, and, earlier in the evening, ladies, gentlemen, and all the children not in bed, were down in the billiard room."

During the summer season ferns are here found in great abundance, and in equally great variety. In the fall, autumn leaves in all their glory of crimson, scarlet and gold, are gathered.

Baraboo, 175 miles from Chicago. Here are the headquarters and offices of the Superintendent of the Madison Division, which extends from Harvard Junction to Winona. The city is built on both sides of the Baraboo river, and contains about 4,000 people. It is a place of large trade and important manufactures; contains many fine residences, business blocks, school houses, one of which cost $40,000, and churches; a woolen mill, a furniture factory, flour mills, saw mills, and foundries, employ over 400 men. Three hotels accommodate the transient guest as well as the summer tourist. Sauk county has many Indian mounds, caves, gorges, etc., which can be reached from this point by carriage. *Sauk City*, 6 miles, and *Prairie du Sac*, can be reached daily by stage. *The Narrows of the Baraboo*, 9 miles west, *The Dalles of the Wisconsin*, 14 miles distant, and *The Pewit's Nest*, on Skillet creek, are romantic places accessible from Baraboo. For many years this was the home of the lamented Icabod Codding, and here may yet be found many of his devoted adherents.

Kirkwood, 178 miles from Chicago, is an unimportant station.

North Freedom, 181 miles from Chicago, is on the north side of Baraboo river, has a population of 200, and is noted for the fine quality of the maple sugar that is made here in great abundance. Hops are a staple article of farm produce in this vicinity.

Ableman's, 184 miles from Chicago. This village, with a population of 400, is by the inhabitants called *Rock Spring*, and is so named from the many springs of pure cold water that is found flowing from crevices in the rock along the banks of the Baraboo river. The station was named after Col. S. V. R. Ableman, who was especially prominent in assisting in building the road through this wild

valley. In the village are a good graded school, two churches, a stave and heading factory, employing 20 men; a flour mill and a saw mill, each employing 10 men, and one hotel. The country near the railway is broken, but beyond it is level and highly cultivated.

Reedsburg, 191 miles from Chicago. This is an important city of some 3,000 people, located in the midst of the "hop region" of Wisconsin, and controlling most of that trade. *Ironton*, six miles west, has iron mines that have been worked for many years. *Cazenovia*, 10 miles west, has large iron furnaces. *Logansville*, eight miles south, and *Spring Green*, 20 miles south, are reached semi-weekly by stage. In the city are six churches, one newspaper, good schools, and two hotels.

La Valle, 198 miles from Chicago. *Ironton*, 8

"The Buttes," near Winona, Minn.—page 98.

miles; *Valton*, 10 miles west; *Lime Ridge*, 6 miles south; *Sandusky*, 12 miles south; *Loyd*, 18 miles southwest; *Rockbridge*, 20 miles southwest, and *Sentinel*, 7 miles north, are tributary, and reached by stage.

Wonowoc, 205 miles from Chicago, is in Juneau county, 16 miles from *Mauston*, the county seat. The surrounding country is broken and covered with timber, but offers fine hunting to the sportsman. Deer are abundant, and bears are not unfrequently shot. The population of the village numbers about 600; it has one hotel, one school, and one church.

Union Centre, 208 miles from Chicago, has a population of 200, and is on the headwaters of the Baraboo river. *Mauston*, the county seat, a village of 1,000 people, is 14 miles east. *Spring Valley*, *West Lima*, *Rockton*, *Hillsboro*, population about 800, *Ontario* and *Trippville* are tributary, and are reached from this station. To Hillsboro' there is a double daily stage line, that meets all passenger trains.

Elroy, 212 miles from Chicago. This is comparatively a new place, it having grown only since the completion of this portion of the railroad to the junction with the WEST WISCONSIN RAILWAY here in 1872. In August, 1872, when the first train reached this point, about 100 persons claimed it as their home; to-day it has over 1,200, and is a bustling, thriving place. It has twenty-five business houses, two grain elevators, one public school, three public halls, three churches, one newspaper, saw mills, flour mills, and some manufactures; also five hotels, that, together, can comfortably accommodate 225 guests, at rates varying from $1 to $2 per day. The United Brethren maintain the Elroy Seminary, which has 90 students.

THE WEST WISCONSIN RAILWAY.

This new line of railway commences at Elroy, and forms the northern end of the through route we are describing. While entirely distinct in ownership from the Chicago & North-Western Railway, it is so closely identified with it in its through business and connections, that it is recognized and treated here as an intimate ally. Its most important points are—

Camp Douglas, 225 miles from Chicago.

Wisconsin Valley Junction, 237 miles from Chicago, where it has connections with the WISCONSIN VALLEY RAILROAD, and secures rail connections for *Tomah*, 13 miles west; *Centralia*, and the important lumbering city of *Wausau*, together with several smaller points east.

Black River Falls, 265 miles from Chicago. The earliest account we have of white settlements on Black river, becomes almost traditionary when details are sought after. Enough is known, however, to assert safely that sometime during the year 1818 or 1819, an expedition was fitted out at Prairie du Chien, under the direction of one Rolette, then a prominent trader at that point which succeeded in reaching the present site of the village of Black River Falls, and erecting a small saw mill on Town creek.

Whether the expeditionists proposed to locate permanently at the "Falls," cannot be ascertained, but whatever their intentions may have been, they were prematurely frustrated by the Winnebago Indians, who burned the mill before it was fairly in operation, and drove the lumbermen off down the river.

Here it might be proper to state, that the territory bordering on and contiguous to Black river, then belonged to the Indians, who did not cede their right to it until 1838. The Winnebagoes claimed to own the land from the east fork of Black river, east to the Wisconsin river, west to Beef slough upon the Mississippi river; thence south to the mouth of the Wisconsin river. On the east side of the last named river, were located the Menomonee Indians, with whom the Winnebagoes intermarried and fraternized generally. North of the territory claimed by the Winnebagoes, were the Chippewas, occupying a vast extent of country, bounded on the west by the Mississippi river, and by Lake Superior on the north.

From the time that Rolette's expeditionists were driven off the river, there was no attempt to effect a settlement at the "Falls" until late in the spring of 1839, (the Indians having the year before ceded to the Government all the lands on Black river claimed by them), when an expedition was organized at Prairie du Chien for a permanent settlement and the improvement of the water-power at Black River Falls.

The hotels are—The Jones, The Popham, The Albion, The Falls House, and The Black River House. The population of the city is about 3,000. It is the county seat of Jackson county, and enjoys a large trade with the surrounding country and the adjacent lumber regions.

Green Bay Junction, or **Merrillan**, 276 miles from Chicago, is the point of crossing the GREEN BAY & MINNESOTA RAILROAD, as we have stated elsewhere.

Augusta, 298 miles from Chicago, is a pretty village of over 1,000 people, and is growing rapidly.

Eau Claire, 320 miles from Chicago, is the capital of Eau Claire county, and is built at the confluence of the Chippewa and Eau Claire rivers. It enjoys the larger portion of the vast lumbering trade of the Chippewa Valley, and is rapidly extending its trade into more distant fields.

Among the many flourishing cities and villages of the Northwest, few, if any, are just now attracting more attention than the city of Eau Claire. The approach to it, either by rail, or by almost all of the dozen highways leading hither, is not calculated to prejudice the traveler in its favor. Environed, as it is, for several miles on every side, by sandy plains or sloping hills, which are verdant and pleasant enough in the summer, as they are covered with a slender growth of young trees, but unproductive, in fact, almost sterile in the way of contributing to human wants generally, or to commercial staples, the visitor, when he first beholds, from some adjacent elevation of land, this cluster of pretty villages, situated at the confluence of the Chippewa and Eau Claire rivers, nestling along and between their banks, at the base of the low, picturesque bluffs, between which lies the head of the lower Chippewa Valley;—when he sees the numerous steam mills with their tall chimneys, from which roll volumes of dense smoke and steam;—the streets, broad and straight, some bordered by large business houses, others by magnificent residences of brick, stone and wood, which rise amid gardens redolent with beauty and perfume;—when he notices the proud temples of learning, the numerous churches with their towering spires, and the spacious hotels, all showing the foot-prints of highest civilization, the visitor is astonished and electrified at beholding the contrast presented by this wealth and beauty, to the cheerless regions which he has traversed to reach them.

A United States Senator, when first visiting this place, after coming over the uninviting stage road from Black River Falls, before the railroad was built, to address the people on the political situation of 1871, was so delighted with the sudden change, and the charming loveliness of the scene before him, as from the slope of the hills which bound the city on the east, he caught the first glimpse of the sequestered metropolis of Chippewa's rich valley, that he compared it "to the ecstatic emotions of Mahomet, when, dust-begrimmed and weary with the long march over Arabia's dreary wastes, he first beheld the gorgeous splendor of Damascus, its proud domes and lofty minarets, glittering in the summer sun with gold and sapphire, and declared that heaven could never be more to him, for he now saw and felt all that his imagination had ever pictured of that celestial abode."

The hotels are—The Williams, The Niagara, The Brittons, and The Eau Claire.

A correspondent says of EAU CLAIRE: "This enterprising little city situated on the Chippewa river, at its junction with the Eau Claire, is the most prosperous inland city in the State. It is at the head of navigation on the Chippewa, and is composed of three towns, viz: North, East and West Eau Claire, incorporated under the name of Eau Claire City. North Eau Claire is situated on the point of land between the two rivers, just above their junction. East and West Eau Claire are situated just below the junction, on opposite sides of the river. The three towns are connected by bridges. The situation of Eau Claire is highly picturesque and healthful. Its public buildings are very commodious, and are built in good style, and it has considerable manufactures. The city is connected with a very extensive back country, which is well adapted to agriculture, although that interest is not very well developed as yet. The building of the West Wisconsin Railroad, which passes through the city, has been of material benefit to the agricultural interests. In 1857, the spot where the city now stands, was a mass of underbrush. Where now is heard the busy hum of machinery, and the rush and bustle of manufacturing life, all was silent, save the occasional croaking of a bull-frog, or the mournful call of the whip-poor-will. Few would, at that time, have believed that it would ever attain to its present importance."

Seven churches, and four fine school houses, speak well for the intelligence and enlightenment of the place.

The United States Land office, which is located here, serves to bring thousands to this point who wish to locate government lands.

The population now numbers about 12,000, and is rapidly increasing as new interests develop and as capital accumulates.

A noted place, and one worthy of the tourist's attention, is "The Dalles," which can readily be reached from Eau Claire.

Running from Eau Claire, up the valley of the river, is the CHIPPEWA FALLS & WESTERN RAILROAD, built to connect Eau Claire with the city of Chippewa Falls, 12 miles distant.

Chippewa Falls. A stranger, to look over the present city of Chippewa Falls, could hardly realize the fact that until a comparatively short time since, Indian wigwams stood, and Indian councils were held on the very spot where handsome brick blocks are now erected; that on the site of the Union Lumbering Company's store and office, where $400,000

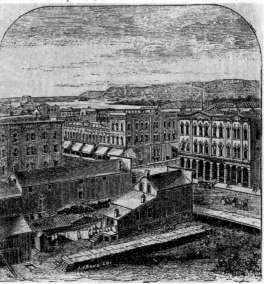

Winona, Minn., from the Bluffs.—page 98.

worth of merchandise is sold, and business to the amount of $1,500,000 is done, the Sioux and Chippewas, in 1850, were drawn up in martial array.

Few places in the Union present better prospects, or have a brighter future. With a population of over six thousand, which is being constantly added to; with the best and most unlimited water-power in the world; with a quantity of enterprising, go-ahead business men, pushing matters along, it cannot fail to have a population of twenty-five or thirty thousand in another ten years.

A Trip to the Falls.

"It was in the evening that the journey was taken, and when the noble bridge, which spans the Chippewa river at this point, was reached, the full autumn moon, that had made only an hour's travel from the horizon toward the zenith, sent its rays aslant the earth and water, forming a picture indescribably grand. The falls of the Chippewa are just above the bridge. The waters came roaring down, catching, and widening, and lengthening the moonbeams, then danced away in white-capped waves, that glistened and sparkled, till suddenly lost among the shadows, and replaced by others just as varied and beautiful. It is worth a day's travel to view the falls of the Chippewa by moonlight.

"The city is situated on the west bank of the Chippewa, on a succession of low hills, rising gradually backward from the river. It is noted for the immense water power, there being a fall of some twenty-six feet in three-fourths of a mile, over a rocky bottom; also for being the heart of the valuable lumber business of the Chippewa Valley. A fine view of the city may be obtained from the Catholic Church. This edifice is reached by a series of steps, ascending through a side-hill grove of magnificent pines to a level table land, lying on the north bank of Duncan creek."

The hotels are: The Waterman, and The Central, on Bridge street, and The Cardinal, on River street.

The Falls of Minneopa, Minn.—page 101.

Menomonee, 343 miles from Chicago, is the capital of Dunn county, and is situated on the east bank of Red Cedar river. It has over 2,000 population, and large manufacturing and lumbering interests. Its hotels are: The Menomonee, The Merchants, and The Central.

Baldwin, 369 miles from Chicago, is a new town with some 250 inhabitants.

Hammond, 372 miles from Chicago, is also a new town, and has over 1,000 people residing in it.

At NORTH WISCONSIN JUNCTION the NORTH WISCONSIN RAILROAD leaves the main line and runs northward towards Lake Superior, is built out about 40 miles, and 16 miles above the junction is the city of NEW RICHMOND, with about 1,200 residents.

Hudson, 380 miles from Chicago, is a city of some 3,000 inhabitants, the county seat of St. Croix county, and built on Lake St. Croix. The largest Mississippi steamers ascend the St. Croix river to this point. Twelve miles southeast is Kinnickinnick river, yielding the finest brook trout, not only in the main stream but on the north and south forks. *Tiffany Creek* also abounds with brook trout. *Bass Lake,* 8 miles northeast, furnishes excellent bass fishing. Four miles from the station is *Willow River* with its beautiful falls, which rival those of the noted Minnehaha. *Taylor's Falls,* at the head of the Dallas, and St. Croix Falls, are worthy of a visit. *Osceola Mills,* having medicinal springs and good hotels, is reached by steamer in the summer and by stage in the winter. *River Falls,* 12 miles southeast, is a thriving village of 2,000 inhabitants, and has a Normal school with 400 students, that is second to no Normal school of its kind in the West. *Pleasant Valley,* 14 miles, *Woodside,* 18 miles, *Brookville,* 26 miles, *Lucas,* 40 miles, *Somerset,* 15 miles, and *Ellsworth,* 25 miles, are reached by stage lines.

Rich Lands at Low Rates.

The WEST WISCONSIN RAILWAY have their general offices here, and at their land office the prospective emigrant can buy any quantity of land he may desire, as the company have a million or more acres along its line to sell. The city is well built, has excellent schools, fine churches, a county court house, town hall, many manufactures, and eleven hotels, one of which is unusually good. The surrounding country is very beautiful, and is full of fine drives, pretty falls and picturesque scenery. The lake and river furnish admirable boating and fishing. Several yachts are owned here, and annually its yacht club has a regatta. Rock Falls, close by, is an unfailing source of pleasure, not only in the summer, but in the winter as well. Game abounds in the woods and prairies surrounding Hudson, and can always be had in quantities sufficient to please and repay the most exacting sportsman. A branch line runs from here to STILLWATER, with its population of 5,000, higher up the river, (see Lake Superior & Mississippi Railway). *The Dalles of the St. Croix* are still farther up, and will at any time amply repay the visitor for the time spent in reaching them.

Four hundred and nine miles from Chicago we reach ST. PAUL, the capital of the State of Minnesota, and a city that has become almost world-renowned for the push, "vim" and energy of its peo-

prairie, or on some of the beautiful lakes which form the characteristic charm of the city surroundings.

Pleasure Resorts.

There are numerous resorts in and within a few miles of St. Paul and Minneapolis, and easy of access. The numerous lakes, with their sylvan associations, form the most prominent charm of the rural landscape. They are scattered in chains, or groups, or isolated gems, all over the State, forming an immense system of reservoirs, which serves a valuable purpose as a guarantee against drouths. Here hotel accommodations are ample and reasonable.

A few miles from St. Paul, close to the base of the almost perpendicular sandstone bluffs, and across the Mississippi, in full view of the scenery up and down the river, is Mendota, the oldest town

Minneopa Falls, in the Winter.—page 101.

ple, and for its admirable climate and healthfulness. In its topographical features and surroundings, St. Paul is one of the most beautiful cities of the continent. Its site is a series of four plateaux rising in regular gradation from the river, of which the first, originally a low bottom, fringing the river for miles, forms the levee, and is occupied by warehouses, railroad tracks, depots and offices, in front of the city; the second and third, with but slight difference in their elevation, about half a mile in width, and stretching for miles to the southwest along and above the river, form the main expanse, on which the business and much of the residence portion of the city rests; while the green slope of the highest encircles this busy scene of metropolitan life and energy like a ring of hills, which are surmounted with many elegant and stately residences; while beyond them, stretches by far the most beautiful residence portions of the city, with fine avenues emerging upon the smooth, green

in this State—a small village, which is said to be inhabited by almost every color, shade and nationality of mankind, and in many cases, a mixture of two colors and races in one. Across, or over, the St. Paul and Sioux City Railway track, and Fort Snelling appears in full view—located upon a commanding eminence at the confluence of the Minnesota (St. Peter) and Mississippi rivers. The scenery on the rivers at this point is exceedingly picturesque and romantic. The white-faced sandstone bluffs along the banks of the rivers, with the charming landscape in either direction, afford a scene of great beauty and interest.

There are points of interest about here which are worth visiting, but too numerous to mention in detail. A short distance above Meeker's Island, close by the roadside, a small stream, from the springs and lakes of the back country, leaps from the limestone rock about forty feet to the bed of the Mississippi. It is known as "Winter Queen," and it is a most beautiful, sparkling cascade, which delights every one who visits it. On about three miles further, and the traveler is at the celebrated "Falls of Minnehaha,"—Laughing Water. These falls are formed by a little stream of remarkable purity and clearness, the outlet of lakes Minnetonka, Calhoun, Amelia, and Rice. In its course to the Mississippi, at a distance of nearly a mile from it, the stream makes a perpendicular leap of fifty-nine feet, the transparent water foaming and sparkling like diamonds in the sunlight. It has a correct proportion of volume to height and breadth; in winter it is covered with pyramids and columns of ice ; in summer a perpetual rainbow is seen ; its fall creates a cheerful music ; it is surrounded by pleasing natural scenery on all sides. Inscribed

Mankato, Minn.—page 101.

on the trees, arbors, benches, bridges, and rocks, are names of tourists from all parts of our own and from many foreign countries, who have been here to see the Falls of Minnehaha, made memorable by Longfellow—"In the land of the Dakotas, where they flash and gleam among the oak trees, laugh and leap into the valley."

On from Minnehaha, in view of one of the most magnificent natural panoramas ever beheld in any country, and soon in sight and hearing of the roaring and foaming cataract, the Falls of St. Anthony, and the massive mills and manufactories of Minneapolis. Across the river, and below the Falls, are the beautiful little cascades—"Fawn's Leap," "Silver Cascade ;" also the Chalybeate Springs, which flow out from the limestone rock on the bank of the river ; they are strongly impregnated with iron, sulphur, magnesia, and other minerals, and the water has proven beneficial in many cases.

Niccolett Island, about 2,000 feet long by 700 wide, is situated in the river, shaded by fine elm, maple and other native trees, and beautified by the residents. It is a charming retreat. Other points of resort here, and near here, are mentioned elsewhere.

The best hotels of St. Paul are : The Merchants, The Metropolitan, The Park Place Hotel, and The International.

Minneapolis.

The city of Minneapolis, (which now includes within its corporate limits what was the city of St. Anthony, one of the oldest settlements west of the Lakes), the county seat of the wealthy and populous county of Hennepin, possesses signal advantages, natural and artificial, which invite the attention of all classes of settlers, and every variety of industry, and must inevitably become a great central point for the production, collection and distribution of the manufactured products, to supply the population which is rapidly occupying the vast extent of country tributary and naturally dependent on it — the home of a progressive people, and the theatre of an important destiny, which is plainly foreshadowed in what has already been accomplished, and what is projected and in course of accomplishment. It has, in a little more than a single decade, acquired a population of over thirty thousand people.

A leading feature of the city, which is especially noticeable, and an attraction, is the chain of beautiful lakes, about three miles out, which, ere many years shall have elapsed, at the present rapid extension of the corporate boundaries, will be within the city limits. For beauty of surroundings, and crystal clearness, one can scarcely imagine more charming bodies of water than *Lakes Harriet* and *Calhoun*, *the Lake of the Isles*, and *Cedar Lake*, (the location of the Oak Grove House), while still further on, some fifteen miles distant, *Lake Minnetonka*, approachable by railroad, and one of the largest and most beautiful sheets of water in the State, offers its charms to the visitor or resident, affording abundance of fish and wild fowl, and sailing and boating. To the east a few miles, is that famed resort, *White Bear Lake*. Minneapolis itself has many features of the picturesque and beautiful, which call forth tributes of admiration from all who chance to visit it.

The principal hotels are : The Niccolett, The Commercial, and Clark's.

Cedar Lake.

This point is four miles, by the ST. PAUL & SIOUX CITY RAILROAD, from Minneapolis. On the shores of the lake, and on the opposite side from the railway station, is The Oak Grove House. The grounds around the hotel, and belonging thereto, cover about one hundred acres of beautifully diversified woodland.

The house is a fine structure, containing seventy rooms, and is located at Cedar Lake Station, fifteen miles from St. Paul ; one hundred and twenty-five feet above the former, and one hundred and ninety-five above the latter ; from its cupola can be had the finest prospect in the Northwest. For home comforts, pure, dry air, fine scenery, good fishing, gaming, boating, bathing, driving, and the neatest pleasure grounds in the Northwest, go to Oak Grove House, on the banks of Cedar Lake. The rules peculiar to this house, are these : 1. No liquor is allowed on the premises ; 2. Sunday is observed as a religious day—a day of rest ; 3. boating and fishing are not allowed on Sunday. It may be said, that near this house is a mineral spring, of powerful medicinal virtues. From the house can be seen Horseshoe and Cedar lakes, the Lake of the Isles, and Lakes Calhoun and Harriet.

Connected closely with our CHICAGO, ST. PAUL & MADISON LINE, are several lines of road running from St. Paul, and over which we send our passengers and freight, and from which large return business is received. Looking towards Duluth, Bismark, or the Manitoba country, we first reach

THE LAKE SUPERIOR & MISSISSIPPI RAILROAD.

The line of this road extends from St. Paul, the head of navigation on the Mississippi river, to Duluth, at the head of Lake Superior, a distance of 155 miles; also a branch to Stillwater, on the St. Croix river.

White Bear Lake, 12 miles from St. Paul, is a popular summer resort, with excellent hunting, fishing and boating. The principal hotels are—Williams', Leip's, and Dunn's, which are surrounded by beautiful groves and lawns. Connections are made here for Stillwater and Minneapolis.

Stillwater, 24 miles from St. Paul, is situated on the St. Croix river, where connections are made with steamers for the famous " Dalles of the St. Croix." The principal hotel here is The Sawyer House. *Forest Lake*, 25 miles from St. Paul; *Wyoming*, 30 miles; *North Branch*, 42 miles; *Rush City*, 54 miles; *Pine City*, 64 miles; *Hinckley*, 77 miles, are small towns surrounded by a fine section of country, and are resorted to by parties desiring quiet locations during the summer months, also by sportsmen in the fall, when deer and other game are abundant, the numerous lakes in the vicinity adding to the attractions.

Northern Pacific Junction, 131 miles from St. Paul, and 24 miles from Duluth, is the point of connection with the NORTHERN PACIFIC RAILROAD for *Brainerd, Moorhead, Bismark, Fort Garry*, and all points in Montana.

Thomson, 23 miles from Duluth, is situated near the head of the Dalles of the St. Louis river, and is the resort of tourists and pleasure seekers. The scenery along the river to Duluth is of a most varied and picturesque character, unsurpassed in the Northwest.

Fond du Lac, 14 miles from Duluth, is beautifully situated on the St. Louis river, and as a summer resort has many attractions in scenery, hunting and fishing. Chambers' Hotel, just completed, is pleasantly located, and offers excellent facilities for summer tourists. There is a mineral spring here which is said to be unsurpassed for its medicinal properties.

Duluth, the lake terminus of the road, is beautifully located on an eminence overlooking Lake Superior. The principal hotel here is The Clark House. Connections are made here with all the lines of steamers traversing the lakes, viz. : Beattys, Windsor and Lake Superior, (Canadian) for *Silver Islet, Thunder Bay, Prince Arthur's Landing, Fort William, Neepigon Bay, Michepicoton Island*, (800 feet high), on the north shore of the lake, and principal points in Canada; with Ward's Central & Pacific, Lake Superior, People's, and Duluth Lake Transportation Co.'s Steamers for *Bayfield, Ashland, Ontonagon, Hancock, Houghton*, and *Marquette*, on the south shore of the lake ; also, *Sault St. Marie, Mackinaw*, and all points east, affording the tourist an opportunity of visiting the numerous points of interest in this romantic and beautiful region.

THE NORTHERN PACIFIC RAILROAD,

Is now in operation from Duluth to Bismark, Dakota, on the Missouri river, a distance of 450 miles. From Duluth to Brainerd, on the Mississippi river, a distance of 115 miles, the road passes through a gently undulating country, covered with a rich forest growth, embracing several varieties of pine, cedar, tamarac, ash, elm, maple, oak, and other woods.

Coming out from Duluth, the tourist traverses the shores of the *Bay of Superior*, St. Louis Bay, and passing up the *Dalles of the St. Louis river*, has in constant view for some 25 miles, some of the most beautiful pictures of natural scenery that can be found in the Northwest.

From Brainerd westward, the country gradually becomes more open, until, arriving at Detroit, some 90 miles west of the Mississippi river, the traveler finds himself in what has been appropriately named the Park Region of the Northwest, so called on account of the many picturesque parks and groves, which, with the intervening lawns, and undulating prairies, waving in the summer with luxuriant native grasses, and now dotted with the dwellings and fields of the new settler, present a beauty of landscape hardly surpassed by any on the continent.

The far-famed valley of the Red River of the North, is reached at a point 120 miles west of Brainerd. This great valley is about 40 miles wide, and some 350 miles long, surface generally level, well watered by numerous streams on both sides of the Red river. The soil is a remarkably rich alluvial mold, from eighteen to twenty-four inches deep, with retentive subsoil of clay, peculiarly adapted for the growth of wheat. The Red river is the boundary line between Minnesota and Dakota, and from here westward, the road passes for 200 miles over an open, undulating prairie, broken only by the valleys of the Shayenne and James rivers to its present terminus at Bismark, on the Missouri river.

Near Evanston, Ill.—page 103.

The Northern Pacific R. R. Co. have an extensive land grant from the Government, for the greater part very attractive for settlement, having, as expressed by a gentleman passing through the country, "a soil whose luxuriant products prove the richest fertility; an ample provision of oak and other timber, growing in charming groves, lakes and streams affording abundant water privileges, in every locality. If Ceres herself should seek a home for prosperous agriculture, her choice might well be here." To these natural attractions, the Company are adding a very liberal policy, and offering fine inducements by low prices and easy terms for their lands, to all settlers desiring location on their line, and the country is rapidly filling up with an energetic, industrious class of people.

The principal towns on the road are—

Aiken, the main point of shipment of lumbermen's outfits and supplies, for the Upper Mississippi river pineries. During the season a small steamboat runs from here to *Pokegama Falls*, a distance of some 150 miles.

Brainerd, on the banks of the Mississippi river, is the headquarters for the general offices of the road, and the location of the Company's shops. Has a good hotel, and the surrounding country affords fine inducements for sportsmen. The lakes are filled with black and rock bass, pickerel and pike, and in the season the woods afford fine shooting; deer, partridge, ducks and geese are found in abundance. The town now has a population of about 1,000.

It is the point of junction with the St. Paul & Pacific R. R., now built and running from St. Paul to *St. Cloud*, now connecting here by daily stage line from St. Cloud.

Also, a stage connection and mail route north,

to *Leech Lake Indian Agency*, *Wadena*, a thriving young village, with stage connections to *Long Prairie*, Todd Co., *Parker's Prairie*, and *Alexandria*.

Perham, a rapidly growing village of some 600 inhabitants, supported by rich agricultural surroundings, with stage connections to *Otter Tail City*, *Fergus Falls*, and *Campbell*, on the St. Paul & Pacific R. R.

Frazer City, a thriving place of but few months' growth, with a fine saw and grist mill, in the midst of a good agricultural country, and now opening roads for connection with *Otter Tail City* and *Fergus Falls*.

Detroit, the county seat of Becker county, near the shores of Detroit Lake, of Minnesota, one of the finest sheets of water on the road, and on the borders of the "Park Region," having about 1,200 inhabitants, mostly New England people, is already becoming a popular place of resort by those who admire beautiful scenery, and enjoy the sports of hunting and fishing.

From here stage connections are made with the *White Earth Indian Reservation* on the north, and southward through the *Pelican Valley* to *Fergus Falls*, and *Campbell*, on the St. Paul & Pacific Railroad.

Audubon, and **Lake Park**, in Becker county, and *Hawley*, in Clay county, are thriving young villages, supported by the trade of the surrounding rich agricultural country, and are becoming quite important wheat shipping points.

Glyndon, located in the Red River Valley, is the point of crossing of the *Pembina Branch of the St. Paul & Pacific R. R.*, now built and running north 60 miles to the *Red Lake river*, there connecting by boat to *Fort Garry*.

Moorhead, on the east bank of the Red river, a bustling, active town of several hundred people, with a large grist mill, having a daily capacity for 600 bushels of grain, fine church and school buildings; is already attracting settlement by its sure promise of continued growth.

Fargo, on the west bank of the Red river, in Dakota, the county seat of Cass county, has the shops and engine houses of the Company for the Dakota Division, one of the best and largest hotels in the Northwest, outside of St. Paul, a fine brick court house, costing $5,000, stores, grain warehouses, lumber yards, etc., and is developing a large trade with the rapidly increasing settlement of the surrounding country. Has stage connections to the north with *Caledonia*, *Grand Forks*, *Pembina*, and *Fort Garry*; northwest with *Devil's Lake*, of Minnesota; southwest to *Norman* and *Owego*; south to *Fort Abercrombie*, and *Breckenridge*, the present terminus of the St. Paul & Pacific R. R. main line, and *Fort Wadsworth*, and during the navigable season, is the shipping point by steamers, of the immense trade carried on by the Red river with the British Northwest, at *Winnipeg* and *Fort Garry*.

Jamestown, in the valley of the James river, adjoining the *Fort Seward Military Reservation*, is a small town of some 200 inhabitants with stores, hotels, etc., doing considerable business with *Fort Totten*, and the *Devil's Lake Indian Reservation*.

Bismark, the present terminus of the road, is beautifully located on high grounds on the east bank of the Missouri river, has a population of about 1,000, with the usual number of stores, hotels, churches, etc., and a heavy trade with the numerous military posts and Indian Agencies on the river. From this point the Missouri river is navigable for 1,200 miles to the northwest, and during the season a regular line of boats is run to *Fort Benton*, and by the Coulson line of steamers, and the Diamond river overland stages, via *Carroll*, an established route is made to *Helena*, in Montana.

The Seminary, Lake Forest, Ill.—page 105.

THE ST. PAUL & PACIFIC RAILROAD.

Leaving St. Paul in a northwesterly destination, we have the first Division of the St. Paul & Pacific R. R. Its lines of road are from St. Paul, Minn., to Sauk Rapids, Minn., 76 miles, and from St. Anthony, 10 miles north of St. Paul, to Breckenridge, Minn., 272 miles. The west line was completed to Breckenridge, on the Red River of the North, in the latter part of October, 1871.

From St. Paul to Sauk Rapids, and from St. Anthony to Breckenridge, the Company have a land grant of ten sections for each mile of road completed, viz.: six sections per mile under act of Congress, approved March 7, 1857, and four sections additional under act of March 3, 1865. The total length of line entitled to these grants, is about 400 miles, and the estimated amount of land accrued and accruing, will be about 1,800,000 acres.

St. Anthony, 10 miles from St. Paul, is at the junction of the main and branch lines. The far-famed water power of St. Anthony Falls furnishes thousands of people with employment in the various mills located here, and the products of these mechanical enterprises add largely to the business of the railroad. The State University, now in successful operation, and an excellent high school, are located here.

The main line crosses the Mississippi river here, on a substantial bridge, to Minneapolis, and thence, in a northwesterly direction, to the valley of Red river.

Wayzata, 28 miles from St. Paul, is a railroad station on Lake Minnetonka, the largest and most beautiful lake in Minnesota, estimated to have a shore line of one hundred miles. It is dotted with beautiful islands, and its shores are mostly covered

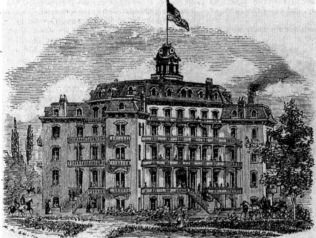

Collegiate Department, Lake Forest, Ill.—page 105.

with heavy timber, among which appear numerous openings, with the farms of industrious settlers. Wayzata contains several good hotels, filled during the summer season with tourists from the East. Two steamboats run between Wayzata, Excelsior, and other points on the lake.

Litchfield, 85 miles from St. Paul, a railroad station, is one of the most important points on this line. It is the county seat of Meeker county, and the site of the U. S. District Land Office. In the fall of 1869 there was a grain crop harvested on the land that is now the site of about two hundred buildings. The town contains several churches, and good schools, hotels, agricultural warehouses, a grain elevator, and other railroad buildings, besides many fine residences. Two newspapers are published in this town. *The Railroad Company has an emigrant house here, where emigrants can obtain all the information they desire in regard to the surrounding country, and a temporary home for their families, while they go forth in search of a farm, or more permanent residence.*

Willmar, 104 miles from St. Paul, the county seat of Kandiyohi county, is situated on the south side of Foot Lake. The village now contains six hotels, also an immigrant house. Willmar is the half-way station between St. Paul and Breckenridge, on the Red river. It is the nearest railroad point for a large extent of country on the Upper Minnesota river. The settlements of *Yellow Medicine*, and *Red Wood Falls*, on the Minnesota river, are only thirty and thirty-five miles distant from Willmar, and connected by lines of stages. North of Willmar are the old settlements on *Eagle Lake, Lake Nevaden*, and the large chain of *Norway Lakes;* all these are tributary and easy of access. For the purpose of experiment, and also to encourage others, the railroad company has planted several thousands of young forest trees around the shores of the lake, which has also added much to beautify the town site.

Morris, the county seat of Stevens county, 160 miles from St. Paul, in the valley of the *Pomme de Terre river*, has attracted the attention of farmer capitalists. There are now ten large 1,000 acre farms opened there; the first crops of some of them have averaged not less than 22 bushels per acre, which average increases in succeeding years. The soil of this county appears peculiarly adapted for wheat culture.

Breckenridge, 217 miles from St. Paul, the present western terminus of the main line of this road, is situated at the confluence of the *Bois des Sioux* and *Otter Tail* rivers, forming at this place the Red River of the North. Breckenridge is the county seat of Wilkin county, and is becoming a place of much importance, being at the head of navigation of the Red River of the North, which flows northward through the British Province of Manitoba.

The branch line of this road, extending from St. Anthony Junction north, is completed, and opened to *Sauk Rapids*, and the extension to *Brainerd*, at the crossing of the Northern Pacific Railroad, a distance of 60 miles, was located, put under contract, and graded during the year 1871. The extension of this line from *St. Cloud*, northwest to

St. Vincent, on the borders of Manitoba, 314 miles, is completed, and operated to *Melrose*, 34 miles. This extension crosses the Northern Pacific at *Glyndon*, and is completed and operated from *Glyndon* north to *Crookston*, a distance of 60 miles.

The principal places of importance on the branch line, are—

Anoka, the county seat of Anoka county, is situated at the mouth of Rum river, 30 miles from St. Paul. It contains about 2,000 inhabitants, has five churches, four saw mills, one flouring mill, and a sash, blind and door factory. Two weekly papers are published here.

Itasca Station, six miles above Anoka. Opposite Itasca, at the mouth of Crow river, is the thriving town of *Dayton*.

Elk River Station, is 5 miles from Itasca.

The flourishing town of *Orono*, situated at the mouth of Elk river, 1½ miles from the station, contains churches, schools, five saw and grist mills. There is also at the station a hotel, school house, two stores and a saw mill. A stage leaves here tri-weekly for *Princeton*, Minn.

At *St. Francis*, a thriving village on Rum river, a saw and grist mill is in successful operation. The town of *Princeton*, 19 miles north of Elk river, is a pleasant village of about 500 inhabitants. It is the headquarters of the lumbermen on the upper Rum river. A fine school house has been built, at a cost of $5,000; it also contains two hotels, grist and saw mills.

Big Lake Station, is 50 miles from St. Paul. It is beautifully situated on the borders of a lake, after which it is named. It is the nearest station for the German and Swedish settlements near *Eagle Lake;* a good road is constructed, (*Elk River* is crossed by a substantial bridge near the mouth of the *St. Francis river*) to *Groton*, where it intersects the State road from *Sauk Rapids* to *Princeton*.

At *Santiago*, in *Baldwintown*, a water power on the St. Francis river has been made available by the erection of a good saw mill.

Becker Station, 7 miles above Big Lake. The surrounding country is largely rich meadow and grazing land.

Clear Lake Station, 7 miles northwesterly from Big Lake.

At both the above named stations, houses have been erected for the accommodation of immigrants; they are capable of holding several hundred persons at a time. They are provided with cooking stoves and other conveniences. Here the immigrant can leave his family in perfect safety, and at little expense, while he goes forth into the country to select his future home. The Company does not make any charge to the immigrant for the use of these buildings. There are grain elevators at each of these stations.

The beautiful town of *Monticello* is located on the west bank of the Mississippi river, 3½ miles from Big Lake. It contains about 700 inhabitants, two churches, school houses, and a saw mill. There is a weekly newspaper published here.

Clearwater, at the mouth of Clearwater river, and 3 miles from Clear Lake station, contains school houses, churches, a good hotel, and good saw and grist mills. Clearwater Lake is particularly attractive, on account of its large and many small lakes. A stage leaves here three times a week for *Fair Haven, Kingston,* and *Forest City.*

Buffalo, the county seat of Wright county, is a new town on the large, beautiful lake of the same name, and now has a hotel, a school house, county buildings, and two saw mills.

Fair Haven, is 17 miles southwest from Clear Lake station. It contains a hotel, a church, school house, and a saw and grist mill.

East St. Cloud Station, is 74 miles northwesterly from St. Paul. Near this station are extensive granite quarries, which are now being worked, and will produce an unlimited supply of the finest building stone in the State. There is a grain elevator at this station, and a fine wagon bridge spans the Mississippi, leading into the centre of the city of St. Cloud.

Sauk Rapids, the present terminus of this road, and the county seat of Benton county, is 2 miles above East St. Cloud. It is a town of considerable importance, and rapidly growing in population and business. It is located on the east bank of the Mississippi river, at the falls of Sauk Rapids, from which it derives its name. The Mississippi river at this point is 600 feet wide, and has a fall of 18 feet in one mile, affording a water power surpassed only by the Falls of St. Anthony, and equaled by no water power in the Northwest. Sauk Rapids already

Ferry Hall, Lake Forest, Ill.—page 105.

contains two spacious hotels, churches, and school houses. The same granite ledge referred to at East St. Cloud, also extends to this place, and quarries were opened for the purpose of constructing the dam of the Water Power Company. In the course of this work it was discovered that the granite reached several feet below the surface, and improved so much in quality that it equals, if not surpasses, the famous Quincy granite.

Near *Watab*, 5 miles above Sauk Rapids, new quarries have been lately opened, containing a white granite almost equal to marble.

St. Cloud, the largest commercial town above St. Anthony, contains about 4,000 inhabitants. It has several hotels, school houses, five churches, two saw mills, sash, blind and door factories, etc. Three weekly papers are issued here. The St. Vincent extension of the branch line starts from this point. It is over 300 miles long. It passes through the fertile Sauk Valley, touching nearly all the principal towns therein, viz.: *St. Joseph, Melrose, Sauk Center. Osakis, Alexandria*, and many others, the trade of which will largely increase the business of St. Cloud.

There is, in connection with this Company, a Land Department, for the disposal of the lands acquired by the act of Congress. These lands have been reserved from sale since 1857, and are now offered to actual settlers. They are the odd numbered sections, situated on either side of, and within twenty miles of, the lines of railroad. The even numbered sections have been, for the most part, disposed of under the homestead and pre-emption laws. The railroad lands are offered at low prices and upon easy terms.

TO SPARTA, WINONA, AND BEYOND.

We have to retrace our steps, and find our way back to Elroy, but in this case there is no hardship, for we step into a magnificent Pullman Palace car at the depot, used by the West Wisconsin Railway at Minneapolis or St. Paul, and in ten hours are back to Elroy. Here we change cars if we come from the north, but if from Chicago we do not, as we have been in one of the Pullman Palace cars that runs through from Chicago to Winona on each through train. It should be borne in mind that the Chicago & North-Western Railway is the only road that runs these cars between Chicago and Sparta and Winona, and *any* point in Wisconsin or Minnesota. Do not overlook this fact when you are selecting your route by which to visit any of these northwestern points. Comfort and safety are always secured if you are securely fixed in a Pullman Sleeper. We must push westward. After leaving Elroy, and passing westward, we find—

Glendale, 217 miles from Chicago. This village of 200 people, is in the midst of a fine trouting country. Many streams, almost alive with brook trout, are found within 4 to 6 miles. Game is quite plentiful. The Glendale House, by W. R. Hart, offers good fare to the sportsman. Large quantities of manufactured wagon stock are shipped from here.

Kendalls, 219 miles from Chicago, is not an important, but is a growing station. It has three hotels. *Lake Torrence* is half a mile distant, and is stocked with brook trout. *Albinville*, 4 miles distant, *Homewood* and *Clifton*, each 10 miles, are reached daily by stage.

Wilton, 228 miles from Chicago, population 500, is built at the head waters of Kickapoo creek, which, with lateral streams, are full of brook trout. Bear, deer and squirrel are found in the surrounding forests, while prairie chickens, partridge, pheasants, quail and grouse are plentiful in the clearings. The village contains good schools, two churches, flour and saw mills, a town hall, and two hotels. *Ontario*, 10 miles south, and *Ridgeville*, 2¼ miles distant, are reached by stage.

Norwalk, 233 miles from Chicago, population 500. Brook trout streams, and many kinds of game, are found in the vicinity.

Summit, 236 miles from Chicago, is at the south end of tunnel No. 3, which is three-fourths of a mile long. On this part of the line will be found three long tunnels through the hills, and much picturesque and wild scenery.

Sparta, 246 miles from Chicago, is an incorporated village of four thousand inhabitants, and one of the finest inland towns of Central Wisconsin. Situated in a fertile valley, entirely surrounded by gigantic bluffs and rocky elevations, near the head waters of the La Crosse river, it presents, with its handsome white painted dwellings and church edifices, its costly business houses and public buildings, with streets adorned with natural and cultivated foliage, the appearance of a prosperous Southern country-seat. Its surroundings are picturesque, and even romantic. To the northwest, and at a distance of five miles, can be seen Castle Rock, towering majestically to a height of seven hundred feet above the level of the river, standing like a silent sentinel on the top of the encircling cordon of bluffs that surround the valley. From its lofty summit can be seen the blue hills of Minnesota, across the "Father of Waters," and an extended panorama of hill and dale is presented to the admiring gaze. Looking back to the southward, the eye rests—in summer—on the verdure-covered plain below, dotted over with its nice farm houses, teeming fields of grain, and crystal streams of pure soft water, abounding plentifully with the finest of speckled trout, affording sport and recreation for the "troutist," in the midst of which Sparta stands, Monarch of the Valley. Pleasure drives and hunting grounds are numerous. Delightful camping places and pic-nic resorts are everywhere to be found beneath the ridges that encircle the town.

In addition to the general natural and artificial advantages and attractions which Sparta presents, it offers special inducements to those in search of health or cure of diseases. To this class, nature, art and science seem to have combined and concentrated here the means for the treatment and successful rejuvenating and curing those suffering from ailments incident to life in less favored localities.

In October, 1867, the boring of an artesian well was undertaken, for the purpose of supplying the village with water. This object was successfully accomplished—a supply of mineral water was unexpectedly obtained at a depth of three hundred and fifteen feet, which is free to all visitors. Several of these wells have since been sunk, and a careful analysis, by accomplished experts, has demonstrated that the water possessed remarkable medicinal and curative properties.

During the year 1875, not less than twenty-five thousand strangers partook of the healing water of these remarkable wells, who, without a single exception, made unreserved acknowledgment of the benefits they had received in consequence thereof. A thorough analysis of it reveals the fact that the water has no superior as a chalybeate and tonic water, on this continent or in Europe.

The hotel accommodations of Sparta are excellent. The Warner, The Ida, The American, The Windship, The Wagner, The Bates, and The Laird hotels furnish ample accommodations. All of the comforts, conveniences and essential luxuries, are to be had for less than half the cost of the same at the Eastern watering places.

Sparta has a large trade in grain—in wheat especially; more than 1,000,000 bushels of grain, and 50,000 barrels of flour are shipped from here annually. It has a paper mill, making 40,000 pounds of paper daily, a county court house, opera house that seats 600 persons, one public hall, The Ida, seating 300, two newspapers, and three banks. Trout are abundant, there being over 250 miles of trout streams in the county (Monroe). Perch Lake was artificially stocked with perch.

Bear in mind that the direct route from Chicago to Sparta, is by the old reliable North-Western road. Do not be deceived in buying tickets to Sparta, by longer and more circuitous routes.

Leon, 4 miles south, *Angelo*, 8 miles, *Cataract*, 12 miles north, *St. Mary's*, 10 miles southeast, *Coon*, 25 miles south, *Viroqua*, 32 miles south, and *Ontario*, 30 miles southeast, are tributary, and are reached by daily stage. HENSEYVILLE, 250 miles, and FISH CREEK, 252 miles from Chicago, are unimportant stations.

Bangor, 255 miles from Chicago, is a village of 600 inhabitants, 16 miles east of the Mississippi river. It has three hotels, one woolen mill, three churches, and a good school. Excellent fishing and shooting can be found close to the village, in the La Crosse river, within a fourth of a mile of the town. Pike, pickerel, black and rock bass, and several other varieties of fish, are found in great abundance. A fine (brook) trout stream flows through the village, and half a mile from it is a large artificial trout pond, fully stocked with fish. In the woods which surround the village, are found deer, squirrel, and wild turkeys. Many bird-dogs are kept here for hire, and there is also a pack of hounds for fox hunting, owned by the Hon. John Bradley, who has a summer residence at this

Highland Hall, Highland Park, Ill.—page 104.

place. The Bangor House, by E. A. De Vau, will be found to be a comfortable home for hunters.

West Salem, 260 miles from Chicago, is in La Crosse county, 1 mile from La Crosse river. *Mindoro*, *North Bend*, and *Melrose*, are tributary. The village contains 600 people, and has a good graded school with four departments, three churches, one hotel, and one public artesian well.

Winona Junction, 267 miles from Chicago. This station is our depot for the city of LA CROSSE, 2½ miles down the river. La Crosse contains over 10,000 inhabitants, and is a fine business centre. We here reach the line of the La Crosse, Trempealeau & Prescott Railroad, now owned by the Chicago & North-Western Railway, and forming from this point to Winona, 30 miles distant, the western end of the present Madison division of the Chicago & North-Western Railway.

Onalaska, 269 miles from Chicago. This village has 500 people; is 5 miles from the city of La Crosse, to which stages run twice daily, connecting with both our passenger trains. A stage also runs from here via *Melrose* to *Black River Falls*, three times each week. Considerable lumbering is carried on at this station. From this point a line of railroad is being built into La Crosse, and soon we shall have our through trains running into that enterprising city.

Midway, 273 miles from Chicago. *New Amsterdam*, 4 miles distant, *McGilroy's Ferry*, 5 miles, *Gale's Ferry*, and *Stevenstown*, 5 miles, are tributary. La Crosse, 8 miles distant, is reached by stage.

Trempealeau, 284 miles from Chicago, is in Trempealeau county, (a large but not densely populated county,) 7 miles from *Galesville*, the capital of the county, and has 600 inhabitants. Pine Creek, 291 miles, Marshland, 292 miles, and Bluff Side, 295 miles from Chicago, are new stations. We have now reached the Mississippi river, and will cross it on a fine bridge, built at a cost of $350,000 by the Chicago & North-Western Railway Co., and at 297 miles from Chicago reach

Winona. This city of 11,000 persons, is the capital of Winona county, Minn., which was organized in 1854, and has 28,000 inhabitants. Lake Winona adjoins the city limits, and in an early day was so noted for its game, that its surroundings were named "*Prairie* aux Isle," or "Prairie of Winged Fowl." Some years after it was named Wabasha Prairie, after the Sioux chief of that name, whose tribe for many generations made this location its home. The county is quite famous for its trout streams. The city of Winona is the largest and most important commercial city in Southern Minnesota, and the third in point of population in the State, and is situated on a beautiful level prairie, on the west bank of the Mississippi river. The first white settlement made in this place was in 1851.

Winona is noted for the natural beauty of its site; for its healthfulness; for the air of taste, comfort, and culture which pervades its residences; for its excellent system of schools; and generally for its thrift, energy, and commercial activity. It has the best system of graded schools in Minnesota, and is, in addition, the seat of the first State Normal School, an exceedingly well conducted and successful institution, for the training of teachers.

The business portion of the town is compactly and substantially built of brick and stone, the streets are wide and regularly laid out, and its whole appearance betokens business activity and prosperity.

It has public school houses that cost $235,000, a Normal School building that cost $82,000, seventeen churches that cost $250,000, six lumber firms that sell 50,000,000 feet of lumber yearly, six flour mills—one being the largest in the State—two foundries, five sash, door and blind factories, two barrel factories, a court house and jail, three fine public halls, seating 2,100 persons, many hotels and manufactories not named above, and a large number of wholesale and retail business houses. Stages run daily to *Alma* and *Fountain City*, three times a week to *Rushford*, and twice weekly to *Houston*.

We have thus briefly sketched the history and business condition of the beautiful and prosperous young city of Winona. Having attained its present growth and prosperity under many adverse circumstances, there is abundant reason to believe that now, with important and increasing railroad facilities secured—with a position admirably adapted to the carrying on of extended commercial and manufacturing operations—and with a liberal minded and energetic population—its future will be as bright and successful as its most sanguine founders ever dared to hope for.

To reach this pleasant and prosperous city, you must take the trains of the Chicago & North-Western Railway Company, as it is the only line that controls the entire route from Chicago to this point.

W. S. Ingraham's Gold Fish Pond, Waukegan, Ill.—page 105.

FINE LAND AT LOW RATES.

The Chicago & North-Western Railway Company has, through the Winona & St. Peter Railroad Company, for sale, in tracts of 40 acres and upwards, at from $3 to $10 per acre (on time), about 1,104,664 acres of choice farming lands in the State of Minnesota, and the Territory of Dakota, along the line of said Winona & St. Peter Railroad, between Winona, on the Mississippi river, and Lake Kampeska, in the Territory of Dakota.

These lands are very desirable for the production of wheat, barley, oats, and other small grain, and all other farm products usually raised in that latitude. They are well watered by springs and clear running streams. The spring seasons are early, and under the warm summer days of Minnesota and Dakota, the warm and friable soil of these lands will richly repay the husbandman for his labor thereon with abundant crops. Minnesota lands, as is well known, produce the greatest number of bushels of wheat per acre, on the average, which is of the finest quality, and commands the highest prices in market of any wheat raised in the United States of America.

Full particulars of these lands can be obtained by addressing GEORGE P. GOODWIN, Land Commissioner of the Chicago & North-Western Railway Company, Chicago, Ill.

Minnesota City, 303 miles from Chicago, is on Rolling Stone river, and has fine water power, on which are two flour mills, one of six and the other of thirteen run of stone, manufacturing 90,000 to 100,000 barrels of flour, and buying over 2,000,000 bushels of wheat yearly. Brook trout in considerable numbers are caught in the streams at the head waters of the river. Population of village, 500.

Stockton, 308 miles from Chicago. Population, 750. Is located in a valley surrounded by timbered bluffs. It contains a flour mill, school, hotel, and two churches.

Lewiston, 316 miles from Chicago, is a pretty village of 400 people.

Utica, 319 miles from Chicago. Population, 200. Has one hotel, three grain elevators, and a good school.

St. Charles, 325 miles from Chicago. Is an active, bustling city of 1,500 people. The city is built in a valley, is surrounded with wooded bluffs, and has one graded school, seven churches, and three hotels.

Dover, 329 miles from Chicago, is in Olmstead county, *is strictly a temperance town*, and has four grain elevators, handling 600,000 bushels of wheat yearly, two hotels, and 200 inhabitants. *Chatfield*, 10 miles south, and *Plainview*, 10 miles north, are reached by stage.

Eyota, 334 miles from Chicago, has a population of 500 persons, a good school of two departments, one church, a public hall that rents at $10 per night, and one hotel. *Elgin*, 11 miles northwest, is reached weekly by stage.

Chester, 341 miles from Chicago, is a village of 200 people.

Rochester, 347 miles from Chicago, is the county seat of Olmstead county, which was organized in 1858, and now has 21,000 people resident therein. The Zumbro (?) and Root rivers run through the county, and besides furnishing ample water power, thoroughly drain the land. Two-thirds of the county is of gently undulating prairie, and the rest heavily wooded with oak, hickory, maple, and other hard woods. The soil is fertile and not surpassed in richness by any in the State. The city of Rochester contains about 5,000 people, and is located in a beautiful valley about two miles wide, through which the Zumbro (?) river runs. Picturesque bluffs lie along the valley, from the crests of which many fine views are obtained. The city has wide streets, fine business houses, large manufactories, fine residences, eleven churches, and several schools; one school building cost $75,000, and two others $7,000 each. The court house is a fine brick structure, and cost $50,000. Two public halls, seating 1,500 people, furnish ample facilities for theatres, concerts, and other shows. Three hotels furnish first class fare for transient guests. At the depot is a first class eating house, by C. C. Morrill, at which all passenger trains stop for meals. Four stage lines centre here, viz.: *High Forest*, via *Stewartsville*, 15 miles, fare $1.00; *Spring Valley*, via *Marion* and *Pleasant Grove*, 34 miles, fare $1.50; *Lake City*, via *Oronoco, Mazeppa, Bear Valley*, and *Lincoln*, 40 miles, fare $2.50; *Red Wing*, via *Oronoco, Pine Island*, and *Zumbro*, 47 miles, fare $3.25. Game is abundant on the prairie around the city.

Olmstead, 352 miles from Chicago, an unimportant station.

Byron, 356 miles from Chicago. Population, 200. Is 3 miles from Zumbro (?) river, has a school, two churches, and one hotel.

Kasson, 362 miles from Chicago. This is a handsome village of 1,500 people. It has doubled its population in the last two years. Is surrounded by one of the largest wheat growing districts in the State. It has a fine hotel, four churches, and two schools.

Dodge Centre, 368 miles from Chicago. Is in Dodge county, 8 miles from *Mantorville*, the county seat, which has a population of 1,000, and with *Wasioga*, 6 miles, and *Concord*, 2 miles distant from Dodge Centre, are reached by daily stage. The village has 900 inhabitants, has wide, shaded streets—in fact, there are so many shade and ornamental trees within the limits, that the citizens call their place "The Park City." The principal hotel is The Kinney House.

Claremont, 375 miles from Chicago. Population, 200. Is in the midst of a fine farming country. Wild land sells from $6 to $25 per acre.

Havana, 382 miles from Chicago. An unimportant station, opened in 1875.

Owatonna, 387 miles from Chicago. The name is from an Indian word, "Ouitunya," meaning straight, hence Straight river is the official name of the stream on which this city is built. This is the capital of Steel county, which was organized in 1854, and has 11,000 inhabitants. This city is in the centre of a very fertile county, and has a large trade in grain, merchandise, and agricultural implements. It has fine schools, two churches, a cheese factory, using the milk of 400 cows, stone-ware factory, flour mills an opera house, three banks, with $200,000 capital, three newspapers, and a number of large manufactures. It has eight hotels, three at least being first class. The court house is well built, and adapted for county business. Mineral springs have been discovered 1½ miles from the city, and are being developed by a company who own the land on which nine of the springs are located. The water of one of the springs is said to resemble that of the celebrated Vichy. *Dodge City*, *Morton*, *Albert Lea*, and *Freeborn*, are reached by stage from this station. *Rice*, *Beaver*, and *Oak Glen* Lakes are 2 to 4 miles distant from the depot. At this point we cross the IOWA & MINNESOTA division of the Milwaukee & St. Paul Railway, and find direct rail connections for *Medford*, 6 miles, *Faribault*, 15 miles, *Dundas*, 26 miles, and *Northfield*, 29 miles distant. Passengers for these points should see that their tickets read via the Chicago & North-Western Railway, *all the way* from Chicago to Owatonna.

Meriden, 396 miles from Chicago, is a village of 100 people.

Waseca, 402 miles from Chicago, is the county seat of Waseca county, which was organized in 1857. This is one of the best wheat counties in the State. The name is Dakota Indian, and means "The Land of Plenty." In the early history of this county are some features that will bear repeating. The first settlers reached here February 7, 1855, and found the snow five feet deep. They built a house of logs, "chinked" it with grass, and "banked it up" with snow. The nearest settlement was in Iowa, 100 miles south. In 1857 the credit of the county was so poor, and money so scarce, that the county authorities in borrowing money on the credit of the county, had to pay interest at the rate of five per cent. *per month*, and that for fifteen months at a time. The winter of 1858–'9 set in early, and was of unusual length and severity. Family supplies and food of all kinds became scarce, and before spring were exhausted. *Corn bran* alone was left, and for weeks was the only food used by the people. When the snow melted, wild roots were dug, which with milk, served the people for many weeks. Finally the plant ginseng was found in the woods, and farmers, lawyers, doctors, priests, and all the people, dug up its roots and sent them to Dubuque, Iowa, over 200 miles, for a market, and from the proceeds managed to live until the next harvest was ripe. What a change time has wrought! Now the county is thickly settled with a rich population, does not owe a dollar, and is in every way prosperous and prospering. The village was laid out in 1858, and now contains a population of 1,500 persons. Its court house is of

Glen Flora Hotel.—page 106.

brick, and it has good schools, seven churches, brick business blocks, banks, public halls, flour mills, grain elevators, and good hotels.

Janesville, 413 miles from Chicago, a village of 700 people, in Waseca county, on the outlet of *Lake Elyrian*, a beautiful body of pure, clear water, 7 miles long. The lake is stocked with many varieties of fish. Salmon have recently been introduced. *Okaman* at the head of the lake, and *Alma*, 6 miles south, are reached by stage. The village contains a grain elevator, holding 45,000 bushels, schools, three churches, a flour mill with four run of stone, and two hotels. The celebrated Lake Elyrian farm of Col. Charles De Graff, adjoins the village, contains 2,700 acres, and is thoroughly stocked with blooded animals, amongst which is a large herd of Alderneys.

Eagle Lake, 421 miles from Chicago. This station is in Blue Earth county, and in the centre of "The Big Woods," which runs along the Minnesota river for over 100 miles. The village contains 300 people, four schools, one church, saw and flour mills, one grain elevator, and one hotel. The village is built on the shore of Eagle Lake, which is 5 miles in circumference, and is "full of fish." No better water-fowl shooting grounds can be found in the country. Reed birds are found in countless numbers. *Madison Lake*, 40 miles in circumference, is 3 miles north, *Jamestown*, 1¼ miles east, *Tivola*, 3 miles east, *Winnebago Agency*, 5 miles distant, are tributary. The La Sueur river is 5 miles east.

Mankato, 432 miles from Chicago. This is one of the finest, largest, most thriving and growing cities in the State. It is the county seat of Blue Earth county, and contains over 5,500 inhabitants. Five rivers converge here, and empty into the Minnesota river; they are the Blue Earth, Maple, Cobb, La Sueur, and Wautonwan, and cause the vicinity to be called the "Undine Region." In the county are also 30 lakes: Loon, Crystal, Jackson's, Eagle, Rice, Madison, Laura, Wilte, and Minneopa, being the largest. The Falls of Minneopa, on the outlet of lakes Crystal and Loon, are very fine, and are claimed to be finer than Minnehaha in many respects. We give two views of these falls. One, a winter scene, shows the beautifying effect of winter-work on the cataract and its surroundings. La Sueur, a French voyageur, built in 1700 Fort L. Hillier, on the site of Mankato, and a portion of the ruins are still preserved. Wild land 6 to 12 miles from Mankato, can be bought for from $10 to $15 per acre, while cultivated farms sell for from $30 to $50 per acre. In 1875, 1,500,000 bushels of wheat were sold from this county. In the city are three schools, each having 500 scholars, Catholic and Lutheran church schools, twelve churches, oil works, woolen mill, two plow factories, two iron foundries and machine shops, fifteen hotels, an academy of music, that cost $20,000, Turner's hall, that cost $10,000, several flour mills, a paper mill, and a driving park. Ten or twelve flowing artesian wells supply ample water for public uses. The Jesuits are erecting a fine college building. Sportsmen can have rare sport here, game and fish abounding. The ST. PAUL & SIOUX CITY R. R. here gives us rail connections for the country traversed by that line.

Kasota, 434 miles from Chicago. This village is 8 miles west of *Cleveland*, the county seat of La Sueur county, which is reached by stage, fare 75c.

The McAllister Springs, Waukegan, Ill.—page 105.

Around the village are many beautiful little lakes, from which fish may be taken in any season of the year. The Minnesota State insane asylum is one mile north, and a State prison is being erected adjacent. The Kasota House, by J. W. Babcock, is the best hotel.

St. Peter, 437 miles from Chicago. In Nicollet county, 134 miles from St. Paul, by river—the Minnesota, or as once called, the St. Peter—may be found this city of 3,500 souls. It is built on terraces, on the left bank of the river, and has a very attractive and picturesque location. Many lakes are near the city, and one of them, Lake Emily, has recently been stocked with Atlantic salmon. The city contains three hotels, a fine brick school house, that cost $28,000, and seven less costly ones. The Swedish Lutheran church has a college here, the buildings and grounds costing over $50,000, of which $5,000 was given by the county, and $5,000 and the land by the city. The State asylum for the insane, situated between Kasota and St. Peter, occupies buildings that cost $470,000; they are very complete, and are heated by steam.

Oshawa, 447 miles from Chicago, is a village of 300 persons.

Nicollet, 451 miles from Chicago, has a population of 300, was laid out in 1874, has a grain elevator, holding 60,000 bushels, one hotel, and a plow factory. Swan Lake, one mile northwest, is 15 miles long by 10 wide, and is full of heavily timbered islands. The Waupeton band of Sioux Indians claim this lake as their home, and twice yearly return to its shores to offer sacrifices to their gods, or to the dead in their burial place, on the shores of the lake.

sent here for that purpose. That loop-holed house still stands. *Redwood Falls,* 45 miles, and *Beaver,* 40 miles distant, are reached by stage. In the summer a steamer also runs to *Beaver,* via the Minnesota river.

We now leave the older settled part of the line, and reach the border.

Sleepy-Eye Lake, 480 miles from Chicago. The lake and the village are named after a celebrated Dakota Indian, by name "Ish-tahm-ba," or Sleepy-Eye. The village has 300 inhabitants. Game abounds in the vicinity, and many varieties of fish in the lakes, of which, besides Sleepy-Eye, there are several. *Golden Gate,* 7 miles, *Iberia,* 5 miles, and *Leavenworth,* 7 miles, are tributary post-villages, and are reached by stage. Running west 65 miles, we pass through a beautiful prairie country, that is but now being settled. Three years ago no settler had made a home beyond Sleepy-Eye Lake, and not until the railroad was completed through this section could any lands be secured.

Burns, Cottonwood, Walnut Grove, Lake Shetek, and **Saratoga,** are stations without agents.

Marshall, 543 miles northwest of Chicago, is the most westerly station having an agent. It is the county seat of Lyon county, which has less than 4,000 people in it, all told. The village has a population

Milwaukee Previous to 1835.—page 108.

Courtland, 459 miles from Chicago, is a new station.

New Ulm, 467 miles from Chicago, is the county seat of Brown county, which was organized in 1855, and immediately received from Chicago over 300 Germans, who have since attracted many hundred families of their countrymen to the city and county. The city shows many marks of German thrift and care, and is noted for its stability and conservatism. Turner Hall, and Arbities Hall, together cost over $80,000, and serve as gathering places for the sociable inhabitants. St. Michael's academy has the best building in the city. It is occupied by the Sisters of the Congregation of Christian Love, who, on being expelled from Prussia by order of Prince Bismark, were invited to settle here. In 1862 the city having 200 houses and 2,000 people, was besieged by Sioux Indians, who had ravaged the county for many miles around. After abandoning their homes, the people took possession of and held a large brick house, and successfully withstood the attacks of the Indians, until they were relieved by soldiers

of 500, and is built on Redwood river. It has a school, two churches, two hotels, and is growing rapidly. *Camden,* 9 miles southwest, *Lake Benton,* 25 miles, *Granite Falls,* 30 miles, *Nordland,* 12 miles, *Redwood Falls,* 40 miles, *Lac Qui Parle,* 28 miles, *State Line,* 40 miles distant, are reached by stages weekly. *Forts Thompson* and *Sully,* on the Missouri river, about 165 miles distant, are also reached by stage from this station. With the opening of the Black Hills to the gold hunter and emigrant, this must prove a good outfitting point, as it is well known that the entire route from this point to the Missouri river is over a fertile prairie, heavily covered with nutritious grasses, with plenty of wood and water. The railroad is built from here through Lac Qui Parle, State Line, Dakota, Coteau, and Prairie, to Lake Kampeska, 624 miles from Chicago, but as the country is as yet unsettled, these stations have no agents. No finer country can be found anywhere than lies along this line, and now that these lands are in the market, they will soon be settled as thickly as any other part of the line.

THE MILWAUKEE DIVISION, AND ITS CONNECTIONS.

Leaving Chicago from the depot at the corner of West Kinzie and Canal streets, this line follows along the western shore of Lake Michigan, and so close thereto, that the lake, with its steamers and sailing vessels, are almost always in sight from the trains. It passes through a succession of beautiful and flourishing towns and villages, amongst which will be found Evanston, Highland Park, Lake Forest, Waukegan, Glen Flora, Kenosha, Racine, and Milwaukee. These are all pleasant summer resorts, and offer to the summer resident many facilities that cannot be found further away from the great cities. Besides the above named, along this line are a large number of pretty villages, in which the summer can be spent pleasantly and quietly. Bear in mind that all of these places enjoy the breezes from the lake, and from most of them the lake is but a few minutes walk distant. To reach any of these places, you must take the Chicago & North-Western Railway, as it is the *only* line that reaches them, or that runs along the lake shore.

Suburban trains are run from Chicago, so as to accommodate those living on this line, but doing business in Chicago. Below will be found a tabular statement, showing rates of fare, in effect June 1st, 1876, (liable to change):

COMMUTATION RATES — MILWAUKEE DIVISION.

Distances from Chicago.	BETWEEN CHICAGO AND	Single Ticket.	10 Ride Ticket, unlimited.	30 Rides, Family Ticket, good for 4 Months.	100 Rides, Individual Ticket.	Number Months 100 Ride Tickets are good.	Annual Ticket.	First Half-Yearly Ticket.	Second Half-Yearly Ticket.
5.3	Belle Plaine	.20	1.40	3.20	7.20	3	40.00	24.00	19.00
5.8	Ravenswood	.21	1.55	3.50	7.20	3	43.00	26.00	20.00
6.7	Summerdale	.25	1.80	4.00	7.20	3	48.00	29.00	22.00
7.7	Rose Hill	.27	2.05	4.60	9.30	3	55.00	33.00	25.00
9.1	Rogers' Park	.30	2.40	5.50	12.00	4	65.00	39.00	29.00
10.2	Calvary	.35	2.70	6.10	12.70	4	66.00	40.00	30.00
10.8	South Evanston	.40	2.85	6.50	14.00	4	71.50	42.50	32.50
11.8	Evanston	.42	3.15	7.10	14.70	4	72.00	43.00	33.00
13.1	North Evanston	.45	3.50	7.90	15.75	4	72.50	43.50	33.50
14.0	Wilmette	.50	3.70	8.40	17.00	4	75.00	45.00	34.00
16.5	Winnetka	.60	4.40	9.90	18.50	4	76.00	46.00	34.00
17.5	Lake Side	.62	4.65	10.50	19.40	4	77.00	47.00	35.00
18.9	Glencoe	.65	5.00	11.40	21.00	4	80.00	48.00	36.00
21.3	Ravinia	.75	5.65	12.80	22.40	4	83.00	50.00	37.00
22.9	Highland Park	.80	6.05	13.80	23.50	4	85.00	51.00	38.00
24.2	Highwood	.85	6.40	14.60	24.20	4	88.00	53.00	41.00
28.0	Lake Forest	1.00	7.40	16.80	28.00	4	95.00	57.00	43.00
30.1	Rockland	1.05	8.00	18.10	30.00	4	100.00	60.00	45.00
35.6	Waukegan	1.25	9.45	21.40	35.50	5	110.00	66.00	50.00
37.3	Glen Flora	1.30	9.90	22.40	37.30	5	112.00	66.00	52.00
39.9	Benton	1.40	10.60	24.00	40.00	5	117.00	69.00	54.00
51.4	Kenosha	1.90	13.65	30.90	51.00	6	150.00	90.00	67.00
61.7	Racine	2.15	16.35 / *13.00	37.00	61.00	6			
85.0	Milwaukee	3.00	22.50	†51.00					

* Family Tickets limited to Four Months. † Family Tickets limited to Six Months.

Leaving the city, 6 miles out we come to—

Ravenswood, a rapidly growing village with 1,000 people, and having good schools, churches, etc. **Summerdale** is 7 miles out. **Rose Hill** with its cemetery, is 8 miles from Chicago. The village is called *Lake View*, and the post office *Havelock*. *Bowmanville* is 1 mile distant. **Rogers' Park** is 9 miles from Chicago; first house built in 1872, and is now a pleasant village. **Calvary** with its cemetery, is 10 miles from Chicago. **South Evanston**, **Evanston**, and **North Evanston**, are 11, 12 and 13 miles distant from Chicago, and together have about 10,000 inhabitants. Evanston was founded in 1853, by the North-Western University. The village was named after Dr. John Evans, since Governor of Colorado. It is strictly a temperance town, no liquor being allowed to be sold within four miles of the station. It is the site of the Union Theological School and Woman's College. Sixteen hundred students are being educated here. In the city are gas works, water works, twelve churches, one newspaper, banks, and many fine business houses.

Wilmette, (Indian, Ouilmette) is 14 miles from Chicago, and has 500 residents. It is located in a natural grove of hard wood trees, which lend their attractions to the place.

Winnetka. The name is said to be Indian, for "Beautiful Land," which well describes the village. It has a population of 900 souls, four churches, fine schools, one of 600 scholars, a hotel for 100 guests, and business houses enough to supply all the commercial wants of the people. This also is a temperance village. LAKE SIDE, 18 miles out, is a growing village. GLENCOE, 19 miles from Chicago, was first settled by W. S. Gurnee, in 1869, and has now 500 residents. The village is half a mile from the station, and has natural groves, good water, schools, and churches. RAVINIA, 21 miles from Chicago, is pushing itself into notice as a pleasant suburb of Chicago.

Highland Park, 23 miles from Chicago, has a charming location, on high bluffs overlooking Lake Michigan. The town was laid out by a company that has spent much money in building streets and walks, and otherwise improving it. It has several good schools, four churches, and excellent society. Highland Hall was built for a hotel, and is used for that purpose from May to September, while, during the rest of the year, it is occupied as a Collegiate Institution for the education of young ladies, with the following broad and comprehensive curriculum:

A Preparatory Department—with the usual Elementary Branches, pursued with great thoroughness ; a Department of Literature—including Grammar, Ancient, Medieval and Modern History, Rhetoric, Composition, Literature, and Criticism ; a Department of Natural Science—including Physics, Chemistry, Astronomy, Mineralogy, Geology, Zoology, and Botany ; a Mathematical Department—including Algebra, Book-Keeping, Geometry, Trigonometry, and its applications ; a Department of Hygiene—including Physiology, Anatomy, Calisthenics, and Practical Lessons in care of the Health; a Department of Languages—Latin and Greek, French, German, Spanish, and Italian ; a Department of Philosophy—Mental and Moral, Logic and Civil Government ; a Department of Music—the Piano, the Organ, the Guitar, Harmony and Thorough Bass, Individual Vocal Training, and Class Drill ; a Department of Fine Art—Drawing in all styles, Painting in Oils and Water Colors, Modeling and Sculpture ; a Department of Practical Art—including Telegraphy, Wood Engraving, etc. ; an Optional course — selected from the foregoing studies, to suit individual wants ; with careful instruction in Morals and the Manners of Good Society ; all under the instruction of able Professors and Teachers.

President Weston, who will have charge, says : "In transferring our educational work from Lake Forest to Highland Park, it is proper to state to the public the reasons of the change. The trustees of the Lake Forest University having revived the long-cherished project of building up a grand institution in the interests of the Presbyterian church, have determined to unite the Ladies' Seminary (Ferry Hall), and the Boys' Academy, under one presidency, and thus to lay the foundation of their projected University for young men and women. Having ourselves undertaken a different enterprise, and carried it forward thus far with gratifying success, we purpose to continue that work at Highland Park, with a college corporation organized under the laws of the State, for the education of young ladies, without connection with any school for young men, and conducted in the special interests of no one religious denomination. This we do on the plain common sense principle of demand and supply, without wasting time in discussing the merits and demerits of co-education, or the propriety of denominational schools. We know that most of our patrons prefer to send their daughters to institutions intended for young ladies only ; and are not anxious that the school education of their children should be impressed with any sectarian features. Surrounded by an enterprising and cultivated community, organized into different religious societies, and dwelling together in the spirit of unity, the Institution will provide for the Sabbath worship of its members with such churches in town as the parents of each may select—Episcopalian, Baptist,

Lake Dells, Milwaukee, Wis.—page 110.

or Presbyterian—and for such religious exercises in the College itself as shall contribute to their generous Christian culture. The facilities for such an institution at Highland Hall are unusually excellens. The building is new and capacious, the rooms large and handsomely furnished, and the location well known for its beauty and healthfulness, and its general fitness for the purposes of a Ladies' School."

Half Day and *Deerfield* are tributary villages, and are reached by stage daily.

Highwood is the next station north, and is 24 miles from Chicago.

Lake Forest, a city of 1,500 persons, is 28 miles from Chicago, and is the seat of educational institutions, with a national reputation for excellence. A male academy, patterned after the celebrated Phillips Academy, of Andover, Mass., and a female seminary, are especially noted. Lake Forest University received in 1875 $80,000 to found professorships, and it has over $295,000 worth of assets. The city is on the highest ground between Milwaukee and Chicago, is a temperance town, and has one good hotel.

Rockland is 30 miles from Chicago.

Waukegan, 36 miles from Chicago, is the county seat of the county of Lake, so called because of it possessing *fifty-six* beautiful lakes within its boundaries. The city has between 7,000 and 8,000 inhabitants ; is situated on a bluff overlooking Lake Michigan, on the western shore of that body of water. The town proper, stands about one hundred feet above the lake, and in point of attractiveness as a summer resort, stands unrivaled in all the Western States. Its acknowledged beauty, fine drives, society, schools, picturesque scenery, ravines, brooks, and general loveliness, as fashioned by Nature's own hands, aided by liberal outlays of money, combine to make it a place which will be sought for by the thousands of private families who yearly, more and more, seek the health-giving quiet and retirement of the country, in order to avoid the heat, dust and noise of a busy metropolis.

Waukegan offers attractions far superior and more meritorious than hundreds of other points, which, by systematic newspaper puffery and advertising, have become more or less celebrated and popular to the seeker after health and quiet enjoyment. Its numerous mineral springs have attracted thousands of people here from our great commercial metropolis, Chicago, and other parts of the country. The most important of these springs, in a medical view, are the McAllister, Glen Flora, and Powell's, each of which claims advantages peculiarly its own. The city has three schools with twenty teachers, nine churches, two public halls, and three hotels. *Deep Lake*, 15 miles north, has summer hotel, *Libertyville*, 10 miles off, *Wauconda*, 21 miles, *Antioch*, 20 miles, *Milburne*, 12 miles, and *Hainsville*, 12 miles distant, are reached by stage. The largest evergreen tree nursery *in the United States*, is within the city limits of Waukegan.

Glen Flora, nearly one mile north of Waukegan, is so intimately connected therewith, that we must treat it as a portion of that city.

Let us mention here, that we have no intention of detracting from the merits of other watering places; our only desire is to show, by a fair and candid comparison, that we have, within thirty-five miles of Chicago, all the attractions, and valuable

Elkhart Lake, Wis.—page 115.
From "Swartz."

mineral springs, which can be reached with far less expenditure of time and money, than can other like attractions offered in this country. The Glen Flora Mineral Springs have not until lately been submitted to thorough analysis. The waters, which have been for perhaps untold ages gurgling from their cool, rocky depths, and flowing in miniature rivulets into Lake Michigan, have been, in a quiet way, doing good to many inhabitants of this place ; but not until last year was the true nature of these waters proven beyond question by scientific analysis. Let us compare this analysis with that of the, so far, most noted mineral spring of the West—the Bethesda, of Waukesha, Wis. It will be seen by the figures of Prof. Blaney, who has made several most minute and careful calculations, that the Glen Flora Mineral Springs are, in all the valuable health-giving, restorative ingredients, far superior to the "Bethesda." Here are the two analyses:

Analysis of the Glen Flora Spring Water.

The following is the result of the analysis by Prof. Jas. V. Z. Blaney & Son, of a specimen of water from "Glen Flora" Mineral Springs. One U. S. gallon of 231 cubic inches, contained—

Chloride of Sodium	.183 grains.
Sulphate of Soda	1.852 "
Bicarbonate of Soda	6.447 "
Bicarbonate of Lime	15.568 "
Bicarbonate of Magnesia	11.091 "
Bicarbonate of Iron	.115 "
Alumina	.151 "
Silica	.907 "
Organic Matter	.100 "
Sulphur, a trace.	
Total	36.414 grains.

The State Capitol, Sacramento, Cal.—page 39.

Analysis of the Bethesda Spring Water.

Chloride of Sodium	1.160 grains.
Sulphate of Potassa	.454 "
Sulphate of Sodium	.542 "
Bicarbonate of Lime	17.022 "
Bicarbonate of Magnesia	12.388 "
Bicarbonate of Iron	.042 "
Bicarbonate of Soda	1.256 "
Phosphate of Soda, a trace.	
Alumina	.122 "
Silica	.741 "
Organic Matter	1.983 "
Total	35.710 grains.

The Glen Flora Springs are easy of access. About sixteen trains pass and repass between the cities of Chicago and Milwaukee daily. The railroad station named "Glen Flora," now completed, is only about one-quarter of a mile from the springs, which are reached by a newly graded road, leading up the bluff in close proximity to the springs. The location of Glen Flora Mineral Springs, for picturesque beauty and romantic surroundings, is unsurpassed in this country, and, indeed, in the world. They are nestled in a beautiful ravine or glen, originally named "Floral Glen," because of the profusion of beautiful wild flowers which grow and thrive spontaneously from end to end of its labyrinthian traceries. This glen has been, and is being, carefully sodded and terraced for long distances, by one of the most experienced of our western landscape gardeners, and while Nature has done wonders to make "Glen Flora" beautiful, Art and a liberal expenditure of money, are daily adding to the attractiveness of this soon-to-be most fashionable of watering places and summer resorts.

An elegant and commodious hotel is now being erected, adjoining the springs, and will be ready for occupancy early in the summer of 1876. (See cut of hotel.)

The Waukegan Magnesian Mineral Springs.

For a long time Waukegan has been the scene of singular cures, which have from time to time been effected through some unknown agency, and for the most part attributed to the general healthfulness of the place. These undoubted restorations to health, coupled with certain legendary stories in which Waukegan was, according to Indian tradition, the seat of certain medicine waters, led John F. Powell to submit some of the magnesia spring water for analysis, to the well known analytical chemists, Professors Jas. V. Z. Blaney & Son, of Chicago, when it was proved that one U. S. gallon of 231 cubic inches, contained 48.811 grains of solid matter, as follows:

Chloride of Sodium	1.876 grains.
Sulphate of Soda	5.796 "
Sulphate of Lime	7.412 "
Bicarbonate of Lime	15.537 "
Bicarbonate of Magnesia	17.276 "
Bicarbonate of Iron	.136 "
Alumnia	.230 "
Silica	.359 "
Organic Matter	.189 "
Chloride Potassium	traces.
Grains per gallon	48.811

To those acquainted with the properties of mineral waters, the above statement will be a sufficient proof of the excellence of Magnesia Springs, as it shows them to be in many respects the best yet analyzed in America. To those unacquainted with the nature of the different ingredients which, when combined, give to water its wonderful curative virtues, we would briefly say that all authorities agree in recognizing bicarbonates as the most important elements in the medicinal combination of mineral waters, and that by comparing for themselves the Magnesia with other springs, they will find that the Waukegan has a far larger amount of bicarbonates than any other spring yet analyzed. In organic matter, Bethesda Springs have 1 grain and 983-1000, or nearly two grains of this undesirable ingredient, to Waukegan Magnesia's 189-1000 of a grain.

These springs are three-quarters of a mile southwest of the depot at Waukegan.

The McAllister Springs.

The McAllister Springs are situated in the southern part of the city, one mile south of our depot at Waukegan, and are the property of Judge W. K. McAllister; they consist of a cluster of five springs, all in close proximity, and remarkable for showing a vast difference in their analysis, and consequently adapted to various diseases. The grounds about the Springs are beautiful and the location desirable.

Spring No. 3 is in its mineral combinations almost identical with the celebrated Bethesda Spring of Waukesha, only that it contains more of the sulphates of soda and potassa, more iron, and less organic matter, which must add to, rather than detract from, its value.

Spring No. 5 contains sulphureted hydrogen, in addition to its other valuable ingredients.

Spring No. 1 is recommended for the cure of rheumatism, Bright's disease, gravel, kidney complaints, dyspepsia and gout.

No. 2 for liver complaints, dyspepsia and chronic constipation.

Nos. 3 and 4 for costiveness, general debility, dyspepsia, heartburn, etc.

No. 5 for diseases of the blood, scrofula, blotches, eruptions, acidity of the stomach, etc.

The water is entirely free at the Springs.

Analysis of the McAllister Mineral Springs, Waukegan, Illinois. The analysis of Springs Nos. 1 and 2 made by Prof. Bartlett, and Springs Nos. 3, 4 and 5, by Prof. Blaney, of Chicago. One U. S. gallon, expressed as anhydrous compounds, contains:

	Spring No. 1.	Spring No. 2.	Spring No. 3.	Spring No. 4.	Spring No. 5.
	GRAINS.	GRAINS.	GRAINS.	GRAINS.	GRAINS.
Chloride of Sodium			1.462	0.737	0.354
Chloride of Magnesium	0.943	1.401			
Sulphate of Soda	1.193	0.451	3.665	0.859	2.268
Sulphate of Potassa	a trace	0.416	0.581	0.253	0.320
Sulphate of Lime			0.470	1.605	
Bicarbonate of Lime	18.810	19.597	17.574	15.511	12.737
Bicarbonate of Magnesia	9.561	9.961	11.541	10.988	6.537
Sulphate of Magnesia	2.229	2.877			
Bicarbonate of Iron			0.108	0.162	0.091
Oxide of Iron and Alumina	0.094	0.071			
Bicarbonate of Soda					4.357
Silica	0.659	0.842	0.870	0.940	0.950
Alumina			0.146	0.100	0.215
Organic Matter			0.530	a trace.	0.180
Total	33.489	35.616	36.947	31.155	28.009

Spring No. 1 contains 1 cubic inch free carbonic acid gas. Spring No. 5 contains .019 cubic inch sulphureted hydrogen.

The *Sag-au-nash Springs* are located in the central part of the city. Their analysis shows a large amount of magnesia and other valuable properties.

Benton, 40 miles from Chicago, and **State Line**, 45 miles, are not of large importance as stations. At State Line, Spring Bluff post office, there are two cheese factories, a butter factory, two churches, and one hotel. Before the consolidation of the Milwaukee & Chicago and the Chicago & Milwaukee railroads, as the two lines that now form the route between Milwaukee & Chicago were formerly called, State Line was the junction, and here all passengers were forced to change cars, and all freight to be transferred.

Kenosha is 51 miles from Chicago, and across the State line in Wisconsin. It is the county seat of Kenosha county, which was separated from Racine county, and organized in 1850, and now has 20,000 population. It is a county of lakes, and has many, from one to two miles wide. Silver, Paddocks, Camp, Centre, Lily, Powers and Twin lakes are the largest. On Twin lake is a pleasure steamer —The Lady of the Lake—that during the summer season carries tourists around its shores. The city of Kenosha has 6,000 population, and three American and one German public schools. Kemper Hall school, for boys, an Episcopal educational institution, is on the lake shore, and has a girls' school connected with it; it has a beautiful location and is in a flourishing condition. Kenosha Water Cure is a noted water cure hotel, with 80 rooms. The Sanitarium of Dr. Gatchell, a noted curative institution, is 1½ miles from the station. Kenosha is the headquarters of several large manufacturing establishments, among which the Bain Wagon Company employs 200 men, and makes 16 complete wagons each working hour. Flour, leather, hay presses, tow, malt mills, wind mills, telegraph insulators, etc., are largely manufactured here. The fisheries off Kenosha give constant employment to 300 men.

Racine Junction, 60 miles from Chicago, and **Racine**, 62 miles, form a flourishing city of 14,000 people. Racine is the county seat of Racine county, which has a population of 29,000. As a manufacturing point Racine is not excelled by any in the State. J. I. Case & Co.'s threshing machine works, cover 11 acres of ground and employ 375 men, and make 1,700 threshing machines yearly: they pay for wages, $350,000; for cast iron, $130,000; wrought iron, $115,000; lumber, $90,000; belting, $50,000, and for postage stamps $2,000, yearly. Fish Brothers, in their wagon works, employ 220 men, and make 7,000 wagons yearly. Mitchell, Lewis & Co. employ 200 men, and make 6,000 wagons yearly; the Racine Woolen Mills employ 90 men; Blake & Co. in their mills manufacture cloths and shawls;

Freeman & Smith, and the Racine Hardware Company, manufacture florists' iron goods and light hardware; Stephen Freeman manufactures engines, castings, etc.; Driver & Son make sash, doors and blinds; Windship & Co. make pumps and washing machines; John Beck has a large boot and shoe factory, and two other concerns also employ a large number of men in the same line. In the city are six ward schools; Col. J. G. McMynn has a fine academy; the Roman Catholics have several good schools, one by the Sisters of the St. Dominico Order being especially noted. Racine College, under Episcopal government, has 200 students. Twenty-five churches furnish sectarian variety to please all. The Taylor Orphan Asylum is a meritorious enterprise of Racine. Two public halls—The Belle City and The Garner—present ample seating accommodations for the visitors to theatre, concert or show. Congress Hall, The Huggins House and The Bouton House are the leading hotels. The citizens of Racine have $800,000 invested in sailing and steam vessels on Lake Michigan. Root river, which is crossed by two bridges, flows through the city; three miles from its mouth are the Rapids, on which are located flour mills, and, near by, extensive lime kilns.

Ives, County Line, and Oak Creek, are unimportant stations to the stranger making a tour over the line. At the last-named station millions of the celebrated cream-colored, Milwaukee brick are made; it also has a butter factory, a good school, and a fine farming country around it.

St. Francis, 81 miles from Chicago, is the seat of a thriving and unusually popular Roman Catholic college. It has a full corps of professors and tutors, and a large list of students. Its popularity is so great that large additions are now being made to its already ample buildings.

Bay View, 83 miles from Chicago, is merely a suburb of Milwaukee, and is the seat of vast iron mills, furnaces, etc.

Milwaukee.

Cities, says an eminent writer, have always been

View of Cliff House and Seal Rocks, off San Francisco.

the fire-places of civilization, whence light and heat radiated out into the dark, cold world; and the union of men in large masses is indispensable to the development and growth of mankind.

Fifty years ago, and all there then was of the now prosperous and beautiful city of Milwaukee—lowland, shore and forest—was in the undisputed possession of the red man. It seems truly incredible. We look upon the picture and try vainly to realize that here he chased the wild deer in a right royal hunting ground, as boundless as the West itself, and fished about the wide bay or floated with the current through the crooked ways of the rivers that still run like the tangled threads of a knotted skein, and in his crude fashion made war continually on the teeming life about him; and the Indian woman prepared for the midday or evening meal of her master a primitive dish, and he ate with a zest born of the healthful breezes grown pure and tonic in their wide sweep over the waters of Lake Michigan.

The first white man to invade this beautiful retreat of the Indian was Solomon Juneau. He came here in the autumn of 1818, and built him a log cabin, which gradually assumed the distinctive features of a store, in which he kept a few goods suitable for barter. For seventeen years he was not only the only merchant in the place, but the only white settler. A few Indian traders occasionally came, but none made a permanent location.

Unquestionable evidences of the wonderful changes that have been wrought in a few short years are shown in the illustrations published herewith. (pp. 102, 103).

Milwaukee is the commercial emporium of the State of Wisconsin, and one of the most important cities, in many respects, in the Northwest. It has a population of about 100,000; built largely of the famous cream-colored Milwaukee brick, which are produced here in large quantities. The situation of the city at the mouth of Milwaukee river, is very pleasant and attractive. The river furnishes one of the best and most commodious bays and harbors on the lakes.

As a place of residence, this city has become noted for its healthful climate and the medicinal qualities of its springs, which invalids avail themselves of. The residence portion of the city is from fifty to one hundred feet above the level of the lake, overlooking that beautiful sheet of water, and with its clean, dry streets, beautifully laid out grounds and yards, presents an attractive appearance to the traveler as he approaches it on this railroad. Many of the public buildings and business blocks are massive and elegant, and many of the residences fine—all indicating wealth, enterprise and refinement.

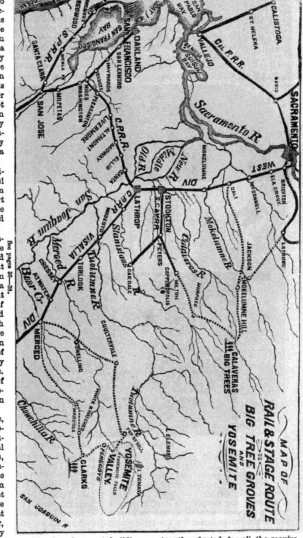

This city is most delightfully situated on the western shore of Lake Michigan, on a magnificent bay, formed by two projecting headlands, which make a safe and extensive harbor. It is regularly laid out; the streets are wide, and are lined with buildings eminently adapted for all the requirements of so extensive a place. The business part of the city lies on either side of the river, and follows it up closely for over two miles. As you go back from the river you find yourself gradually ascending, till you stand on an elevation of considerable height, and can see the city spread out at your feet. The streets have a gradual rise, therefore, as you recede from the river, and when you come to the lake shore you stand on a high bluff. The healthfulness of the city is something remarkable. Its location, the cleanliness of the streets, the admirable sanitary regulations, which are stringently enforced, and the intelligence of the people, all combine to prevent any disease from obtaining a foothold, and to keep at a distance those epidemics which so frequently prevail in large cities. The cream-colored bricks, together with the width of the streets, give the place a most charming and delightful look, affording a pleasing variation to the monotonous rows of glaring red bricks met with in the large Eastern cities. As a summer resort, Milwaukee possesses many peculiar attractions, that are every year becoming more widely known, and that specially commend it to those who seek rest and recuperation during the hot months of the year. Situated on the banks of a beautiful lake, it is fanned by the invigorating breezes that pour in an almost continual current over the broad waters. These bring relief and comfort, even in the hottest seasons. The hotel accommodations are of the very finest character.

The Newhall is centrally located in the heart of the business part of the city, on Broadway, corner of Michigan street. The house contains three hundred rooms, airy and spacious, and fitted up in the most thorough and complete manner. The Plankinton House is another of Milwaukee's first class hotels. It is pleasantly located on Spring street, and will be found by visitors to be unexcelled by any house in the country. It can accommodate three hundred visitors.

Lake Dells, a beautiful summer place, with its charming little Swiss cottage and arbor on the shore, will give the reader but a faint idea of the peculiar beauty of this section, towards which so much attention has been recently directed by those in search of sites for suburban residences or summer homes. During a few years past numbers of residences and cottages have been built upon the summit of the bluff, or on the plateau beneath. The illustration is from a photograph from Lake View, looking north, and embraces Ferny Brae, Lake Dells, Fern Ravine, and Rocky Point—all beautiful places. Lake Avenue, the famous drive of Milwaukee, runs through and by these places, to Whitefish Bay, five miles or more from the city, and most of the distance upon the high bluff overlooking the lake, making a most charming summer drive. For much of the distance the hill-tops above these lowlands are covered with growths of wood, partially hiding from the avenue the beauties of the low grounds, with the exception of an occasional opening made by the crossing of a ravine.

In the Yosemite.—pages 36-38.

No place can be more favorable for a summer residence than the plateaus of the north shore. Shut out from the afternoon sun by the high wooded hills in the rear, with the charming and extended sea-view in front, with cooling lake breezes throughout the day, and every opportunity for sailing, fishing or bathing, enchanting rambles on sandy beach or through wild ravines, and unsurpassed drives, with the bustling city only a few miles away, yet as entirely isolated from it as if in the Adirondacks. The sea-view from early dawn to sunset is beautiful, changing with the hours of the day, caused by the varying direction of the sun's rays upon the water, giving them a variety of brilliant tints or sombre back upon the lake, tinge the waters as well as the sail in the offing with their own brilliant colors, making a picture so beautiful we wish it might never fade.

During the late summer and early fall months, the temperature of the water is delightful for bathing, averaging in the shallow bay off Lake Dells, by actual test and record, 68° to 72°, while the descent of the shore is so gradual, that at two thousand feet out, the sounding showed but eleven feet of water, the whole distance being a gradually sloping sandy bottom. No dust or mosquitoes are found upon the lower ground, from the fact that the avenue is too far distant to furnish the former, and the

In the Yosemite.—pages 36—38.

hues. The picture is greatly enhanced by the large number of sail and steamers constantly in sight, engaged in the commerce of the lakes, the course of most of the passing vessels being but a mile distant. The splendor of the morning sky as the sun rises from the lake, is only surpassed by the beauty of our Western sunset, whose golden hues, reflected breezes of the lake too cool for the latter. Another attraction of this location consists in the many drives descending the hillside, on the margin of the lake, or winding under the overarching trees through ravines, affording from various points new and extended lake views.

If you do not desire to remain at Milwaukee, you can, in the same cars that brought you from Chicago, push on to or towards Fond du Lac, by the Fond du Lac Air Line, an extension to the Milwaukee Division, that was opened for business two years ago. It shortens the distance between Chicago and Fond du Lac, and points north on the Wisconsin Division, many miles, and secures to passengers a choice of routes—to come via the line we have just described, and via Milwaukee, or to take the old route, via

Janesville. Tickets to Fond du Lac, or beyond, are good by either route. Leaving Milwaukee from our depot on the lake front, at the lake end of Wisconsin street, where is found an admirably well kept hotel, The Lake View, and a dining hall and eating house, under the management of J. Y. Ross, that vies with any in the land, we pass LAKE SHORE JUNCTION and LINDWERM, and reach, at 100 miles from Chicago, the village and station of GRANVILLE. *Menomonee Falls* is 3 miles distant, and is reached by stage; fare, 25 cts.

Salt Lake and Vicinity.—pages 33, 34.

West Bend, 119 miles from Chicago, has a population of 1,500, and is the county seat of Washington county, which has a population of 23,000. The village has good schools, one bank, two newspapers, two grain elevators, several breweries, making lager beer that rivals that made at Milwaukee; two flour mills, each with four run of stone, and seven churches. Its court house is built of wood; it has a good public hall, and one hotel that can accommodate 200 guests. The village is built on the west bank of the Milwaukee river, and the station house is on the east bank. *Young America, Mayfield, Filmore, Boltonville, Kohlsville,* and *Aurora,* are tributary villages.

Barton is one mile from West Bend, and is built in a valley between two high hills. It has many picturesque aspects. The village contains three hotels, a fine school, two churches, and a lodge of Good Templars.

Kewaskum is 127 miles from Chicago, and has a large grain trade. Three elevators are kept busy, one of them being the largest in the State, outside of Milwaukee. The population of the village and surroundings is largely German.

New Cassel, 133 miles from Chicago, is situated

Rockfield, lately *Germantown,* is 107 miles from Chicago, and has two grain elevators, and a fine business in building stone. *Dheinsville* is 1½ miles off, and is the headquarters of the Germantown Insurance Company, which has $300,000 capital, and writes 3,000 policies yearly. *Menomonee Falls,* a pleasant summer resort, is 6 miles off.

Jackson is 112 miles from Chicago, and has 500 inhabitants, most of whom are Germans. It has three flour mills, a woolen mill, and two churches. *Mayfield,* 1½ miles, and *Clear Creek,* on a lake of the same name, 3 miles distant, are tributary villages.

in the southeast part of Fond du Lac county, 16 miles from Fond du Lac, and 47 miles from Milwaukee, in a rich farming country. The Milwaukee river passes through the eastern part of the village, furnishing good water power; the railroad passes through the western part. Surrounded by a beautiful forest on the north, and a chain of gentle elevations on the south, among the hills and valleys lies one of nature's parks. Its population is 500, a gain of 300 since the railroad started. There are four churches, a convent, and an academy for young ladies, and a good district school. The manufactories of the place are unimportant, except the flouring mills of J. H. Reysen, the brewery of John P. Husting, and cheese factories of H. Schrooten and Robert Miller. There are three good hotels—The Adams House, by A. Holzhoure, The Railroad House, by J. Degenhardt, and The New Cassel Hotel, by P. Schoofs. The villages of *Dundee* and *Eblesville* are each 7 miles, *Waucousta* 5 miles, and *Lomira Centre* 8 miles from the station; *Lake Fifteen* is 3 miles, and *Long Lake* is 7 miles distant. They have many attractions, and will soon become justly popular as summer resorts. A large variety of game and fish are found in those sections. On Bannon's farm, as also on Dierrenger's, one mile from New Cassel, may be found Indian mounds, embankments, ditches, etc., laid out with great precision, showing that the builders had considerable knowledge of military science. Around New Cassel the country is gently undulating, with ascents and declivities of various heights and depths. The forests are composed of sugar maple, basswood, elm, black and white ash, red oak, hickory, and butternut. The soil is a deep, black, sandy loam, with a mixture of marl, and subsoil of reddish clay. The first house was built in New Cassel in 1843, and the first school taught in 1848. The surroundings of New Cassel are admitted by all who have seen them, to be unrivaled. Its rolling and fertile land, dotted with neat farmhouses, and the rich foliage of its woods and skirted hill-sides, presents a scene more resembling the fine tints and groupings of a splendid picture, than the substantial reality that is here.

Eden is 140 miles from Chicago, and by this route Fond du Lac 148 miles, or 28 miles less than via Janesville.

Hanging Rock, on Chicago, Dubuque & Minnesota Railway—page 16.

UP THE LAKE SHORE.

On reaching Milwaukee, you can proceed up the lake by taking, at our depot on the lake front, at the lake end of Wisconsin street, the cars of the MILWAUKEE, LAKE SHORE & WESTERN RAILWAY that passes through *Port Washington, Belgium, Sheboygan, Manitowoc,* to *Two Rivers.* All these are active business cities, and besides having the railroad, are on the lake shore, and thus have unusual facilities for shipping their products.

Sheboygan, Wisconsin, the county seat of Sheboygan county, is a thriving manufacturing city of about 7,000 inhabitants. It is the eastern terminus of the Sheboygan & Fond du Lac Railway, and is the most important station on the line of the Milwaukee, Lake Shore & Western Railway north of Milwaukee. The former of these roads makes close connections with the Wisconsin Division of the Chicago & North-Western Railway at Fond du Lac, and the latter is practically an extension of the Milwaukee Division of the Chicago & North-Western Railway.

Sheboygan is one of the most delightful summer resorts in the West. It is beautifully located upon a bluff overlooking Lake Michigan, whose azure waters, moving perpetually, and here and there dotted with sails, are a constant source of amusement to the eye; while in the background lies a landscape of rare beauty—hills clad with the richest verdure, groves of native forest trees, and fields of waving grain. The Sheboygan river flows down one of the most picturesque valleys in the State, winds nearly half way round the city, and finally empties into the lake south of the residence portion of the place, affording a safe and convenient harbor. The city itself presents a most attractive appearance. It is tastefully laid out; its streets are wide and well shaded with oaks, maples and evergreens; its business houses are mainly built of cream-colored brick. The court house is one of the finest structures of the kind in Wisconsin. In walking about the city, one is struck with the scrupulous neatness of the streets, and the evidences of thrift, prosperity and refinement that are beheld on every hand. The society of Sheboygan is excellent, and (especially during the summer months) parties, concerts, and entertainments of various kinds are frequent. The city is well supplied with churches, and boasts several talented preachers. The river affords unsurpassed opportunities for rowing, while the lake is a favorite resort for those who enjoy sailing. Pleasure boats of all kinds may be had here. The fishing is good; the fisheries off Sheboygan are among the most important on Lake Michigan, and a summer day can hardly be more pleasantly spent than in visiting them in one of the steam fishing smacks. The drives in the vicinity of the city are fine. This is especially true of the drive up the river five miles, to the charming village of Sheboygan Falls. But, after all, the chief attractions which Sheboygan holds out to the summer tourist, are the healthfulness and coolness of its climate. Lying, as it does, ten miles out in the lake, it is fanned by deliciously cool and invigorating lake breezes from the north, east and south, and consequently, the intensely hot weather that prevails in the interior during the summer months, is unknown here. The Beekman House is Sheboygan's principal hotel. It is well furnished, and is capable of accommodating one hundred guests.

A recent acquisition is the discovery of unusually valuable remedial qualities in the waters of an artesian well that has been sunk here. Its waters are strongly impregnated with various salts, and an analysis shows elements of rare value. The water is free to all comers.

This well is located in the public park of the city of Sheboygan, and is 1,475 feet deep—92 feet being through the drift. It has been tubed a distance of 450 feet, below which no rifts were found in the rock. The well discharges two hundred and forty gallons of water per minute, at a temperature of 58 deg. Fahr.

An analysis of the water shows that it is remarkably rich in salts; nothing of the same character having been found in the West. During the short time it has been used it has been found beneficial, as a bath or internally.

Annexed is an analysis as made by Prof. Bode, of Milwaukee, in December, 1875. An analysis of the waters of the Congress Spring, Saratoga, Sharon Springs, New York, Kissingen and Kreuznach, of Germany, is also added for the purpose of comparison, to which your attention is called.

COMPARATIVE ANALYSIS.

ONE WINE PINT CONTAINS SOLIDS	SHEBOYGAN, Wisconsin. Temperature, 58 deg. Fahr.	CONGRESS, New York. Temperature, 52 deg. Fahr.	SHARON, New York. Temperature, 48 deg. Fahr.	KISSINGEN, Germany. Temperature, 51 deg. Fahr.	KREUZNACH, Germany. Temperature, 54½ deg. Fahr.
Soda, Carbonate		0.934			
" Phosphate		0.002			
" Nitrate				0.07	
Sodium, Chloride	45.956	50.055	0.28	44.71	72.883
" Iodide	0.003	0.017		Trace.	
" Bromide	0.132	1.069		0.06	
Magnesium, Bromide					0.278
" Iodide					0.035
" Chloride			0.30		
Magnesia, Carbonate	0.048	9.019		4.50	0.106
" Sulphate	11.166		5.30	2.33	
" Chloride				0.24	4.071
Iron, Carbonate		0.031			
" Sulphate	0.093				
Lime, Carbonate	0.187	12.449		8.14	1.693
" Sulphate	9.518		13.95	2.99	
" Phosphate				0.04	
Calcium, Chloride	13.663				13.389
" Fluoride		Trace.			
" Hydro Sulphuret			0.28		
Potassium, Chloride	1.238	1.006		2.20	0.624
" Sulphate		0.111			
Lithia, Carbonate		0.374			
" Chloride	0.003			0.15	0.613
Strontia, Carbonate		Trace.			
Baryta, Carbonate		0.095			
Alumina	0.137	Trace.			0.025
" Phosphate					
Silica	0.091	0.105		0.09	0.129
Organic Matter		Trace.			
	82.235	75.267	20.11	65.52	93.846

The Chicago & North-Western Railway.

From Sheboygan, the popular summer resorts along the line of the Sheboygan & Fond du Lac Railway may be easily reached. It is only an hour's ride from Sheboygan to beautiful Elkhart Lake; a three hours' ride to the famous mineral springs at Fond du Lac; and a five hours' ride to that gem of Wisconsin scenery, Green Lake.

Elkhart Lake.

Wisconsin is famous for her beautiful lakes, the annual resort of thousands of people in quest of health and pleasure. Among the loveliest of these is Lake Elkhart, acknowledged to be one of the healthiest places in the West. It is fifty-seven miles north of Milwaukee, and can be reached by the Chicago & North-Western Railway and its immediate connection, the Sheboygan & Fond du Lac Railway. The station, Glenbeulah, is three miles from the lake. Omnibuses run to the hotels from all the trains arriving at this station.

Elkhart Lake covers about eight hundred acres, and is pleasingly diversified by bays, which coquettishly wind around jutting bluffs, beneath whose shades the crystal water slumbers, so pure and clear that the white sand and gravel of the lake bottom can be plainly seen at a depth of twenty to twenty-five feet. All the brilliant colors of the rainbow are reflected on the smooth and sparkling surface of the water, and bordered by a beautiful green, reflected from the foliage of the hillside. As viewed from the elevated veranda of Marsh's Swiss Cottage, the scene is beautiful beyond description. The hills that surround the lake are verdant with pine, spruce, maple, basswood, red and white cedar; while wheat fields now and then peep through forest vistas, affording to the eye, as it feasts upon the varying charms, a most pleasing variety. The Swiss Cottage is a large hotel, and has 400 feet of wide veranda, and pleasant walks and drives. A steamboat and barge, sail and row-boats, are run to convey passengers to any part of the lake desired. About twenty rods from the hotel is a pavilion for dancing. There are neither house flies nor mosquitoes here to trouble the visitor. —— Talmage, —— Davison, and —— Sharp, have, in this vicinity, good farm houses, well adapted for boarding summer visitors.

Dubuque's Grave, near Dubuque, Iowa.—page 16.

FROM KENOSHA, WIS., TO ROCKFORD, ILL.

Running across the northern portion of the State of Illinois and a part of Wisconsin, is a line of railroad owned by this Company, that is known as the Kenosha and Rockford Division. It is 40 miles long, and runs through a charming farming country. It traverses the famous dairy district of Illinois, and its trains pass within a short distance of many beautiful lakes, full of fish, and surrounded by a highly cultivated country. Leaving Kenosha, we successively pass PLEASANT PRAIRIE, WOODWORTH, BRISTOL, SALEM, FOX RIVER, BASSETTS, GENOA JUNCTION, where it crosses the Fox River Division, as before related ; HEBRON, ALDEN, HARVARD, where it crosses the Wisconsin Division ; CHEMUNG, CAPRON, POPLAR GROVE, SOUTH CALEDONIA, where it crosses the Madison Division ; ARGYLE, and HARLEM, and reach ROCKFORD and the Freeport Line. In most of these villages are cheese and butter factories, and more or less of other manufactures. Near Fox RIVER are Silver and Lily lakes. *Wilmot* and *Munster* are tributary, and reached by stage. *Brighton* is two miles from Salem, and is reached by stage. *Twin Lakes* are one and a half miles from BASSETTS. ALDEN is a strict temperance village, of 200 people. *Parks Corners* and *Russellville* are tributary to CAPRON. A Scotch settlement surrounds ARGYLE, which was named for the Scotch duke of that title. Although off the main line of tourist travel, these villages are well worth a visit. They are mostly inhabited by New England people, and would strongly remind the Eastern visitor of the many similar, pleasant, homelike, quiet villages he has passed through in New England.

CONCLUDING REMARKS.

We have traversed with you the country along and tributary to most of the lines that together make up this great railway and its immediate allies and feeders, and we trust we have given you a not unfavorable opinion of its capabilities, usefulness, nay, indispensability, in its sphere, as one of the great roads that does its full share in conducting the vast transportation interests of this Western Continent.

After digesting the foregoing pages, brimful of facts as they are, and fully grasping the mileage of the road, the country that it covers, and the vastness of its resources, we feel sure that you will join with its older friends in desiring its future prosperity, and assisting in carrying that desire into fruition by lending to it your aid, comfort, and patronage.

You can confidently recommend it for the following reasons :

1st. Its great extent—its own lines covering important parts of five great States and one Territory, and its immediate connections covering an equally large area. It can carry you or your stores to a larger number of points than any other road in the country, and can serve you better on the journey than can other lines where you have to be subjected to changes of cars, changes of train men, and changes of local management, as is the case when passing over many short lines or circuitous routes.

2nd. Its well-known and everywhere-acknowledged excellence as regards its superb track, its safety in road bed, bridges, and everything that goes together to make up a perfect road ; its steel rails, full complement of ties to the mile, rock and gravel ballast, the constant vigilance of its employees, the courtesy and kindliness of its train employees—all tend to make it deserve and retain its good name, Pass along its main lines day or night, and especially at night, in fogs and storms, and you will see, of its army of 15,000 employees, ever-present sentinels watchful for your safety, and for the safety, comfort and well-being of all its patrons. On no road in the world is the axiom, Eternal vigilance is the price of safety, more fully believed in and acted upon than on this.

3rd. In the excellence of its steel track, perfect equipment, and thoroughly educated train force, positive assurance is given of great speed, coupled with great safety, comfort, and certainty of arriving on time at destination. So great has been the certainty of trains being on time, that along its lines it has become a common saying, that you can set your watch by their prompt arrival and departure at given points as per the time tables. To the business man, or to him who has to make certain connections at junction points, the promptness of moving trains is of great importance, and on no road is this point kept more in view. The standing orders are, first, absolute safety, and second, making schedule time.

4th. Its equipment is always kept abreast with the improvements and inventions of the day. For comfort its day coaches are unexcelled anywhere, and but seldom equaled. Its palace drawing room sleeping cars are the best in every sense that can be procured for money, and are as well served as years of experience have dictated

THE CHICAGO & NORTH-WESTERN RAILWAY.   117

the means or way. Between Chicago and several of its terminal stations, it is the only road that runs the celebrated Pullman palace drawing room sleeping cars, in which women and children can have a room to themselves, and be as isolated as in their homes. This is the case on its lines between Chicago and Council Bluffs, Chicago and St. Paul, Chicago and Milwaukee, Chicago and Freeport, Chicago and Dubuque and McGregor, Chicago and Madison, Sparta and Winona, and Chicago and Green Bay and Marquette. No matter what inferior and competing lines may advertise, by statements expressly prepared to deceive, yet this fact stands unquestioned, none of them control or run them on their lines.

5th. Miller's Patent Safety Platform, Coupler and Buffer, are considered to be indispensable to the safety of the trains on this line. The Platform is an invention which stiffens the platforms of passenger cars so that they cannot be doubled up, and forms a safe path from one car to another. The Coupler admits of cars being firmly and quickly joined together without the aid of pins or links or any of the old appliances which required a man to place himself in a dangerous position whenever a coupling was to be made. The Buffer is a contrivance which softens the shock when cars are joined together and holds them firmly joined, so that the engineer cannot "get the slack" or "jerk" the train as he can with the old style of coupling. On trains fitted with these appliances "telescoping" is impossible. The Westinghouse Air Brake with which this road is equipped, is an invention by which all the brakes on the train

Eagle Point, near Dubuque.—page 16.

may be, set and loosened in an instant by the hand of the engineer. A small air pump on the engine keeps constantly filled with compressed air a cylinder (also on the engine), from which cylinder run flexible tubes connecting with a smaller cylinder under each car, in which a piston is fitted which connects directly with the brakes. With the aid of this invention the engineer can stop a train so suddenly that collisions are almost impossible. On this road heavy safety chains are placed in pairs between the cars, and between the body and trucks of each car; the former to keep the train together in case anything should happen to the coupler; the latter to prevent the car from leaving the trucks in case the latter are off the track. The "Angle Bar Joint" adopted by this road is the latest and best known invention for joining together the ends of the rails, so that that they may be passed over as smoothly as any other part of the rail. It is a very expensive joint, but it is the BEST, and this road spares no expense that is necessary to procure the best of everything. Many other appliances looking towards the safety of its trains or the comfort of its patrons, are in daily use on the various lines of this road.

6th. The almost ubiquity of its agents—general, local, or traveling—makes it extremely easy to get any information about its trains, its running time, the places it reaches, etc., etc. This is of no little importance to the traveler in a strange country, or to the one expecting to travel into an unfamiliar locality. Ask almost any of the many thousands of railway ticket agents in the land for tickets via this road, and he will supply you, and give you valuable information. Ask for its advertising maps, time cards, pamphlets or books and you can get, freely and without cost, stores of facts that may be of great value to you. To those persons who are anticipating a trip overland from the Atlantic or the interior to the Pacific, or *vice versa*, and to those expecting to pass between Chicago and St. Paul, in either direction, we would especially commend the routes owned by this Company. With the shortest lines, the best equipment, the most perfect track of steel rails, and the beauty of the country they pass through as compared with that of any other route, it is acknowledged that this stands head and shoulders above them all. On the map attached to this little book will be found full and elaborate time cards of most of the lines controlled by this corporation. The "time" there given is correct at the printing of these pages, but is liable to be changed at any time, and is now given only to show the present time that is made between the points named. Correct time cards are issued monthly or oftener.

Turkey River Bluff.—page 16.

RATES OF FARE BY THIS LINE.

The rates of fare charged by or over this line for the transportation of passengers are and always will be as low as those given by any other line to the same points. On first class, second class, or emigrant tickets this is true, as well as with prices charged for any cars that may be chartered for the transportation of passengers. Between local stations of this line, as a rule, the following rates are charged per mile traveled: In Illinois, 3½ cents; in Iowa and Wisconsin, 3 cents; in Minnesota and Dakota, 4 cents; and on the line of the northern peninsula of Michigan, 4 cents. To the more prominent through points, the *present* rates from Chicago are as follows:

From CHICAGO to	First Class.	Second Class.	Emigrant.	From CHICAGO to	First Class.	Second Class.	Emigrant.
Ackley, Iowa	$10.40	$9.75	....	Milwaukee, Wis	$3.00	$2.50	$2.50
Albany, Oregon	145.00	117.00	....	Mankato, Minn	16.30	12.20	....
Albert Lea, Minn	14.00	11.25	....	Marquette, Mich	15.10	11.55	....
Austin, Nev	136.00	113.00	$80.50	Marysville, Cal	116.00	88.00	55.50
Austin, Minn	12.85	10.20	....	Mason City, Iowa	11.95	10.95	....
Battle Mountain, Nev	111.00	88.00	55.50	Menasha, Wis	6.75	6.25	....
Black Hawk, Col	56.20	48.40	....	Mineral Point, Wis	6.55	6.05	....
Blair, Neb	15.60	13.30	....	Minneapolis, Minn	15.50	11.25	....
Boise City, Idaho	135.50	121.50	90.50	Moorhead, Minn	30.50	23.25	....
Breckenridge, Minn	25.25	21.00	....	Negaunee, Mich	14.55	11.00	....
Carson, Nev	117.00	91.00	58.50	New London, Wis	9.10	8.60	....
Central City, Col	56.70	48.90	....	New Ulm, Minn	17.70	13.60	....
Cedar Rapids, Iowa	7.40	7.00	....	North Platte, Neb	30.55	27.55	....
Cheyenne, Wyo	47.00	37.00	....	Ogden, Utah	93.50	73.00	53.00
" " (Special)	41.00	33.00	25.50	Omaha, Neb	16.00	13.00	10.50
Colfax, Cal	115.00	88.00	55.50	Owatonna, Minn	14.50	10.40	....
Colorado Springs, Col	52.20	....	....	Palisade, Nev	111.00	88.00	55.50
Corinne, Utah	95.25	74.75	54.75	Portl'd, Or., via San Fr.	141.00	113.00	67.50
Council Bluffs, Iowa	15.50	12.50	10.00	" via Sacram'to	156.00	128.00	95.50
Denver, Col	52.20	44.40	84.40	Prairie du Chien, Wis	8.75	7.50	....
Detroit, Minn	29.45	25.20	....	Pueblo, Col	52.20	44.40	34.40
Des Moines, Iowa	11.20	10.75	....	Reno, Neb	114.00	88.00	55.50
Duluth, Minn	21.75	17.50	....	Ripon, Wis	5.85	5.35	....
Dubuque, Iowa	7.25	5.75	....	Sacramento, Cal	116.00	88.00	55.50
Elko, Nev	110.35	88.00	55.50	San Francisco, Cal	116.00	88.00	55.50
Elk Point, Dakota	17.50	14.25	....	Salem, Oregon	144.00	116.00	....
Evans, Col	56.80	49.00	....	Salt Lake City, Utah	95.50	75.00	55.00
Fort Dodge, Iowa	12.20	11.50	....	Sioux City, Iowa	16.25	13.00	....
Fort Garry, Manitoba	40.50	26.25	....	Sheboygan, Wis	5.00	4.50	....
Fremont, Neb	16.80	14.50	....	Sparta, Wis	9.20	8.50	....
Galena, Ill	6.30	5.25	....	St. Cloud, Minn	18.80	14.55	....
Golden City, Col	53.20	45.40	....	Stevens' Point, Wis	9.25	8.75	....
Grand Island, Neb	23.70	20.70	15.50	Stockton, Cal	116.00	88.00	55.50
Greeley, Col	57.20	49.40	....	San Jose, Cal	116.00	88.00	55.50
Helena, Montana	142.75	114.75	91.50	St. Paul, Minn	15.25	11.00	....
Hancock, Mich	17.85	14.30	....	St. Peter, Minn	16.50	12.40	....
Houghton, Mich	17.85	14.30	....	Truckee, Cal	115.00	88.00	55.50
Idaho Springs, Col	57.20	49.40	....	Umatilla, Ore	141.00	126.50	90.50
Ishpeming, Mich	14.65	11.10	....	Virginia City, Mont	134.50	110.00	86.50
Kearney Junction, Neb	25.80	22.80	17.00	Virginia City, Nev	117.50	91.50	59.00
Kelton, Utah	101.00	80.50	55.50	Walla Walla, W. T	141.00	126.50	90.50
La Crosse, Wis	10.25	8.50	....	Waterloo, Iowa	9.20	8.55	....
L'Anse, Mich	16.60	13.05	....	Winona, Minn	11.35	9.50	....
Lincoln, Neb	18.75	15.75	....	Wisner, Neb	19.35	17.05	....
McGregor, Iowa	8.75	7.50	....	Yankton, Dak	19.90	16.65	....
Madison, Wis	4.90	4.40	....				

To points on the Union Pacific Railway and Burlington & Missouri River Railway in Nebraska, Round Trip Land Explorers' Tickets are sold from Chicago at two (2) cents per mile each way.

SYNOPSIS OF GAME LAWS.

The following table gives the time when it is lawful to shoot game or to take fish in the States this line of road runs through or is tributary to:

COLORADO.

Quail, or Virginia Partridge..October 1st to November 15th.
Prairie Chickens...September 1st to October 31st.
Wild Turkeys and Mountain Grouse.............................September 1st to November 30th.
Goose, Duck, Curlew, Snipe and Plover.......................May 15th to August 15th.
Elk, Deer, Antelope and Mountain Sheep......................August 1st to January 1st.

SYNOPSIS OF GAME LAWS—continued.

MICHIGAN.
Elk, Buck, Doe, or Fawn..December 15th to August 1st.
Wild Turkeys..October 1st to December 31st.
Woodcock...July 5th to December 31st.
Prairie Chickens, Ruffled Grouse, Pinnated Grouse, Partridge, Pheasant,
   Wood, Teal and Mallard Ducks, or any Water Fowl...................September 1st to December 31st.
Quail, or Virginia Partridge..October 1st to December 31st.
Pigeons, not within five miles of nesting grounds...........................At any time.
Speckled Trout..May 1st to September 1st.
Grayling..June 1st to November 1st.
In Diamond and Stone lakes, fish may be taken only from May 1st to November 1st.

CALIFORNIA.
Partridge, Quails, Grouse and Ducks..September 15th to March 15th.
  Do.   do. in San Bernardino and Los Angeles counties, April 1st to August 1st.
Elk, Deer and Antelope...August 1st to January 1st.
  Do.   do. in Eldorado, Placer, Sierra and Siskiyou counties, August 1st to February 1st.
Several other counties have special game laws.

IOWA.
Prairie Chickens..August 15th to September 1st.
Woodcock..July 1st to January 1st.
Ruffled Grouse, or Pheasant...September 12th to December 15th.
Wild Turkeys..September 1st to February 1st.
Deer..September 1st to January 1st.
Quail, not at all on enclosed grounds, except with consent of owner, and
   then only from...October 1st to January 1st.

OREGON.
Deer, Elk, Moose..July 1st to January 31st.
Wild Swan, and all kinds of Ducks...July 31st to March 31st.
Grouse, Pheasant and Sage Hen...June 15th to March 31st.
Quail, or Partridge...July 31st to March 31st.

ILLINOIS.
Deer, Wild Turkey, Prairie Chickens, Ruffled Grouse, Partridge, or
   Pheasant...August 15th to January 1st.
Quail...October 1st to January 1st.
Woodcock..July 1st to January 1st.
Wild Duck, Goose, Wilson Snipe, Brant, and other Water Fowl.................August 15th to April 15th.

NEVADA.
Grouse, Sage Chicken, Prairie Chicken, Partridge, Pheasant, Woodcock,
   Wild Goose, Teal or other Ducks, Brant, Swan, Sand Hill Crane,
   Plover, Snipe, Curlew and Bittern..September 1st to April 1st.
Deer, Antelope, Elk, Mountain Sheep and Mountain Goat.......................July 1st to January 1st.

NEBRASKA.
Buffalo, Elk, Mountain Sheep, Deer and Antelope.............................October 1st to January 1st.
Grouse..August 1st to January 1st.
Wild Turkey and Quail...October 1st to January 1st.

MINNESOTA.
Woodcock..July 3rd to October 31st.
Prairie Chickens and Grouse...August 14th to October 31st.
Quail, or Partridge...September 1st to October 31st.
Ruffled Grouse or Pheasant..September 1st to November 30th.
Deer and Elk..October 1st to December 15th.
Speckled Trout..April 1st to August 31st.

WISCONSIN.
Woodcock..July 4th to November 15th.
Prairie Chickens, or Grouse...August 15th to November 15th.
Quail, Ruffled Grouse and Pheasant..September 15th to January 1st.
Ducks...September 1st to February 1st.
Deer..August 15th to December 15th.
In Brown county, Prairie Chickens cannot be shot until the 15th of August, 1877. In Eau Claire, Chippewa, Dunn, Pepin, Buffalo and Trempealeau counties, Prairie Chickens and Partridges may be killed from August 10th to November 15th.
In Council House, Deer and Deep creeks, and in Runkle & Freeman's Mill Pond, in Monroe county, fish must not be taken until March 10, 1877.

DAKOTA.
The Game law says, that it shall be unlawful for any person, except on his own premises, and for his own use, and not for sale, trade or traffic, to kill, ensnare, or trap, or in any way or manner destroy or pursue with such intent, any Quail, Prairie Chicken, or Grouse, between the 1st day of March and the 1st day of August, in each and every year.

PULLMAN PALACE CARS.

These cars are so constructed as to combine the convenience and elegance of a private parlor by day, and the comforts of a well-furnished bed-chamber by night—clean bedding, thick hair mattresses, thorough ventilation, etc., etc. Conductors and porters accompany each car, to provide for the wants of passengers.

The following Prices are charged for Double Berths:

New York to Chicago	$5.00
Omaha to Ogden, Utah	8 00
Ogden to San Francisco	6.00
Chicago to San Francisco	17 00
Chicago to Green Bay, Wis.	1.50
Chicago to Milwaukee, Wis.	1.50
Chicago to Madison, Wis.	1 50
Chicago to St. Paul, Minn.	2 00
Chicago to Winona, Minn.	2.00
Chicago to Omaha, Neb.	3.00
Chicago to Council Bluffs, Ia.	3 00
Chicago to Cedar Rapids, Ia.	1.50
Chicago to Clinton, Iowa	1.50
Chicago to Freeport, Ill.	1.50
Chicago to Dubuque, Iowa	1 50
Chicago to Elroy, Wis.	2 00
Chicago to Fond du Lac, Wis.	1.50
Chicago to McGregor, Iowa	2.00

PULLMAN PALACE CARS.

These celebrated cars are run on all night trains on all the lines of this road. They are run between—

Chicago and Omaha; Chicago and Cedar Rapids; Chicago and Dubuque and McGregor, Iowa, via Clinton; Chicago and Freeport; Chicago and Marquette; Chicago and Green Bay; Chicago and Milwaukee; Chicago and St. Paul; Chicago and Sparta and Winona.

This is the Only Line running these cars between Chicago and St. Paul or Chicago and Milwaukee.

At Omaha our Sleepers connect with the Overland Sleepers on the Union Pacific Railroad, for all points west of the Missouri River.

Pullman Palace Chair Cars are run between Chicago and Milwaukee, via this Line, and via this Line only.

All Express Trains on this Route are equipped with *Westinghouse Patent Air Brakes and Miller's Patent Safety Platform and Couplers.* The most perfect protection against accidents known.

This popular route is unsurpassed for Speed, Comfort and Safety. The smooth, well-ballasted and perfect track of steel rails, the celebrated Pullman Palace Sleeping Cars, the perfect telegraph system of moving trains, the regularity with which they run, the admirable arrangement for running through cars from Chicago to all points West, North and Northwest, secure to passengers all the *comforts in modern railway traveling.*

Interior View of a Pullman Drawing Room and Sleeping Car, such as are run on this popular route.

Interior View for Day Travel of a Drawing Room Chair Coach, such as are run on this popular line.

Printed in the USA
CPSIA information can be obtained
at www.ICGtesting.com
LVHW010215230823
756037LV00011B/773